W9-AVK-864

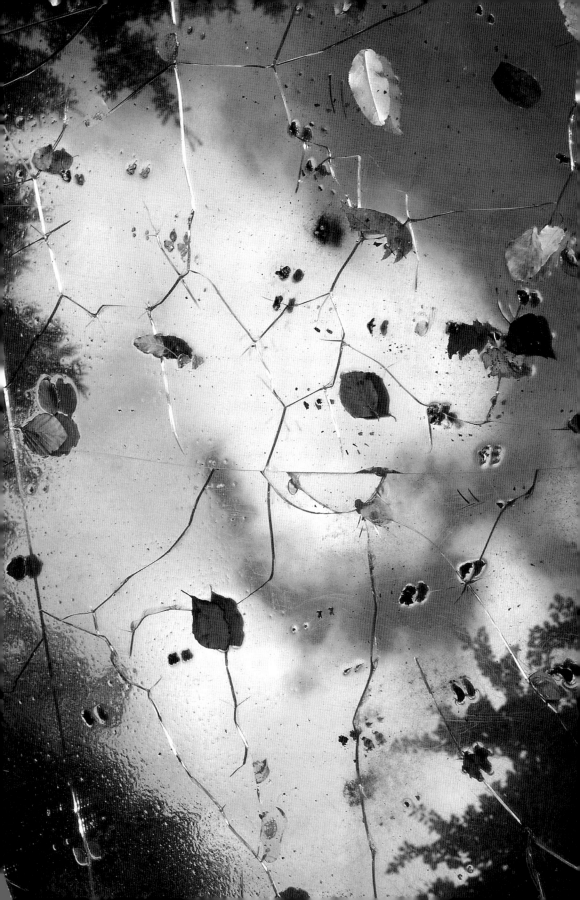

Jan Stoutenbeek / Paul Vigeveno
Translation: Wendie Shaffer

Photography: Sjaak Henselmans

Jewish
Amsterdam

Ludion Amsterdam-Ghent

CENTRE

OLD JEWISH QUARTER

PLANTAGE

JEWISH CANALS

19TH-CENTURY NEIGHBOURHOODS

SOUTH

RIVER NEIGHBOURHOOD

BUITENVELDERT

AMSTELVEEN

Groot
Duivendr
polder

TABLE OF CONTENTS

FOREWORD

Jewish Amsterdam is here again. It's here as a guidebook, having been out of print for many years; and it's here as a reality. Not that there are huge numbers of Jews in Amsterdam – it's something like 20,000 inhabitants out of a total population of around 700,000. But the Jewish presence is making its mark on the city. In the Amsterdam of the twenty-first century you can hear Jewish songs, see plays with Jewish themes, buy books on Jewish subjects or CDs of Jewish music and attend public lectures on many aspects of Judaism. If you like, you can visit one of its synagogues or enjoy an exhibition in the Jewish Historical Museum. Indeed, in certain districts of the city, such as South Amsterdam or Buitenveldert, you could almost say that Jews have become part of the street scene. Of course, Amsterdam is no New York, where a quarter of the population is Jewish; nor is it comparable with London or Antwerp, which have entire Jewish neighbourhoods. The city of Amsterdam still bears deep scars, memories of the persecution during the Second World War, when almost all its Jewish inhabitants were deported and killed. But Amsterdam respects its past and learns from it. Despite all the horrors of the Second World War, the city and its Jews live on. And Amsterdam continues to be the place where, as this guidebook shows, aspects of Jewish culture are integrated into the colourful city scene. Historic synagogues, no longer used for worship, have been restored to their former glory and now contribute to a revival of interest in Jewish culture. These and other listed buildings serve to remind us both of a vivid past and the many-facetted Jewish contribution to the Amsterdam life of yesterday and today. This guidebook, with its powerful and sensitive descriptions and apt citations, conjures up the spirit of Jewish Amsterdam. I have great pleasure in recommending it to anyone who wants to find out about Jewish Amsterdam: it's a new updated edition, packed with information and insights.

Rabbi Edward van Voolen,
Curator, Jewish Historical Museum Amsterdam

Ijar 5763 / May 2003

INTRODUCTION

There is no city in the Netherlands with so strong a Jewish tradition as Amsterdam. Indeed, this is born out by the city's nickname of 'Mokum', which is the Yiddish word for 'place'. Down the centuries, about half of all Dutch Jews have lived in Amsterdam, at one time forming almost 10 percent of the city's population. Amsterdam was called the Jerusalem of the West. At the outbreak of the Second World War in 1939 there were over 70,000 Jews with their own unique lifestyle, shaping the character of their city, 'Mokum'.

The book *Jewish Amsterdam* sets out to recount this history in a manner that is as comprehensive as possible. Thus it examines not just specifically Jewish features such as synagogues and cemeteries, but also considers the many-facetted nature of Jewish life. Often the Jewish tint is just a fraction of a shade different from that of other Dutch people. In the section on the history of the Jews in Amsterdam a general outline is provided and where necessary the story is set against a broader backdrop. This book centres round the history of the Jews in Amsterdam, using the many buildings and other visible memorials of former times. In this way, the book may also serve as a city guide. We decided to use contemporary photographs, since we only describe places and objects that can still be seen today. So we have resisted the temptation to include historic pictures. The broad nature of the work is expanded by the use of relevant citations, often by well-known Dutch authors writing about a particular place or subject. It is impossible to talk about Jewish Amsterdam and ignore the Second World War. The anguish of those years cannot be forgotten. Indeed, the very fact that the subject repeatedly recurs bears witness to the immeasurable suffering of the Jews.

This book, titled in translation *A Guide to Jewish Amsterdam*, was published in 1985 and later incorporated into the volume *Joods Nederland* (Jewish Netherlands) published in Dutch. Since then a great deal of new information has become available in Dutch, including the comprehensive *Pinkas, Geschiedenis van de joodse gemeenschap in Nederland* (A history of the Jewish community in the Netherlands, by J. Michman, H. Beem and D. Michman, in Hebrew and Dutch) and *The History of the Jews in the Netherlands* (edited by J.C.H. Blom, in English). Furthermore, several monographs have appeared in which the years of the Second World War are the main topic; and various literary works have also been published by Jewish authors, among which *Verhalen uit Joods Amsterdam* (Stories from Jewish Amsterdam, in Dutch and German), *Ochenebbisj* (Nebbish, the Yiddish word for 'a loser') and *Levie in de Lage Landen* (Levy in the Low Countries). In addition, a growing awareness of the fate of the Amsterdam Jews has meant that many buildings in the city have been given memorial plaques, making them more easily recognized. All this means that the present new edition of *Jewish Amsterdam* has been thoroughly revised and expanded. The two authors are especially grateful to the following: the staff of the library at the Jewish Historical Museum Amsterdam for their assistance in researching for this book; and Luc Stranders, Jaap van Velzen, Edward van Voolen and Ilja van Nes who read the manuscript and offered invaluable suggestions.

A HISTORY OF THE JEWS IN AMSTERDAM

THE ARRIVAL OF THE JEWS IN AMSTERDAM

Well before the Christian era, Jews were living throughout much of the Middle East. In 70 AD/CE the Romans suppressed a Jewish uprising in Palestine and drove the Jews out of the area. They became scattered throughout the Mediterranean lands, spreading in later centuries to west and eastern Europe. From the close of the 16th century the city of Amsterdam, in what was then known as the Low Countries, became an important centre for the Jews of this diaspora. The first Jews to arrive in Amsterdam came from the Iberian peninsula and are called Sephardim. For centuries they had lived in Spain and Portugal, making a valuable contribution to the economy and cultural life of those countries. But during the 15th century the Roman Catholic Church put increasing pressure upon Jews to convert to Christianity. From 1479 onwards the Spanish Inquisition kept a beady eye on these *conversos,* as the Jewish converts were called. Then in 1492 came the decree from Spain's 'Catholic monarchs' that all Jews must either convert to Christianity or leave Spanish territories. This was the signal for severe persecution of the Jews and most of them who could, including the *conversos,* fled from Spain to neighbouring Portugal – at that time still an independent kingdom – and to the countries of north Africa, Italy and the Ottoman empire.

Although in 1496 the king of Portugal issued a similar decree regarding conversion to Christianity, initially this was not implemented. Not until the Portuguese Inquisition was set up in 1548 did things grow really difficult for the (converted) Jews. So there was a new stream of refugees – this time to nearby Italy and the flourishing harbour city of Antwerp, in the Low Countries. This port on the river Schelde became the centre of a vigorous trading diaspora.

When in 1580 Spain and Portugal were united under one monarch there was yet another flood of refugees. In the meantime, the Dutch provinces had risen in revolt against their Spanish Habsburg overlords and hostilities broke out. In 1585 the city of Antwerp fell to the Spanish, resulting in a blockade of the harbour by the Dutch rebels. So the centres shifted and now Amsterdam and Hamburg became the cities where trade and (relative) tolerance prospered. Indeed, Amsterdam was to become the major city of the Sephardi diaspora. It became especially attractive to these Sephardi merchants when it developed into the international staple market for a large number of products. With the Twelve Year Truce of 1612 bringing a temporary halt to the fighting, trade with the Iberian peninsula once again picked up and the Jews with families still in Portugal made the most of their contacts to promote business.

It would not be true to say that the Golden Age of Amsterdam was thanks to the arrival of Sephardi Jewish merchants. The city was already enjoying a boom in trade when the newcomers appeared. Furthermore, the Sephardi Jews didn't bring any capital to speak of; what they did have were useful business contacts whereby in the course of the 17th century several of them could build up considerable fortunes. They also introduced new elements to the entrepreneurial world, such as the trade with Brazil and the West Indies, and the diamond import trade. One of Amsterdam's major trading activities in the mid-17th century was the sugar business. In this the Sephardi Jews played an important part and were partially responsible for the ongoing upswing in the Amsterdam economy and its rate of development. And for most of the impoverished Jews, Amsterdam's prosperity was indirectly important since it affected the general spending power of the population, which meant that the turnover of the Jewish petty tradesmen and hawkers was greater here than elsewhere.

The fact that Sephardi Jews settled in Amsterdam was connected with the city's religious tolerance. In the 1597 Union of Utrecht, the Dutch Republic of the United Provinces stated that no one could be persecuted because of their religious faith. Although this clause was not written with Jews in mind, the principle was extended to include them – after a little initial hesitation. The Protestant Dutch Provinces were also free from the Inquisition, Jews were free to marry, they were not forced to wear a distinguishing badge or sign proclaiming that they were Jews, they could acquire and inherit property and they were not obliged to live within a ghetto. There was hardly anywhere in Europe where Jews enjoyed these fundamental freedoms.

The Portuguese merchant families who first settled in Amsterdam were so-called New Christians, that is, they had been forced to convert to Christianity sometimes as much as a hundred years previously and since then had adopted Christian customs. Jews were persecuted and oppressed and it is not clear to what extent they still honoured their Jewish heritage. They presumably continued to observe Jewish practices within the closed family circle, but in practice this must have varied greatly. Initially the Sephardim in Amsterdam could not practise the Jewish religion openly. Furthermore, they arrived as nominal Christians baptized into the Roman Catholic faith – an added complication in Protestant Amsterdam. In practice, however, the Amsterdam government showed remarkable flexibility. Indeed, in 1597 one Emanuel Rodriguez Vega was able to take the oath as citizen of Amsterdam. In the following year the regents (members of the wealthy ruling Dutch families) of Amsterdam announced that Sephardi merchants could buy the citizenship of the city:

> trusting that these people be Christians and that these same people will live honest lives in this place as good citizens' and 'that here in this city no other religion can nor may be practised or admitted apart from that which is already practised in public in the churches of this place.

It was to be several decades before the Sephardi Jews living in Amsterdam once more openly observed the traditions and practices of Judaism. Moreover, the magistracy of Amsterdam needed time to adjust. In 1602 we have the first mention of a Jewish religious service in the home of rabbi Uri ha-Levi. Others soon followed without interference from the city government. Apparently it was only the public observance of the Jewish faith that met with disapproval. In an age of vicious religious intolerance Amsterdam showed itself remarkably mild.

However, in 1612 the Jews were not granted permission to build a public place of worship. The first actual recognition of Jewry came in1614, when Jews were granted permission to buy a plot of land in Ouderkerk on the Amstel, just outside Amsterdam, for a Jewish cemetery. Despite this, two years later it was decreed that Jews:

> could not by spoken or written word…bring our Christian religion to even the smallest degree into contempt nor attempt to convert or to circumcise any Christian person' and further that Jews could not 'have any carnal contact with Christian women or daughters outside wedlock notwithstanding that these same women might be of ill repute.

Then in 1639 the first public Sephardi Jewish place of worship was consecrated, to be followed in 1672 by the splendid building still in use today, known as the *Esnoga*.

The Portuguese synagogue about 1675

Meanwhile, Jews from eastern Europe, called Ashkenazim, had arrived in Amsterdam; they had a different background and tradition from the Sephardim. Initially, their community consisted of impoverished Jews who had been expelled from or persecuted in certain German cities or principalities. Most of them fled eastwards from Germany, but a certain number turned towards the Dutch Republic. Once in Amsterdam, the majority found service with the more well-to-do Sephardi Jews. Thus a new Jewish community developed, consisting of down-and-out Ashkenazim. Their first registered religious service dates from1635. In 1671 the 'Great Synagogue' in Amsterdam was consecrated.

More Ashkenazim streamed in around the mid-17th century as a result of persecutions in Poland, Lithuania and the Ukraine. These Jews had their own language, Yiddish, and a distinct cultural tradition. The refugees from eastern Europe had not shared in the western European developments but instead had led a somewhat isolated existence. Although not compelled to do so, the Jews in Amsterdam lived for the most part in a close community, in one of the least salubrious quarters of the city, close to the shipbuilding and industrial neighbourhood in the east. Also, many Jews wished to live within walking distance of a synagogue. With their own language and customs they created their own Jewish world, which comprised all the buildings and bodies important in everyday Jewish life. In the course of the 17th century the number of Ashkenazim in Amsterdam grew to surpass that of the Sephardim. The latter community had expanded rapidly to reach about 3,000, after which it stabilized. The Ashkenazim, on the other hand, continued to expand until they exceeded 20,000 at the end of the 18th century.

It is remarkable that the municipal government of Amsterdam did not try to stem the tide of destitute refugees. Undoubtedly, cheap labour was in high demand during Amsterdam's Golden Age, but the attitude of the Amsterdam regents would also seem to reflect a tolerance virtually unique for those days. Furthermore, the wealthy classes weren't bothered by the masses of Jewish paupers, since the Jews had their own system of caring for their poor.

THE ECONOMIC POSITION OF JEWS UNDER THE DUTCH REPUBLIC

For the Jews in Amsterdam it was the same old story – it proved almost impossible to avoid a life of poverty, due to crippling restrictions about what jobs they could pursue. True, Jews could purchase the position of 'citizen' but this didn't mean they had entry into the trades and industries or any of the crafts that were controlled by the guild system. This was made patently evident in an ordinance of 1632:

> 'The burgomasters and governors of the city of Amsterdam hereby declare that it be understood
> that the Jews within the city who have been or who shall be accepted as citizens, shall not there-
> by have the right to practise any sort of citizen's trade.'

A few exceptions were made to this rule, for instance by the apothecaries' and surgeons' guilds. Since the majority of professions were organized through the guild system, very few openings were possible for Jews. They had to resort to the 'un-organized' trades and professions, such as hawking and peddling or business and banking activities. There were also a few new trades and industries, some indeed introduced by the Jews themselves, such as diamond cutting and polishing, sugar refining, silk production and the tobacco industry. But here again the Jews were hamstrung, since they weren't allowed to own a shop. However, in the course of time a few exceptions were made and Jews were able to become grocers or *comenys, vettewaaiers,* and barkeepers, or run tobacco shops. Furthermore, the regents would often turn a blind eye – after all, this small fry didn't bother such lordly merchants. But the Christian shopkeepers regularly protested and in order to preserve the peace their complaints would sometimes be listened to.

Although regulations to the Jews' disadvantage weren't followed all too strictly, there was neverthe-less extreme poverty among this group of Amsterdammers. The small number of well-to-do Sephardim formed an exception. And in the course of the 18th century this group shifted their activi-ties increasingly to (international) trading, living off investments and trading on Amsterdam's Stock Exchange, which had been founded in the 17th century. Most of the Sephardim and almost all the Ashkenazim were deeply affected by the economic exclusion laws. As early as 1621 the Sephardim imposed a tax upon their own members in order to assist the poor of their community. By the close of the 17th century, for every family who gave charity there were two other families who lived from this poor relief. And it must have been far worse among the Ashkenazim. With the economic deterio-ration of the 18th century the poverty among the Jews of Amsterdam became appalling. Even the municipal tax on flour and peat (for heating) had to be lifted. During the Corn Crisis in 1771 to 1772 the death rate among Jews doubled, while among non-Jews it rose to 30 percent. The figures relat-ing to poor relief in the year 1795 speak volumes. Of the total population, 37 percent were on poor relief. Among the Sephardim it was 54 percent while for the Ashkenazim it reached the horrifying percentage of 87. At the same time the few wealthy Jews were hard hit by the crises on the Amsterdam stock market in 1763 and above all in 1773.

JEWISH SELF-GOVERNMENT DURING THE DUTCH REPUBLIC

During the 17th and 18th century the Jews were considered to be a people apart, called the 'Jewish nation'; they had their own languages – Yiddish, Portuguese or Ladino, and their own culture, dominated by their many laws such as those regarding the food they could eat, and the observance of their Sabbath. All this was expressed in a comprehensive state of autonomy enjoyed by the Jewish communities, adapted to an age-old tradition of Jewish self-government within a non-Jewish state. In this way the national government managed to ensure the responsibility of Jewish authorities for their own communities, particularly that they cared for their own paupers. Consequently, the Jewish community was a thing apart, with a strong internal discipline. It had its own religious leaders (rabbis), leaders of the community (parnasim), synagogues, cemeteries, ritual baths, ritual butchers, kosher bakers, system of poor relief and other forms of charity, and societies for the study of the Torah. It was above all through study, or *lernen*, that the Jewish values were passed down from generation to generation. Together with the Torah, the teachings of the rabbis played an essential role. In this way the Jews lived as far as possible according to their own laws, while at the same time recognizing the laws of the land in which they lived.

This internal organization was maintained through financial independence. The local communities received their income from taxes, contributions, donations and fines, which could be imposed by the parnasim. These heads of the community were thus very powerful figures. The Jewish communities were on the whole highly dependent on a few wealthy members who could provide the necessary funding for the many needy instances and especially for poor relief.

THE EMANCIPATION OF THE JEWS IN 1796

During the 18th century, influenced by Enlightenment ideas, attitudes of tolerance gradually spread. There was increased interest in the common, or shared, morality of different religions, which helped promote the acceptance of Judaism by the Christian majority. Within the Jewish community there was a growing interest in integration (equal participation in a dominant culture while preserving one's own identity) and assimilation (being absorbed into a dominant culture with loss of individual identity). Assimilation was a much-debated question in those Jewish circles that saw the preservation of Jewry and Jewish identity as a sine qua non. It was partly because of this that only a small elite of the Jews in the Netherlands can be termed followers of the Enlightenment. This enlightened, or politically liberal, Jewish elite regarded Judaism principally as a religion and being Jewish a matter of personal choice. This attitude was opposed both to those who wished to exclude Jews from Dutch society and also to the fact that the some powerful Jews (in particular the parnasim) controlled the lives of the members of their community.

Those who opposed emancipation were strongly attached to the autonomy enjoyed by the Jewish community under the traditional structures. As they saw it, being Jewish was not a matter of individual choice, but a communal phenomenon. The isolated position of Jews within the diaspora would only end with the coming of the Messiah. Seen this way, Judaism included both the people (Jewry) and the religion, so that the distinction between church and state, which the followers of the Enlightenment wished to introduce, was considered unacceptable and un-Jewish.

The emancipation, or Act of Civic Equality, was finally achieved under the French occupation with the official introduction of the concepts of Liberty, Equality and Fraternity into the Netherlands. In 1796 the National Assembly of the Batavian Republic, as the Netherlands was temporarily called under French rule, decreed:

> No Jew shall be deprived of any right or advantage that is attached to the right of citizenship in the Batavian Republic and which he might desire to enjoy, provided he possess all the necessary requirements and meet all the necessary conditions which the general constitution requires of every active citizen of the Netherlands.

As one of the few European sovereigns to do so, Dutch king Willem I continued the policy towards the Jews that had been introduced under the French in Napoleonic times. Thus the emancipation of 1796 forms a distinct watershed in the history of Dutch Jewry. It signified the end of autonomy for the Jewish communities and a severe pruning of the powers of the parnasim. This power had gone hand in hand with great organizational involvement in matters concerning Jewish education, culture and administration. Now in its place came greater individual freedom. Jews were able to set up businesses where they chose and in principle all professions were open to them. Countless discriminating regulations were abolished and Jews even had, in theory, the right to vote (although this right was very restricted in the Netherlands of those days and in fact only the wealthiest could vote). Furthermore, Jews could now be granted government appointments. In practice, however, the new rights did not mean that from then on Jews actually functioned as equals in Dutch society.

JEWISH AMSTERDAM UNDER THE DUTCH MONARCHY

The turnabout that the Napoleonic period signified for the Jews of the Netherlands had significant repercussion during the 19th century. During the first half of the century there was on the one hand continued poverty among the Jews and economic exclusion, while on the other hand formally they had equal rights and there was a high measure of (Dutch) government interference in Jewish questions. The Dutch state, through its Ministry of Religious Affairs, controlled many aspects of Judaism. Government policy aimed as far as possible to limit Judaism to being a religion, not a social or cultural phenomenon. The decision of 1817 to introduce the Dutch language into Jewish education and religious services had far-reaching results. Within a few generations Yiddish had disappeared as the main language of the Jewish community, although Jews continued to speak with a strong Yiddish accent and retained a great many Yiddish expressions. A further point was that education was now available for girls and this would in due course have a huge impact on the emancipation of Jewish women in the Netherlands. Incidentally, it should be noted that due to lack of means the Dutch government supervision of Jewish education was of remarkably poor quality.

Although initially only a small Jewish elite belonging to the political, social and cultural middle class promoted emancipation of the Jews, it was not long before the Jewish proletariat came under the influence of this government-sponsored integration. In contrast, Orthodox (religious) Jews tried to continue living as they had always done. Thus the foundations were laid for the later alienation of the proletariat from both the middle-class and Orthodox ways of life.

The second half of the 19th century saw further far-reaching changes. The Dutch constitution of 1848 drew a sharp distinction between church and state, whereby the Ministry of Religious Affairs was no longer responsible for Jewish matters. The result was a marked decentralization, which left the separate Jewish communities more or less independent. Equally significant was the Education

Act of 1857 which, although stating that it was permitted to establish independent (religious) schools, also abolished any form of school subsidy. Thus Jewish schools lost their – at best limited – financial support and before long disappeared entirely. From then on, Jewish children attended state schools and this was a further reason for the decline of Yiddish as a spoken language. What did continue was religious education, which was given after school hours; but this tended to be of a pretty poor standard, nor did it attract large numbers.

Another sign of integration was that the religious services in the shuls were adapted to Dutch customs. Besides the use of the Dutch language, increasing adjustments were made to the order of service, which was thought to be too 'un-churchly'. Choirs were introduced to lead the singing and it was forbidden to wear caps and clogs. Also frowned upon was too much noisy thumping and jeering when the name of Haman was uttered – he was one of the earliest biblical persecutors of the Jews, known in Yiddish as *Homon Horooshe*, or Haman the Wicked. This traditional Jewish custom was abolished in the attempt to get rid of the picture of the synagogue as a place filled with uncivilized goings-on. All these adjustments could not, however, prevent attendance at synagogue from gradually declining; the observance of the Sabbath and the Jewish dietary laws also slowly became watered down and the traditional Jewish way of life came under threat. Such developments meant that in the course of the 19th century the Jews became steadily more integrated into the Dutch society around them while the ties with Jewish traditions and culture grew steadily weaker.

THE SOCIAL AND ECONOMIC POSITION OF THE JEWS UNDER THE DUTCH MONARCHY

With the occupation by the French under Louis Napoleon the position of the city of Amsterdam as a major trading centre was lost forever. Indeed, it initiated a long spell of malaise. It would seem that the number of emigrants rose as a result, for the number of Jews in Amsterdam stayed the same and even dipped in the early 19th century. Since the Act of Civic Equality made it possible for Jews to settle where they wished in the Netherlands, sizeable numbers of them left the impoverished Mokum and settled in the Mediene, that is, the provinces. There in the course of the 19th century, flourishing Jewish communities were to arise.

Despite their emancipation, many Jews in Amsterdam remained in the traditional trades. They still lived in a Jewish district, often speaking a distinct language or dialect and following the laws of their religion; these things hindered swift emergence into a new way of life. Consequently, extreme poverty prevailed among the Amsterdam Jews until well into the 19th century. Among the Ashkenazim in 1820 at least 78 percent lived on poor relief – a figure which dropped to 55 percent by 1849. During those years the figure for the Sephardim actually rose to 63 percent. In comparison, among the non-Jewish population, under 20 percent lived from poor relief.

The economic recovery of Amsterdam took off in around 1860. Generally speaking, Jews were not immediately involved in this process. They profited indirectly since people's spending power increased, whereby the turnover of Jewish wares could also increase. As a result of the economic recovery the traditional Jewish activities once again flourished. A remarkable phenomenon was the development of several Jewish retailers dealing in textiles and haberdashery who blossomed into such elegant emporiums as the *Maison de Bonneterie*, Gerzon and the *Bijenkorf*. Jews were also active in many intellectual professions and in the ever-expanding government services. One result of this expansion was that Jews returned from the provinces, the Mediene, to make Mokum more than ever the centre of Dutch Jewry. By 1900 over 50 percent of all Dutch Jews were living in Amsterdam.

The real break-through of the Jewish proletariat came because of the diamond trade. In 1870 with the discovery of large quantities of diamond in South Africa the industry took a sharp upturn; those years are known as the Cape Age. The demand for skilled diamond workers grew rapidly and wages rose phenomenally. Although the Jews didn't actually hold a monopoly they dominated the diamond trade, and so it was that thousands of families could at last enjoy a measure of prosperity. The social consequences were enormous. Many families could now afford to let their children study or could set up their own small businesses. The significance of the diamond trade for the Jews of Amsterdam is revealed by the fact that in 1908 there were still 29 percent of Jewish families dependent upon it.

SOCIALISM AND ZIONISM

With the decline in poverty towards the close of the 19th century the dependence of the Jewish masses on poor relief and zedakah (literally meaning 'righteousness' or 'justice', in common usage, 'charity') declined sharply. New societies developed to provide social aid and these in turn grew into the trades unions. An important date in this development was the 1894 strike initiated by the Christian diamond workers, which soon spread. The success of this strike led to the founding of the first Dutch trades union, the General Dutch Diamond-Workers Bond (ANDB). In the wake of the union movement the Jewish proletariat marched forward towards Socialism. With the developments in the diamond industry, as well as the tobacco and textile trades, a Jewish proletariat had developed towards the close of the 19th century. These people became increasingly aware of their working-class position, which went hand-in-hand with declining religious observance. This foreshadowed the break with both Orthodox Judaism and the liberal Jewish leaders (mainly middle-class intellectuals). Around 1900 there were already 60,000 Jews living in Amsterdam. The old Jewish quarter was bursting at its seams and people began to settle in new working-class neighbourhoods on the east and south sides of the city. Here, for the first time since the 18th century, new synagogues were built at the turn of the nineteenth-twentieth century. Partly because Jews were members of socialist housing societies they tended to live in these new complexes. The housing societies constructed blocks of buildings and rented then out at a not-too-exorbitant price. The poorest Jews, of course, remained behind in the slums of the old Jewish quarter, which became more and more dilapidated. The wretched living conditions in the neighbourhoods of Vlooyenburg, Uilenburg and Marken led to the organization of the first slum-clearance programmes by the municipality of Amsterdam.

One result of the increasing number of Jews and their consequent distribution throughout the city was to end their isolation. Also, their participation in the Socialist movement strengthened their inte-gration. With all these various developments, Jewish Amsterdam became characterized by a well-integrated Jewish elite, religious leadership tending towards Orthodoxy, and a large mass that was growing ever more secular and ever more Socialist. Politically active Jews tended to be either Liberals or Socialists. (Note that Dutch speak of 'liberals' meaning those with a somewhat right-wing attitude; different from the British or American usage.) In the Amsterdam political parties they made a valuable contribution. One noteworthy outcome of all this was that the highly-assimilated Dutch

Jews had little in common with Jewish communities elsewhere in Europe. Towards the end of the 19th century there was an outbreak of violent anti-Semitism throughout Europe, partly caused by feelings of nationalism, partly in reaction to Jewish assimilation. This in turn sparked off Jewish feelings of nationalism; for the first time in centuries of living in the diaspora some Jews dreamed of a nation state of their own as the answer to many problems. It would solve the decline of Jewry, and the recurring threat of persecution: Jews could return to their original homeland from which they had been expelled by the Romans. In the main, such ideas by-passed the Netherlands, and thus Amsterdam. The Dutch Zionist Bond, founded in 1899, had a very small following. The Orthodox Jews opposed the strongly secular nature of Zionism and rejected a political solution in the form of a homeland for the Jews, because they believed that the coming of the Messiah would be the salvation of the Jewish people. And the assimilated elite in the Netherlands saw Zionism as a threat to their hard-won position within Dutch society. Above all, the Dutch Jewish proletariat were unmoved by Zionism. This group was mainly Socialist and Socialism was by its very nature international (that is, non-nationalistic). Furthermore, most Jews had grown accustomed to ignoring problems. Nevertheless, Zionism certainly provoked passionate discussions and increased awareness among Jews of their specific identity, at the end of a century dominated by assimilation, integration and secularization. Undeniably, these were radical changes, but we should never forget that most Amsterdam Jews earned their living as peddlers, barrow-boys or buyers-up of second-hand garments and metal goods. At the beginning of the 20th century the diamond trade offered well-paid jobs to a skilled elite. One rung down from them came the tobacco and textile workers. Hawkers and small retail traders stood at the bottom of the social ladder. The economic Depression of the 1930s sent the whole world into a crisis, including the diamond trade. At its worst, 80 percent of the diamond workers were unemployed. Many types of trade and business suffered in those years. The decline in spending power inevitably affected the Jewish retailers, who sank into abject poverty. Poor food (and the poor housing) encouraged contagious diseases such as typhus and tuberculosis. Many sought to make a living from the traditional hawking and peddling. In the mid-1930s Amsterdam had thousands of street-sellers and about 1,200 rag-and-bones men; in 1935 the municipality took measures to prevent any further increase. The general decline in spending power meant that there was scarcely anything for these junk dealers to earn anyway.

THE 1930s

It will remain an unanswered question how the Dutch Jews would have continued the centuries-long process of integration in the Netherlands. The Second World War caused a dramatic hiatus in this story. What was happening in Germany in the 1930s brought Dutch Jews face to face with questions they had never posed before. What did being Jewish mean? The age-old Christian prejudices against Jews now gained a 'scientific' slant in Germany. It was 'proven' that the Jew was inferior and a threat to the culture of Germany and indeed western Europe. Historical attitudes of a religious or economic nature were called as evidence. In Germany Adolf Hitler (1889-1945) stated:

'I have been attacked for the manner in which I treat the Jews…For fifteen hundred years the Roman Catholic church has regarded the Jews as parasites and banished them to a ghetto. That church knew what Jews were good for. … I am simply following a tradition that is fifteen centuries old. Possibly I am doing Christianity the greatest service.'

Although there doesn't appear to have been such blatant anti-Semitism in the Netherlands the 'Jewish question' was undeniably a hot topic and it became clear that this country was by no means free from anti-Jewish tendencies. For instance, in 1924 the Roman Catholic Church forbade (Catholic) young women to go into service in Jewish families. The arrival of thousands of Jewish refugees from Germany in the 1930s put more strain on the situation. The Dutch government left the care of these refugees to the Jewish communities. This was putting the clock back to before the Act of Civic Equality and the 1796 emancipation. A special body was set up – the Committee for Special Jewish Interests – in 1933, and after discussion it was decided that the refugees were not to be a financial burden on the state of the Netherlands.

A camp for German-Jewish refugees was build in Westerbork and paid for by the Jewish community. Ironically Westerbork later turned into a deportation camp. Incidentally, the Dutch government made a clear distinction between Jews who were seen as a welcome addition to the community in the worsening economy, and those who would only be a burden on the state. Thus refugees were only admitted if it could be shown that they might in some way contribute towards the country's econo-my. Furthermore, refugees should be encouraged to move on to other countries. In brief, what the Dutch policy amounted to was: 'Who is paying for you, what can we get out of you, and what's the quickest way to get rid of you.' Generally speaking, the Jewish leaders supported this policy. On the one hand there was a sense of solidarity with other Jews, but on the other hand they were afraid of spoiling the relatively good relations between Jews and non-Jews in the Netherlands, by accepting thousands of 'communists and paupers'. Only if it were a matter of life and death could Jews be allowed in. The Dutch Minister of Justice Gosseling stated that this was not the case when it became known that in Germany Jews were being imprisoned in concentration camps. Postscript: later on Gosseling was to die as a hostage in a Nazi concentration camp.

THE DESTRUCTION OF JEWISH AMSTERDAM

In May 1940 German troops invaded the Netherlands. A few days later they occupied Amsterdam. Although some Amsterdam Jews contrived to escape abroad, the majority waited to see what would happen, anxiously, but as yet unaware of the full horror of what lay in wait. Initially, things didn't look too bad. Only gradually did it appear that the Nazi plan was to exterminate the Jews. The Nazis defined what they termed 'the Jewish question' and made detailed plans about how to deal with it; in the years that they were in power they gradually intensified their activities against the Jews. Up until 1939, for instance, compulsory emigration from Germany to somewhere distant like Madagascar was still considered an option. After the German occupation of Poland, where millions of Jews were living, ghettos were set up in the occupied countries, under the aegis of a Jewish Council which was intended to give a semblance of self-government. The next step was the systematic murder of the Jews by special commando groups.

The first measures taken in Amsterdam by the German occupiers dealt with the compulsory regis-tration of all Jews and the isolation of Jewish members of the community. Towards the end of 1940 the so-called Aryan Declaration was introduced, whereby Jews had to declare their racial origins; those who said they were non-Aryan were dismissed from government employment. Personal prop-erty and assets were also registered. In 1941 the Nazis made use of the efficient Dutch registration system to demand that everyone have a personal Identity Card; and if you were a Jew, your card was stamped with the letter 'J'. In rapid tempo, regulation followed regulation. Jews were banned from using public transport and even from riding bicycles, their telephones were cut off and then Jews from smaller communities in the provinces were herded into Amsterdam. Here, for the first time in the history of the Netherlands, a ghetto was created in the old Jewish quarter, bordered by barbed wire.

In May 1942 it was made compulsory for Jews to wear a yellow Star of David sewn onto their clothes. By this time the Nazis had taken the decision to exterminate all Jews, and systematically set about carrying this out. During the Wannsee Conference in January 1942 the Nazis had reached agreement concerning the *Endlösung der Judenfrage* (The Final Solution of the Jewish Question) and had drawn up a plan that they proceeded to implement down to the last detail, '*gründlich*'. They built various concentration camps, soon followed by the extermination camps.

Summer 1942 saw the first roundups of Jews in the Netherlands, followed by deportation. The official German line was that these people were being recruited for labour in Germany. About 12,000 Amsterdam Jews ignored the call-up to set off for the work camps, and went into hiding. Of these, about one third were later betrayed and taken prisoner. Jews who simply stayed in their homes were later arrested during roundups. The Jews in Amsterdam were taken to the former theatre, Hollandsche Schouwburg; here they were loaded onto trains and shunted off to Westerbork concen-

Many departments of the Jewish Council with their revealing names

.ijnbaansgracht 366,	Boekhouding
"	Personeelbureau
"	Interne Dienst
"	Afd. Westerbork
"	„Beirat" voor niet-Nederlandsche Joden
"	Centrale Voorlichtingsdienst
"	Interne Informatie
"	Voorlichtingsbureau
"	Emigratie
"	„Hulp aan Vertrekkenden" (Centraal Bureau)
"	Zakelijke belangen
"	(Landelijk apparaat)
"	Kartotheek Provincie
.ude Schans 74,	„Hulp aan Vertrekkenden" en Kampafdeeling
" "	Kleerenvoorziening en uitgifte kampartikelen
" "	Atelier
" "	Bureau van den financieelen leider van de afd. „Hulp aan Vertrekkenden" en Boekhouding
.frikanerplein 14/16,	„Hulp aan Vertrekkenden" Districtbureau „Oost"
.frikanerplein 19,	Voorlichtingsbureau
.mstel 25,	Reis- en verhuisvergunningen
.mstel 93,	Cultureele Zaken
"	Psychotechnisch Laboratorium der J.C.B.
"	Stichting Joodsche Arbeid
.sterdorp,	Afd. „Asterdorp"
.achstraat 1,	„Hulp aan Vertrekkenden" Districtbureau Zuid-E(uterpebuurt)
" "	Zuigelingenzorg
.amperstraat 17,	Opleidingsschool voor Joodsche Handels- en Kantoorbedienden
.hrist. de Wetstraat 21,	Voorlichtingsbureau
.uterpestraat 35,	Geneeskundige behandeling
.roenburgwal 44,	Zuigelingenzorg
"	Schooltoezicht
.aarlemmermeerstraat 87,	„Hulp aan Vertrekkenden" Districtbureau „West"
.avikslaan 23,	„Hulp aan Vertrekkenden" Districtbureau „Noord"
.emonylaan 27,	Joodsche Centrale voor Beroepsopleiding (J.C.B.)
.ortusplantsoen 1,	E. J. van Detschool
.outmarkt 10,	Sociale Zorg
.ac. Obrechtstraat 53,	Bijstand aan niet-Nederlandsche Joden Contrôle-Commissie
.an van Eyckstraat 11,	„Hulp aan Vertrekkenden" Dépôt Uitrustingsstukken (Afd. Onderwijs)
.ekerstraat 84,	Administratie
"	Financiën
"	Toezicht
.odenbreestraat 63,	Het Joodsche Weekblad Administratie (Afd. Evacuatie)
.odenbreestraat 89,	Bewerking materiaal Het Joodsche Weekblad Redactie
.odenbreestraat 93,	
.ekstraat 150,	Voorlichtingsbureau

Blz.	Address	Department
21	Muiderstraat 21 (gebouw Pigol),	M. B. Nijkerkschool
	Nic. Witsenkade 14,	„Klera"
22	Nic. Witsenkade 41,	Cursuswerk
	Nw. Heerengracht 23,	Blindenzorg
		Broodvoorziening (zie aanvullingsblad)
	" "	Groente-distributie " "
	Oosteinde 14,	Gem. Bureau voor Joodsche inkwartiering
	Oosteinde 16,	Tehuis Oosteinde
23	Oosteinde 24,	(Tehuis Oosteinde)
		Naai- en verstelwerk
	Oude Schans 92,	Bagage-afdeeling
	Plant. Franschelaan 13,	Stichting Joodsche Arbeid
	Plant. Parklaan 9,	Buitenschoolsche Jeugdzorg
24	" "	Sociaal Paedagogische Zorg
	" "	Medisch Sociaal Bureau (Psychiatrisch Consultatie Bureau)
	Polderweg 10,	Zuigelingenzorg
	"	Schooltoezicht
	Rapenburgerstraat 128,	M. B. Nijkerkschool
	Reguliersgracht 109,	Archief „Lijnbaansgracht"
		„Hulp aan Vertrekkenden" Districtbureau „Centrum"
	Roerstraat 75/79,	Zuigelingenzorg
	"	Schooltoezicht
25	Tolstraat 127/129,	Joodsche Vereeniging voor Verpleging en Ve zorging (J.V.v.V.V.)
	Tulpstraat 17,	Onderwijs
	"	Secretariaat
26	Valckenierstraat 39,	A. B. Davidsschool
	Vening Meineszkade 10/11,	Commissie ter Behandeling van Financieele Aa gelegenheden
	" "	Accountantsdienst
27	Waterlooplein 109,	Uitzending Buitenland (zie aanvullingsblad)
	"	Groente-distributie " "
	Waterlooplein 119/121,	Bijstand aan niet-Nederlandsche Joden
	"	Financieele afdeeling
	"	Ondersteuning en Maatschappelijk Werk in buiten Amsterdam
		Voorlichtingsbureau
	Waterlooplein 123,	Vleeschvoorziening
27	Westeinde 17,	M. B. Nijkerkschool
28	Zuider Amstellaan 45,	„Hulp aan Vertrekkenden" Districtbureau „Zuid-R(ivierenbuurt)"
	Zwanenburgwal 33,	„Hulp aan Vertrekkenden" Centraal Dépôt
29		Bestuur van het Joodsche Onderwijs in Nederland
		Commissie van Advies voor onderwijs-technische vraagstukken
		Algemeene Advies Commissie voor het Joodsche Onderwijs
		Commissie ter Behartiging van de Belangen van Geëvacueerden
		Commissie voor Buitenschoolsche Jeugdzorg
		Centrale Commissie
		Centrale Cultureele Commissie voor Joden in Nederland
		Contact-Commissie
		Contact-Commissie
30		Hachsjarah-Raad van de J.C.B.
		Financieele Commissie J.C.B.
		Tarboeth Commissie J.C.B.
		Gebouwen-Commissie
		Juridische Commissie
		Commissie voor Grafische Opleiding „A. B. Davidsschool"
		Commissie voor Jeugdontwikkeling

tration camp. Sometimes they stayed there only a few days, sometimes weeks, but generally this was merely a temporary halt on the journey to the 'East', to the extermination camps.

Although these deportations were ultimately organized by the Nazis, the German policy was to have the Jew themselves do as much of their dirty work as possible. The Dutch civil service carried out the orders of the German occupiers almost without protest. The Municipal Transport Services of Amsterdam carried thousands of Jews by tram to the railway station, where Dutch Rail shunted them off to concentration camps. The Amsterdam police assisted in the roundups and in guarding those who were taken prisoner. Dutch people continued to do their jobs even when it meant assisting in the emptying of (Jewish) hospitals, homes for the elderly, and homes for the mentally disabled – whose inhabitants could scarcely be intended to work in German factories. In particular, the Dutch police under the leadership of the National-Socialist (Nazi) chief commissioner Tulp, appointed in 1941, eagerly complied with the orders of the German occupiers. A special department was created to deal with Jewish Affairs, while to counteract the Dutch Resistance a secret service was set up, which made a substantial contribution to the deportation of Dutch Jews.

The Jewish Council also did its work with a minimum of protest. This body was set up by the German occupiers under the leadership of two prominent Jews, Abraham Asscher and David Cohen, and had as task the registration and supervision of the Amsterdam Jews. The Jewish leaders hoped that by complying with the German regulations they might acquire certain concessions and somewhat mitigate the situation; for instance, the Jewish Council could declare someone to be an 'essential' or 'indispensable' person, and thereby save them from imprisonment, though always with the note in the margin bis auf weiteres (until further notice). The Germans, in turn, made small concessions to lubricate the cooperation. For instance, there were about 17,000 members of staff working for the Jewish council, and they were initially exempt from the call-up. However, in May 1943 the Germans demanded that 7,000 of them be deported. Asscher and Cohen then issued orders to select seven thousand of their staff.

Assisted by this divide-and-rule tactic, the Germans ensured that the majority of Jews in the Netherlands were deported with little protest. This picture of thousands of Jews being sent to their deaths without any struggle has contributed to the notion that there was virtually no Jewish resistance. It should be remembered, however, that initially no one was clear about what the Nazis were actually doing with the Jews – a reality that is still beyond imagination. What was clear to everyone was that resistance could lead to immediate execution. Nevertheless, there was considerable resistance, both from the Dutch Jews and from the refugees who had fled Germany and other countries. One of the Jews who saved the lives of many was the German-born Walter Süskind who worked with a group rescuing children from the crèche across the road from the Hollandsche Schouwburg, the former theatre where Jews were rounded up. Indeed, the Jewish Resistance bears comparison with the organized Dutch Resistance. Alongside this struggle to survive came a different reaction from most of the Orthodox Jews, who saw the persecutions in terms of the Eternal One and his relation to the Jewish People: they adopted an attitude of pious acceptance. In their view, the sufferings of the Jewish people would hasten the coming of the Messiah and that would finally bring about the salvation of the people of Israel. From the early Middle Ages the Jews of Europe had withstood persecution upon persecution supported by this hope.

With hindsight, it would seem that too little was done in Amsterdam to prevent the deportations. The most important act of resistance was the strike held in February 1941 but unfortunately this remained an isolated incident. The Dutch Resistance only really got going in 1943 when the Nazi

Chief rabbi Justus Tal during the first emotional gathering in the Portuguese Synagogue, 7 May 1945.

regulations began to affect the rest of the Dutch population. For most Amsterdam Jews it was already too late. Considering the superior strength of the Germans, resistance was both difficult and dangerous. Nevertheless, it remains extremely painful to realize how little resistance there was and how assiduously the Dutch authorities assisted in the processes involved with deportation. Only 10,000 of the 70,000 Jews living in Amsterdam in 1940 survived the war.

A DECIMATED COMMUNITY

The survivors who emerged from their hiding places and the remnant who returned from the camps were faced with a sense of complete bewilderment at what had happened. They waited for members of their family, for friends and neighbours and beheld the spectacle of Jewish organizations in complete disarray and Jewish buildings and homes looted and plundered. About 10,000 Jews returned to Amsterdam. This figure grew in the 1950s to around 15,000 when Jews who had survived the Nazi terror in other parts of the country moved to Amsterdam because there at least something remained of a Jewish community. The survivors had to cope not only with the total upheaval in their own ranks, they were also confronted by a chilly, formal reaction from both Dutch officialdom and Dutch society. Partly due to the powerful Nazi propaganda of the prewar and war years, during the first postwar years there was a distinctly anti-Semitic wave which, however, did not leave a lasting mark. The Dutch government based its policy after the war on the general idea of being a citizen of the Netherlands, leaving little room to support specifically Jewish needs. Furthermore, it was necessary to rebuild the shattered Dutch country in a general sense, rather than to concentrate on minorities. On the matter of the legal restoration of property to the former Jewish owners, there was much suffering and bitterness. There were heartbreaking legal cases involving the return of children to their natural parents or next-of-kin, after they had been cared for during the war years by non-Jewish foster families. Even these moving stories attracted little attention since for many decades after the war the Netherlands was absorbed by its own suffering under the German occupation, and the role of the Dutch resistance.

In Amsterdam it was a barren climate for Jews but in spite of this before long Jewish life began to emerge once more. Shortly after the liberation of the southern part of the Netherlands in 1944 a Jewish coordinating committee was set up, which initially played a significant part in this re-emergence. In 1946 the Netherlands Israelite Community was refounded in Amsterdam to be followed a year later by the organization for Jewish Social Work. Led by several rabbis and others who had been trained before the war, the Jewish community returned as far as possible to its traditional structures. However, this was not a matter of course. Many people concluded that in view of what had taken place during the war, the only way for Jews to break free from the age-old pattern of persecution and discrimination was by complete assimilation. Yet there were also many who felt that complete acceptance by, and membership of, a fundamentally anti-Semitic Christian culture was a fond illusion. For such people, the only solution was to be found in an exclusively Jewish nation. Important in this context was the founding of the state of Israel in 1948 whereby for the first time in almost two thousand years there was once more a State of Israel. Immediately after the Second World War emigrants flooded into Israel, but this stream soon dwindled. The number of emigrants to America was far larger. In the 1960s the postwar generation of Jews was closely involved with the Jewish homeland, at that time under considerable threat from its neighbours. Emigration to Israel finally settled down to a steady stream, equalled by the return to the Netherlands of disappointed Dutch Jewish emigrants. Since the 1980s the Netherlands has seen an influx of Israelis, often with Dutch backgrounds, and after the fall of the Berlin Wall Jews from Russia and eastern European states have also arrived in increasing numbers.

Thanks to these developments the Jewish community of Amsterdam has on the one hand been partially restored although on the other hand far-reaching changes have taken place. The Holocaust (Shoah) had reduced the sizeable Jewish proletariat to a mere fraction and after the war the age-old vicious circle of poverty was gone forever. Nowadays many Dutch Jews enjoy a relatively high socioeconomic position; they have enjoyed higher education, hold posts in the cultural and academic professions or are successfully employed in branches of business and commerce.

The Jewish community has also had to deal with the secularization process and today we find less than half the Jews living in Amsterdam are members of a religious organization. Furthermore, few of them still pay strict observance to the Jewish laws, such as those regarding kosher food. However, this doesn't mean that the sense of loyalty to the Jewish community and traditions is any the less. Indeed, since the 1980s the sense of having a Jewish identity is certainly on the increase. In family circles Jewish traditions are often respected without there being strict religious observance. The Jewish Social Work organization is important in many social and cultural circumstances where a sense of Jewishness plays a central role. This slots into a general social tendency in which the Welfare State has assumed many tasks that were formerly in the domain of the churches and religious bodies. These include poor relief (charity), education and cultural and leisure activities.

In the case of the Jewish community two further elements should be noted, which are in sharp distinction to the rest of the Dutch population. They are the memory of the Holocaust, the destruction of the Jews in the Second World War, and the creation of the state of Israel. Dutch Jewish writers and historians have recorded the persecutions: Abel J. Herzberg in 1950, Jacques Presser in 1965 and Lou de Jong in his many-volumed history begun in the 1970s. Partly because of these writings the Holocaust has over the years become part of a collective Dutch consciousness; it has developed into one of the major gauges of morality in Dutch society. If one were to put it cynically, the persecution of the Jews has been adopted by the Dutch as their national trauma.

Initially, the Jewish survivors were strongly oriented towards Israel. When the second generation began posing new questions and particularly when Israel turned out to be not just a Jewish dream but a physical state whose politics were open to criticism, this one-sided orientation became more complex. In America, Jewish life was a reality and in Europe it also took shape once more. And in Amsterdam a growing self-awareness came to accompany the Jewish way of life.

The continuation of Judaism, of Jewry, often in new guises, is usually a starting point. One important example of this is the growth of Liberal Judaism. This current within Judaism lays less stress on the ritual practices of the religion and the observance of, for example, the dietary laws, or the many hundreds of prescriptions and regulations. It prefers to emphasize the ethical content of Judaism, as this is taught by the prophets through the Scriptures. In Amsterdam the Liberal Jewish community before the Second World War was a tiny minority; it has in the meantime expanded to become the same size as the Orthodox community. Within the stagnating Dutch Orthodox community the influence of international Jewry has gradually grown stronger partly due to the fact that most of its rabbis have to be recruited from abroad but also through immigration from Israel and eastern Europe. In particular, the Lubavitscher movement has increased in both size and influence. The traditional Jewish groups in Amsterdam have continued, though diminished; among them the relatively stable though small Sephardi community. Together with numerous new, often not directly religious, initiatives of a cultural nature, such as the activities of Amsterdam's Jewish Historical Museum, they give shape to a Jewish community that is once more alive and resilient. As evidence of this, new synagogues have been built, Jewish education has boomed and countless cultural activities are flourishing.

The old Jewish Quarter has only played a small part in this new blossoming. During the Second World War the neighbourhood became totally rundown and after the war ambitious city planners dreamt up all kinds of schemes for it, including building a metro. Not until the end of the 1980s can we speak of a systematic restoration policy. Much of the old Jewish Amsterdam has disappeared and the narrow streets and poky houses where once the proletariat lived their cramped lives have all been redeveloped. But many of the stately old houses are still standing and now fulfil another function in the city. The heart of Jewish Amsterdam has shifted to new neighbourhoods, to the tranquil suburbs of South Amsterdam, in particular Buitenveldert and Amstelveen. Here we find today the only Jewish community in the Netherlands that is enjoying a period of expansion. So here too are the new buildings and centres. They bear witness to the fact that albeit small, Amsterdam's Jewish community is alive and energetic. Today there is still – or maybe once again – a Jewish Amsterdam, a Mokum.

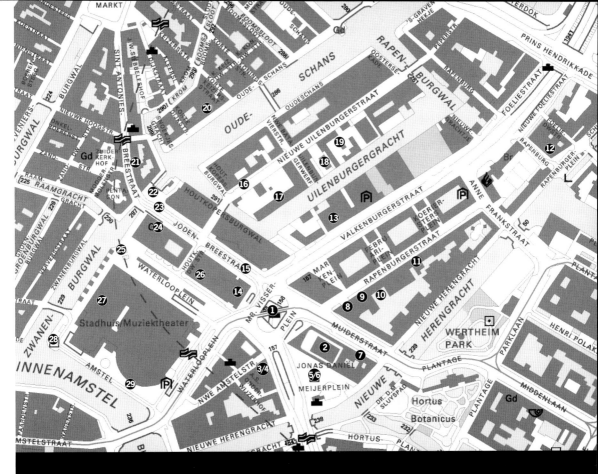

THE OLD JEWISH QUARTER

For centuries the heart of Amsterdam's Jewish Quarter was to be found near Jodenbreestraat (Jews Broad Street) and Deventer Houtmarkt (the wood market), today called Jonas Daniel Meijerplein. This was the home of the Jewish proletariat and the location of the large imposing synagogues. The neighbourhood had its origins in Vlooyenburg, where the first Portuguese Jews, or Sephardim, arrived in around 1600. Nowadays the area is occupied by the comparatively new City Hall cum Opera House but a few centuries ago it was a marshy bog close to the shipbuilding neighbourhood of Amsterdam. Industries related to shipbuilding were housed on the islands of Uilenburg and Marken to the east of the city centre. They moved eastwards in the second half of the 17th century to new artificial islands. The rapidly expanding Jewish proletariat swiftly took over Uilenburg and Marken. With the city extensions of 1662 the city walls as it were shifted outwards, and where formerly bastions and fortresses had stood, there was now open space. In this new free space the rapidly-growing Jewish community was able to construct large synagogues, in full public view. There was almost nowhere else in Europe at that time where Jews could profess their religion so openly. Since the more well-to-do Jews, who were mostly Sephardim, lived on the newly-built canals east of the river Amstel, the synagogues lay at the heart of Jewish Amsterdam, and the old Jewish Quarter gained a strongly proletarian flavour.

This remained unchanged until well into the 19th century. Then the city rapidly expanded and Jews began living in large parts of east and south Amsterdam. Nevertheless, the soul of Amsterdam Jewry nestled in the old Jewish quarter. This only ended with the Nazi terror of the Second World War. Then the homes were raided, the people were deported and killed, and during Amsterdam's bitterly cold Starvation Winter of 1944-45 anything that could be taken was looted from the houses to be used as fuel. As if this were not enough, the sorely deprived neighbourhood fell prey to urban redevelopment schemes in the 1950s and 60s. A huge underpass was designed to link up with the road traffic tunnel under the waters of the IJ, and a station on the new metro line was built close to the Town Hall. The heart was, as it were, carved out of the old Jewish quarter. Happily, the 1990s saw the beginnings of change and reconstruction. New buildings have gone up along Sint-Antoniesbreestraat and Jodenbreestraat. Indeed, some of the city's ugliest postwar monstrosities, such as the so-called Maupoleum building, have been pulled down and replaced by constructions more in line with the historic street plan. Also, the gap created when building the IJ tunnel has now been filled with new buildings. The historic Jewish houses once more stand in a living neighbourhood. The Portuguese (Sephardi) Synagogue is still used; The Ashkenazi synagogue complex has become the city's Jewish Historical Museum.

1 MR L.E. VISSERPLEIN

The Sephardi synagogue and the Ashkenazi complex, unique in Europe, face each other across one of Amsterdam's busiest thoroughfares. The huge roundabout at this point is named after Meester (the Dutch title for a lawyer) Visser. Recently, new buildings have gone up here. The magnificent Jewish buildings no longer stand in splendid isolation as they did for many decades after World War II. Lodewijk Ernst Visser (1871-1942) was a scion of a prominent Jewish family. In 1915 he became a member of the Dutch Supreme Court and in 1939 was appointed President of the highest court of law in the Netherlands. Dismissed from his function by the German occupiers – incidentally there was no protest from the other members of the Supreme Court – he continued to oppose anti-Jewish measures and in particular the stance of the Supreme Court. He worked for the underground press, notably the illegal newspaper *Het Parool*, protested against setting up separate schools for Jews and refused to wear the Star of David sewn onto his clothes, claiming that this form of discrimination was in conflict with the Dutch constitution. When Visser heard about the measures that the Jewish Council were having to take, under instructions from the occupier, he declared:

> *'I am deeply distressed by the humiliations that you, who are well aware of the historical importance of these measures, have brought about by complying with this order.'* A few days later Lodewijk Visser died of natural causes.

2 THE PORTUGUESE (SEPHARDI) SYNAGOGUE

The Portuguese (Sephardi) Synagogue is one of the major Jewish landmark buildings in the Netherlands and is indeed world-famous. Although the Ashkenazi Great Shul is in fact a little older, the Portuguese Esnoga or Snoge, as it is called, has become a symbol for the public profession of the Jewish faith. The building's large size and its imposing architecture reveal the self-confidence of the Sephardi community in Amsterdam as well as the tolerance of the municipal government – for nowhere else in west Europe at that time were Jews able to avow their faith so openly. With the destruction of the Temple in Jerusalem in 70 CE and the subsequent Jewish diaspora the emphasis in Judaism came to lie more and more on the Torah, the written first five books of the Bible, and on the Talmud, the written and verbal commentary passed down by Jewish scholars. The Talmud, begun in the sixth century of the Common Era, continues to be studied and interpreted, thus is not a closed book. The study of these holy teachings, in Yiddish called *lernen*, became the best way for pious Jews to spend their lives. The rabbi became the teacher and the synagogue the place where pious Jews would meet for study and prayer. This also explains the names *scuola* in Italian, in German *Schule,* hence the Yiddish *shul,* indicating that the synagogue was a school, a place where one studied. Thus the actual building housing a synagogue is far less important than what goes on inside it. There the pious learn about every conceivable facet of daily and religious life. A synagogue complex will often contain prayer rooms, study rooms, classrooms and a library. In the Jewish diaspora no one specific architectural style developed and what generally happened was that the forms of local buildings were adopted. The Snoge was constructed under the Amsterdam city architect, Elias Bouwman, between 1671 and 1675. It rose in an empty space formerly occupied by one of the city bastions. Specifically Jewish features were incorporated using symbolic details and can be seen particularly in the front courtyard, which echoes Solomon's Temple in Jerusalem. The low buildings that surround the synagogue comply with the regulation that a synagogue should be higher than the nearby dwellings so that everyone could see it.

The Portuguese *Esnoga* (synagogue) stands out from the surrounding buildings

The impressive interior of the Portuguese Synagogue, showing the *tevah* and Ark, *Ehal*

The Hebrew text above the Snoge entrance is taken from Psalm 5 and reads, 'But as for me, I will come into thy house in the multitude of thy mercy.' The year 5432 (1672) and the name of the rabbi who initiated the Snoge building, Aboab, are woven into the text. The gateway on Muiderstraat dates from the 19th century and is decorated with a pelican feeding its young with the blood of its breast – the symbol of the Sephardi community of Amsterdam. It is the work of the famous sculptor Joseph Mendes da Costa (1863-1939). The interior of the Snoge is almost completely in its original state. People are greatly struck by the remarkable light that floods the building, something one would not suspect from its somewhat heavy classical exterior. The large windows let in ample daylight. Four stone pillars support the vaulted roof. The women's gallery rests upon twelve individual pillars, which represent the twelve tribes of Israel. The interior of the synagogue emphasizes the importance of study. The

seats all face towards the *bimah*, or *tevah* as Sephardi Jews call it, a small platform where the Torah readings are held and prayers are recited. Opposite this on the east side is the richly decorated Holy Ark, inside which the Torah scrolls are kept. During religious services hazzan, or cantor, leads the singing and reading. The rabbi, as teacher and scholar in the Law, occupies a place of honour within the community but does not lead the services. Down the centuries the Portuguese Synagogue has been a symbol for the growth of Jewish Amsterdam and has helped to create a certain image of the wealthy Sephardi Jews. This building was the model for many later Sephardi synagogues, such as those in London, in Parimaribo (Surinam), in Willemstad (Curaçao) and New York. Visiting the Netherlands in 1934 Egon Erwin Kisch, a German author and journalist, was full of admiration for the Snoge, which he expressed in his work *Emigrants: place of residence – Amsterdam:*

The historical Ets Hayyim library, still used for study today

The Portuguese Synagogue is not, for instance, like the Altneu Shul in Prague. In no way could it be described as a shabby, shivering, timorous meeting place for illegal immigrants – no, it is a splendid construction, a Jewish cathedral... The nave, supported by pillars of hewn granite, reaches to the heavens and resembles those churches in Iberia where Jews of yore were dragged in to hear sermons of conversion to Christianity, or to be forcibly baptized.

The synagogue services are illuminated by 613 candles, a costly and old-fashioned method of lighting, to be sure, but it's not going to be changed – that's how it was done in Granada and in Lisbon, and that's how it'll be done here. And because that was the way in Granada and Lisbon, here too the rabbi wears escarpins [shoes like pumps], silk stockings and buckle shoes, the officials wear the flat stiff Jesuit cap with curving brim and those serving in the temple wear a tri-

corne just as formerly the Guardia Reale (royal guard) did in Spain, and today is worn by members of the Guardia Civile.

The synagogue was in continuous use from its opening until May 1943. The Nazis considered using the building as a deportation centre, but decided against this because it had no electric lighting. So the Hollandsche Schouwburg was chosen instead and the beautiful synagogue was left unmolested. Remarkably, it survived all the lootings and plunderings and the dire Starvation Winter of 1944-45. Even the Torah scrolls with their elaborate brocade covers and jewelled decorations were left untouched throughout the war. The Snoge is still used today by the Sephardi community. The building has been twice renovated, in the 1950s and 1990s. During wintertime another building is used – the small winter synagogue in one of the annexes – because the Snoge is too large and difficult to heat. Initially the winter synagogue was a lecture hall for

The Great Shul and the New (*Neie*) Shul, today part of the Jewish Historical Museum

the Ets Hayyim seminary. The 1955 restoration transformed it into an impressive small synagogue. Some of the furnishings came from Amsterdam's very first public synagogue on Houtgracht canal (today Waterlooplein) which was consecrated in 1639.

Beside the winter synagogue you'll find the world-famous library Ets Hayyim (meaning Tree of Life). The brotherhood Ets Hayyim was founded in 1637 to help needy students with their studies. Due to lack of funds, those attending the Talmud Torah (Study of the Law) established in Amsterdam in 1616 often found it difficult to continue their studies. The training course qualified you to be a rabbi, teaching Hebrew and Bible studies. But many were unable to complete the course. Later, Ets Hayyim would also support students at the seminary. Across the years the library here has grown to be one of the finest collections of Sephardi Jewish books and manuscripts in the world and is essential for Jewish studies. In particular, David Montezinos (1828-1916) made an indispensable contribution to the collection. Ets Hayyim-Livraria Montezinos not only had an impressive number of books but also an important collection of manuscripts and engravings. During World War II the chief treasures were hidden, while much was transported to Frankfurt in Germany, to the *Institut zur Erforschung der Judenfrage*. The purpose of this quasi-scholarly institute was to carry out research into Jewish culture and the 'Jewish Question' after the Jews had been exterminated. When the war was over the collection was returned virtually intact and can presently be admired in a good condition in its original home. Finally, the mikveh, or ritual bath, dating from 1891 is still in use, housed in one of the annexes on Jonas Daniel Meijerplein; it replaces an older mikveh.

3 THE ASHKENAZI SYNAGOGUE COMPLEX

Since 1987 the synagogues built for the Ashkenazim have housed the Jewish Historical Museum Amsterdam. The largest synagogue complex of Europe is once more a centre of learning and discovery, after standing deserted and desolate for forty years. The complex consists of two large and two small synagogues, which have been linked using modern architecture.

The oldest of the synagogues, the Great Shul dating from 1671, stands at the corner of Nieuwe Amstelstraat. It is recorded that from 1635 on Ashkenazi Jews held religious meetings in their homes on Vlooyenburg. Soon these developed into small, often secret, shuls. When these became too small the Ashkenazi community was granted permission to erect a large house of prayer on an empty plot of ground. The fine classical building was the first synagogue in west Europe to be built in full public view – no more hiding. The synagogue was designed by the city architects Daniel Stalpaert and Elias Bouwman, the latter also designing the Portuguese synagogue across the road. The architecture is characteristic of its period. The four pillars mark the shape of the Greek cross, a frequently used shape in Amsterdam (church) buildings of the time. The furnishing of the interior emphasizes the building's length. On the east side, which faces towards Jerusalem, lay the Ark, Aron Hakodesh, where the Torah scrolls are kept. On the other sides were the galleries for women (in Orthodox Judaism, women and men sit in separate parts of the synagogue so as not to distract each other). In the centre stood the bimah, the small platform where the Torah is read. The mikveh, or ritual bath, was on the Nieuwe Amstelstraat side of the building. Not long after the consecration of the Great Shul its rapidly growing congregation was splitting the seams. So in 1686 to 1688 a smaller shul was built above the meat market which stood behind the Great Shul. This Obbene Shul (obbene is Yiddish for 'upper') was a compact building with two galleries running down opposite sides. Before long even this building

couldn't cope with the numbers, so in 1700 a third synagogue (Dritt Shul) was consecrated in two houses on Nieuwe Amstelstraat, and in 1777 this was replaced with a new building. Since 1740 the classrooms of Bet Hamidrash Ets Hayyim (College of the Tree of Life) were also located there. For hundreds of years this was the centre of lernen, the place where Jews studied the Torah and the teachings of Jewish scholars. Ets Hayyim thus occupied a central place in the religious culture of Jewish Amsterdam, and this didn't change when in 1883 it moved to Rapenburgerstraat. The crowning glory of the synagogue complex was the Neie (New) Shul in 1730, for which several dwellings were taken over and adapted. The building which stands there today, with its impressive dome designed by the architect G.F. Maybaum, dates from 1752. The Neie Shul is the largest of the four synagogues and with its dome and its entrance flanked by Ionic columns, is certainly the grandest. Above the door are words from Psalm 118:20, This is the gate of the Lord into which the righteous shall enter and above that from Psalm 53, Oh, that the salvation of Israel were come out of Zion. The design strongly resembles that of the Great Shul, the major difference being that the galleries only run down the long sides. The light falling through the cupola creates a wondrous sense of space.

Although the four synagogues form one complex, they in fact belonged to different communities, each having their own rabbi and cantor. The elegant Grote Shul was the seat of the chief rabbi and the parnasim, the leaders of the community. The Neie Shul was one rung down the ladder, while the Obbene and Dritt Shul were typical proletarian synagogues. Within the Jewish community the fact that people could so openly profess their various religion led to a great devotion to the Dutch government and in particular to the royal House of Orange. In his writing titled The Jonas Daniël Meijerplein, Dutch author Jaap Meijer (1912-1993) cites the speech made in 1924 by chief rabbi Onderwijzer on the occasion of a visit by Queen Wilhelmina of the Netherlands to the Great Shul:

'In this manner and according to Jewish tradition the synagogue weaves the unbreakable bond of

love and trust between your Majesty and your Jewish subjects. In accordance with Jewish tradition. For the learned teachers of Israel have taught us most aptly the respect and honour that we owe to our Queen, in the words of the Bible, where it says in the book of Chronicles, 'Solomon was seated upon the throne of the Eternal One'... When the word is fulfilled that is spoken in the Psalms, "Grant, O Lord, to Solomon the King, thy judgements". ... When the king, notwithstanding his power, whereby he could make his will into law, nevertheless chooses the lofty principles of pure justice to be his guide, then his throne becomes a holy seat which, raised aloft, fills everyone with awe and fear. Therefore, Ma'am, those who across the years have attended this synagogue have always served the renowned House of Orange with love and loyalty. In times when elsewhere violent storms threaten the

Torah scroll in the Jewish Historical Museum

House of Jacob, through the years and to this very day the sceptre of Orange was like a holy symbol that guaranteed the strictest and strongest justice here, including for members of the Jewish faith.'

In the course of the 20th century synagogue attendance in the old complex declined, partly due to growing secularization and partly because Jews moved away to live in other neighbourhoods, where they built new synagogues. From 1936 on the Neie Shul was only used on high holidays. The Obbene Shul was used as a classroom for a youth group while the Dritt Shul replaced the one on Waterlooplein, which had to be sold. During the war the synagogue complex fell into disuse. The last service to be held in the Great Synagogue took place in 1943. Later on, the buildings were plundered and at the end of the war presented a spectacle of ruin and desolation. Sadly, all that has survived of the original interior of the Great Shul is the splendid Ark. This is probably because it's made of marble and couldn't be used as fuel in the cold winters of the war. After a long process of negotiation, in 1955 the municipality of Amsterdam bought the empty complex. For a considerable time they weren't sure what to do with the buildings. Finally in 1974 it was decided that this could be the location for the city's Jewish Historical Museum. It was to take another thirteen years to restore the severely damaged buildings, but in May 1987 the new museum was opened.

4 THE JEWISH HISTORICAL MUSEUM

When in the 1920s the slums of Amsterdam's Jewish Quarter were being cleared, the idea was born that aspects of traditional Jewish life in the Netherlands, which at that time was fast changing, should be recorded in a museum devoted to this topic. In 1932 a Jewish Historical Museum was opened by Alderman Emanuel Boekman, housed on the top floor of the Weigh-house on the large market square, Nieuwmarkt. During the Second World War the young museum's collection was removed to Germany and only a small part of it was ever recovered. Since the museum's re-opening in 1955 the collection has grown considerably with acquisitions from the many Dutch synagogues that closed during the war, never to re-open. The museum has also received many donations and objects on permanent loan. The former synagogue complex provides a setting in which these objects can be appropriately displayed. The four separate synagogues have been linked with each other and the small alleyways running between the buildings have been covered in with glass. Every effort has been made to preserve the individual nature of the four buildings. By using modern materials, a clear distinction has been drawn between the historic architecture and the contemporary additions. The mingling of old and new has been consciously planned in order to express the notion of Jewish history – temporarily fractured during the war years – recovering and healing. The Jewish Historical Museum expressly aims to be a museum of the living that presents contemporary developments in Judaism. As well as its function of preserving and presenting the past, the museum is actively involved in organizing lectures, films and activities for young people.

You enter the museum from Shulgasse, a narrow pedestrian way running between the Great Shul and the New Shul. The space inside the New Shul is used for temporary exhibitions. The gallery is home to the youth section of the museum, which was awarded a prize by one of the major Dutch foundations that assists cultural endeavours, the Prince Bernhard Cultural Fund. The Great Shul, with the Ark entirely restored to its original state, retains an impressive atmosphere of a Jewish house of prayer. Here the finest examples of the large collection of Jewish religious objects are on display. Jewish festivals, such as the Sabbath, the New Year (Rosh Ha-Shanah), the Day of Atonement (Yom Kippur), the Feast of Tabernacles (Sukkot) and the winter festival of dedication (Hanukkah) are all given their place. Many of the Jewish laws that the pious observe daily are also recorded, such as the binding on of

Inside the Great Synagogue, view of the women's gallery

the phylacteries before morning prayers, and the rituals observed in connection with birth, marriage and death. Then a section deals with the synagogue and objects used in various ceremonies. The most beautiful of these objects on display date from the 17th and 18th century. The embroidered damask covers for the Torah scrolls, the silver finials, the crowns, shields, pointers (*yadaim*), goblets and platters are displayed in the showcases standing at the centre of the shul. One of these showcases holds modern ceremonial objects. The painting *Interior of the Great Synagogue*, 1935, by the Dutch artist Martin Monnickendam captures the ambience of bygone days.

The gallery houses a display dealing with the topic of Jewish identity. Following the dispersion of the Jews and the destruction of the Temple in Jerusalem, Judaism came to rely on the traditions of the Torah and teachings of Jewish scholars, which were continually adapted to contemporary circumstances. Thus such a thing as uniformity of belief was well nigh impossible. The display examines the three main branches of Judaism: the traditional (Orthodox); the Conservative (moderates) and the Progressive (Liberals). The Jewish dream of a home in Jerusalem and Israel stems from biblical times and has endured through the centuries. Anti-Semitism, especially in the late 19th and 20th century, only served to strengthen this longing. Born in the 19th century, political Zionism had as goal the formation of a Jewish homeland in Israel, which became reality in 1948. Since then Jewish identity has been inextricably connected with contemporary events in Israel. The exhibition illustrates the element of 'persecution and survival' using documents and photographs showing how during the occupation of the Netherlands in World War II, Jews were first isolated as a group within Dutch society, and then deported and killed. There is also a section dealing with the Dutch concentration camp at Westerbork, and the difficulties faced by Jewish survivors in reconstructing their lives after the war. The individual's personal history and its influence on the feeling of Jewish identity is also examined. This is done using written self-portraits, for example the diaries of Etty Hillesum, photographs and written sources. The interaction with Dutch culture is explored by examining the lives of several individuals, which combine Jewish and Dutch influences. The impoverished Ashkenazi Jews tended to hold on longer to their traditions than did the Sephardim, who with their initially higher social status were more quickly accepted into Dutch society. The museum is planning to create a printroom, which will illustrate the work of the remarkable artist Charlotte Salomon (1917-1943), born and trained in Berlin, who escaped to join her grandparents in France in 1939. The suicide of Charlotte's grandmother shortly after her arrival in France prompted the young artist to make a pictorial autobiography, in a series of over seven hundred gouaches titled *Life? or Theatre?* The mikveh, or ritual bath, can be seen close to the former main entrance into the shul on Nieuwe Amstelstraat; it was uncovered during restoration work. The mikveh is important in religious (Orthodox) Judaism, since in that branch women are considered unclean after menstruation and childbirth, and must be purified before they again have sexual intercourse. There are fewer rules for men concerning ritual purification in the mikveh. The bath should be filled with running water and in Amsterdam rainwater was led through wooden gutters to flow through the mikveh. On the wall of the mikveh is a tile picture possibly dating from the 17th century illustrating cleansing or immersion in the mikveh. The Obbene Shul is now a kosher café run by Theeboom's under rabbinical supervision (ORT). It serves lunches and light snacks in accordance with the Jewish dietary laws. Here too is a museum shop with an excellent assortment of books and postcards on Jewish topics. Both café and bookshop can be visited without entering the museum itself. In the new section of the complex is a library containing books, audiovisuals and archival material, which can be accessed through the museum. The Dritt Shul is now the administrative quarters of the museum. At the back of the complex, new apartments have been built to form a courtyard, the A.S. Onderwijzerhof, called after the chief rabbi of Amsterdam from 1917 to 1934.

5 JONAS DANIEL MEIJERPLEIN

Between the Portuguese and the Ashkenazi synagogues lies the large square called Jonas Daniel Meijerplein, where the massive statue of the Dockworker focuses the attention. This square was for centuries the open-air recreation ground of Jewish Amsterdam.
Jonas Daniel Meijer (1780-1834) was a gifted lawyer who gained his doctorate at the tender age of sixteen. Shortly afterwards in 1796, thanks to the Act of Civic Equality, he became the first Jewish advocate in the Netherlands and soon grew to be a renowned legal expert. An important advisor to King Louis Napoleon of the Netherlands, he was one of the driving forces behind the policy of emancipation

Statue of the Dockworker, Portuguese Synagogue in the background

February. During these *razzias*, 425 Jewish 'hostages' were taken prisoner. The roundups were a form of reprisal by the German Occupiers for violent protests by the Dutch against their treatment, in particular the attack on Coco's ice-cream parlour. The Communist Party of the Netherlands in particular called for the strike. In their pamphlets they called for the release of the Jews who had been arrested and urged solidarity with Jewish workers. The first to lay down their tools were those working in the dockyards (the longshoremen), swiftly followed by the public transport workers. The strike spread to the nearby cities of Haarlem, Zaandam and Utrecht, and the region of the Gooi. The Dutch Communist Party tried to give the strike a general character for example by demanding a rise in wages, but the Party lost its grip on the organization. Things turned more and more into an anti-German revolt which was forcefully put down by the Nazis. The Jews who were taken prisoner were deported to Mauthaussen death camp. The strike is commemorated each year on 25 February and there is a solemn march past the statue of the Dockworker. It has grown into a remembrance not only of the Nazi reign of terror but also into a general protest against discrimination and oppression of minorities.

for the Dutch Jews. Under King Willem I of the House of Orange, Jonas Daniel Meijer was the only Jew to be a member of the Committee of Notables and was also secretary of the committee for the Reform of the Constitution. In all these offices he championed the cause of Jewish equality within Dutch society.

6   THE DOCKWORKER

Standing among stately old trees at the centre of Jonas Daniel Meijerplein is the statue of the Dockworker, a powerful determined figure. The statue, made by Mari Andriessen, was unveiled in 1952 by the former queen of the Netherlands, Juliana. It is a memorial to the February protest strikes held in 1941, which were organized after the first roundups of Jews in Amsterdam on 22 and 23

7   THE DE CASTRO APOTHECARY

In one of the small houses built in the shadow of the Portuguese Synagogue, at number 14, Muiderstraat, is De Castro's pharmacy. It was founded in 1832 by Daniel Henriques de Castro (1806-1863), who like his nephew David, was a scion of one of the most notable Sephardi families of Amsterdam. There were frequent cholera epidemics in 19th-century Amsterdam, and many poor Jews living in the crowded slums fell victim to the disease. De Castro fought hard to save as many people as possible and was awarded the silver medal of the Cholera Committee of the City of Amsterdam for his efforts. He was also an active member of the Sephardi community, among other things holding the position of parnas. Interestingly,

Rapenburgerstraat showing the Jewish Seminary, the shul and the Girls' Orphanage

he was also one of Holland's most skilled 19th-century glass engravers. In Amsterdam's Rijksmuseum and Jewish Historical Museum you can see examples of his beautifully engraved glasses. His house was later home to J. Vita Israel, art collector and one of the founders of the Jewish Historical Museum.

8 THE NETHERLANDS ISRAELITE SEMINARY

The training to be a rabbi is considered one of the most important traditions in Judaism. Initially, the training in Amsterdam was given by the Bet Hamidrash Ets Hayyim, where everyone could study Torah and the Jewish law. After 1740 Bet Hamidrash was housed in the Dritt Shul on Nieuwe Amstelstraat. In the 19th century the Dutch government did not officially recognize this internal Jewish training as being the equivalent of a theological seminary and the students were not, for instance,

exempted from military service. Under pressure from the Dutch government it was decided to transform the training school into the independent Netherlands Israelite Seminary. This opened in 1839 in the building at numbers 175-179, Rapenburgerstraat, which was presented by David Hollander.

The Seminary gained an authoritative voice under the leadership of Dr J.H. Dünner (1833-1911). In 1862 Dünner was appointed head of the seminary and ten years later became chief rabbi of Amsterdam. He remained a leading figure in the Jewish community until his death. Following the German tradition, Dünner introduced the Gymnasium (compare English Grammar School) school system, which in due time produced many excellent rabbis. In this way the Netherlands Israelite Seminary made a considerable contribution to the preservation of Judaism in an age of increasing integration and assimilation. However, Dünner's approach was also criticized. Because he laid such emphasis on a thorough classical education the character of official Judaism assumed a highly intellectual tone. This led to an even greater distancing from the proletariat. The Netherlands Israelite Seminary continued until the Second World War. The last sixty students were almost without exception deported and killed. Since then there hasn't been a rabbinical training college in the Netherlands. The fine building has been thoroughly restored and little remains to tell of its former purpose. It is now used as an office.

9 RAPENBURG SHUL

The house at number 173, with its brick picture-frame façade, four huge windows and impressive central steps leading to the front door, is the Rapenburg synagogue. This shul is primarily known for being the seat of the chief rabbi in Amsterdam. Interestingly, it was founded by liberal Jews who in the time of the Enlightenment at the close of the 18th century also founded the society called *Felix Libertate* (Latin, meaning 'Happy in Freedom') which aimed to secure equality for Dutch Jews. This group wished to see certain reforms, such as the use of the Dutch language in Jewish religious services, but these were not accepted by the Jewish community. The conflict eventually resulted in a schism. The liberal Jews formed the so-called Community of Israel, the Neie Kille or Adath Jeshurun. They first met in the home of Lopez Suasso on Nieuwe Herengracht but in 1799 acquired the use of premises on Rapenburgerstraat. The Neie Kille was extremely critical of the power of the parnasim and for that reason their synagogue contained no separate seats for the leaders. This breakaway community had its own cemetery outside Amsterdam in Overveen. Partly due to the negotiations of Jonas Daniel Meijer the two Jewish communities were reunited in 1808 by order of King Louis Napoleon under the central authority of a Supreme Consistory. Then the synagogue became the Rapenburg Shul and later the Supreme

Rabbinate was established there. The building, like so many others, was looted in the war. In 1950 it was converted into offices, thereby losing almost every vestige of its former character. However, a magnificent Star of David still adorns the floor of the entrance hall.

10 THE GIRLS' ORPHANAGE

Early in 2003, sixty years after its desolation, the house at numbers 169 to 171 Rapenburgerstraat had two memorial plaques affixed to the façade. These record that the buildings were once the home of Dutch Jewish orphan girls. The history of the girls' orphanage dates from 1761 when the Netherlands Israelite Orphan Girls College was founded under the motto 'The education of orphan girls is among the good works.' This form of zedakah, or charity, is based on the com-

The elegant gallery in the orphan girls' Home

Former Girl's Orphanage showing stones set in façade and roof ridge-beam

mand in the Torah to care for widows and orphans and distinguishes the Jewish community down the centuries. Traditionally, orphans were cared for by close relatives or neighbours, who would be given a contribution towards their upkeep by the Foundation. The girls were taught Religion until they were eleven years old by a teacher who came to the house, and after that at a state school.

By 1861 it was no longer possible to maintain this system. So the Netherlands Israelite Orphan Girls' Home was opened on Rapenburgerstraat. It only took in children whose parents had been members of the Jewish congregation. Many people couldn't afford the contribution and so weren't members. This explains the small number of orphan girls living in the home. Initially there were thirty girls, who worked in the sewing or knitting room. They were given a strict Orthodox upbringing and taught to be grateful to their patrons. Like Amsterdam's Civic Orphans who lived in what is today the Amsterdam Historical Museum, the girls had to wear uniform. Their lessons were also given in the home; to begin with they were only taught what might be useful to them as a future maidservant, but later they could follow higher education. In accordance with the norms of the day, the girls had a stern upbringing but the kind of extremes that frequently occurred in some orphanages, including children being sold for hard labour and being put under lock and key, do not seem to have happened here.

Following the 1920 Education Act it was decided to close the school in the home and send the girls to schools for Jewish education or to one of the state schools in this largely Jewish neighbourhood. This measure helped to reduce the girls' social isolation. Then in 1926 the building was rebuilt and the now superfluous classrooms were removed, while an attractive entrance hall and staircase were created. On 10 February 1943 the eighty or so girls living in the house were arrested by the Nazis. A few managed to escape through the garden. Almost all the rest of them were taken away and killed. Recently the building was converted into apartments. The façade with the plaques and the Hebrew text run-

ning along the roof ridge-beam, the well-preserved main staircase and the former governors' room – now a café – are the chief reminders of what was once a home for orphan girls.

11 BET HAMIDRASH ETS HAYYIM

In spite of the radical rebuilding that took place in 1973, the former Bet Hamidrash Ets Hayyim (College of the Tree of Life) has retained its imposing exterior bearing the Jewish date for the year 5643 (1883) on the central pillars. The Bet Hamidrash Ets Hayyim was established in 1740 by the Ashkenazi community to promote the study of Torah and the Jewish laws, which form the nub of Jewish religion and culture. The theological centre became a pivot of study in Jewish Amsterdam. For those who wished to become a rabbi a special society was set up in 1760, called Saadat Bachurim,

Bet Hamidrash Ets Hayyim

Jewish date written on building façade

Here the weekly newspaper *Nieuw Israëlietisch Weekblad* now has its headquarters. The NIW is the oldest Dutch weekly in existence. It was founded in 1865 (5625) as a counterpart to the more liberal paper *Weekblad voor Israëlieten*, which had started ten years previously. The motto of the NIW was: *'To inform you about the real truth'*. The paper was supported by Dr Dünner and opposed the many arguments for change that were gradually creeping into Dutch Jewry. The paper also opposed Zionism. It devoted a great deal of attention to everyday events in the Dutch Jewish communities and in this way became the newspaper of the Jewish Netherlands. At the beginning of the 20th century about one third of all Jewish households was subscribed to the NIW. During the 1930s the editorial board of the NIW had great reserves about the arrival of Jewish refugees from Germany because they saw this as a threat to Dutch Jewry. Not until 1938 did the paper evince a positive attitude towards Zionism. After October 1941 the NIW was banned. The newspaper *Het Joodsch Weekblad*, a weekly under the censorship of the Jewish Council, was printed until the end of 1943. Phoenix-like, the NIW reappeared as early as 17 May 1945. Today the paper has around 6,000 subscribers and is generally considered to be a mouthpiece of Jewish Netherlands. All back files of the NIW can be consulted in the Bibliotheca Rosenthaliana.

which later developed into the independent Netherlands Israelite Seminary. Initially, the Bet Hamidrash Ets Hayyim was housed in the Dritt Shul. In 1883 it moved into a building designed in eclectic styles by father and son Salm, at number 109, Rapenburgerstraat. Classrooms, lecture halls, library and a synagogue with richly decorated façade were constructed. The theological college became an important stimulus for Jewish study, or *lernen*, at a time when Dutch culture was playing an increasingly important part in Jewish life. Like almost all Jewish buildings during the Second World War, Bet Hamidrash Ets Hayyim also ceased to function. Afterwards the premises were taken over by a factory and drastically rebuilt. However, it was restored in 1973. The part which had formerly been a synagogue gained an added floor at the level of the women's gallery and is now used as an office. The ceiling on the second floor still bears the wooden shields of David. The main building of the complex has partly regained its Jewish cultural purpose.

12 THE RAPENBURG NETHERLANDS ISRAELITE HOSPITAL

The modest corner house at number 9, Rapenburgerplein has a stone set in its side wall bearing a picture of a pelican pecking its breast and feeding its young with its blood. The picture was used by the Sephardi community to refer to the charitable nature of this building, which housed the first Jewish hospital. In 1804 the hospital was founded with money raised from private sources. It was a small house, nursing both the mentally and physically ill. In 1885 the hospital moved into much roomier premises on Nieuwe Keizersgracht. The

Portuguese Israelite Hospital, with plaque on wall of Pelican feeding her young with her own blood (see page nr. 8)

Moses, one of the wall plaques from the outside of Moses and Aaron Church

then much smaller Sephardi community had the Rapenburgerplein hospital at their disposal. It was at this time that the painted plaque was put up. Then in 1916 the Sephardi community moved from this small hospital to a larger one on Plantage Franschelaan, today Henri Polaklaan.

13 NUMBERS 200-210, VALKENBURGERSTRAAT

The block numbering 200-210 Valkenburgerstraat was built in 1877. Its Jewish background is revealed by a plaque in the façade bearing the Dutch date side by side with the Jewish year of 5638. A further plaque records that the first stone of the house was laid by Mietje W. Speyer and Elisabeth J. Speyer. The building was one of the more well-to-do dwellings in the largely poverty-stricken Valkenburgerstraat, which with its almost totally Jewish population belonged to the very core of Jewish Amsterdam. This dwelling was one of the

few to survive the slum clearances that began in the 1920s and were completed after World War II.

14 MOSES AND AARON CHURCH

At the beginning of Jodenbreestraat stands the church of Moses and Aaron and because it is plumb in the middle of the Jewish quarter people often take it for a synagogue. But it is a Roman Catholic church, dedicated to St Anthony of Padua. Its popular name, the Moses and Aaron Church, comes from the two carved plaques that are set in the back wall, which were taken from the facades of nearby houses where once Jews lived. After the historic 'Alteration' of 1578, when the city of Amsterdam came down on the Protestant side in the religious wars, Roman Catholics were no longer able to practise their religion openly. Many religious minorities had to find hidden places of worship. From 1649 the Catholics had one of their hidden churches in the house called *Moyses* and this later expanded to the house called *Aaron*.

The fact that there was a sizeable Catholic church in the Jewish Quarter suggests that this neighbourhood was never one hundred percent Jewish, but rather, was the home of the poor and minority groups. Evidently, the majority of these were Jews. In 1841 the Catholic church was built in its present classical style and the old stone plaques showing Moses and Aaron were set into the back wall on Jodenbreestraat. The Roman numerals I - X refer to the Ten Commandments. Some Hebrew characters can be discerned by the figure of Aaron.

15 JODENBREESTRAAT

The havoc that has been created in the old Jewish Quarter is nowhere so clearly to be seen as on Jodenbreestraat. From the 17th century on this street, with its famous open-air market, was the centre of the Jewish Quarter. Indeed, for many people it symbolized Jewish Amsterdam. The writer, feminist and trade-union activist Sani van Bussum (1876-1933) caught this atmosphere succinctly in her book *Een bewogen vrijdag op de Breestraat* (A Busy Friday on Broad Street):

> *Friday morning in the wee small hours, people are putting up stalls…there's so much to be done. The boards must be laid out across the packing cases, all the baskets must be lined with clean newspaper, the fruit must be arranged attractively, so that the oranges whose scent wafting towards you makes your heart lift, stand out among the luxuriant bunches of grapes and the soft blushing peaches… Glory be, what a display! It's a work of art! The passers-by just have to stop and gaze and their shopping baskets open of their own accord and their mouths begin to water and out comes their money. Then they buy this and that and the stallholders have a blessed Friday with enough money earned by the end of the day to make a good Shabbat!*

All that has gone. Even before the war the run-down neighbourhood was becoming poorer and those who could afford it were moving to other districts.

During the war almost all the local inhabitants – most of them very poor – were deported and killed. The houses – particularly in the Starvation Winter of 1944-45 – were looted and half demolished. The Dutch poet Ed Hoornik must already have heard the curtain fall when he wrote prophetically in 1938:

> The Jewish Broad Street is a deep ravine,
> I see my shadow dancing on the walls.
> The train to Berlin only takes ten hours.

After the war the most dilapidated house were pulled down. The east side, in particular, disappeared completely to make room for a considerable widening of the street. Thanks to recent redevelopments of the buildings put up in the postwar period, Jodenbreestraat looks a great deal better. The premises at number 140 were extensively renovated and early in 2003 the restaurant *Jerusalem of Gold* was reopened. Once more there is a kosher place to eat in the old Jewish quarter. Like the recently opened *King Solomon* restaurant on Waterlooplein, the menu at *Jerusalem of Gold* is largely Mediterranean and aimed at Amsterdam's many tourists. The new building at number 16 has a stone plaque on the façade inscribed with a Hebrew text, which is repeated in Dutch on the glass below. The words are from Pslam 137 verse 5: 'If I forget thee, O Jerusalem, let my right hand forget her cunning.' All that remains of the textile wholesalers De Vries Van Buren's at number 8 is the façade which has been merged into the new building now used by Holland Experience. In 1829 De Vries and Van Buren started a haberdasher's shop – selling sewing thread, tape, lace and caps. It was one of many such Jewish ventures in the neighbourhood. But De Vries and Van Buren gradually grew into a famous wholesalers supplying wares to the many stallholders working in the Jewish quarter. In 1882 they added a new building and also bought up the adjoining premises at numbers 10 and 12. The business ended in the war. Only the façade survived the postwar slum clearance. Finally, the façade plaque on the corner house at number 2, with the Jewish date of 5649 (1889) is a reminder of its former Jewish inhabitants.

16 NIEUWE UILENBURGERSRAAT

After the slum clearances of the 1920s on Uilenburg we hear mention of the 'new' street, Nieuwe Uilenburgerstraat. The original Uilenburgerstraat, although run-down and poverty-stricken, had a richly textured Jewish street life, which appealed strongly to the imagination. In particular the Sunday market, which straggled through into the nearby streets of Jodenhouttuinen and Jodenbreestraat, largely determined people's picture of Jewish Amsterdam. However, those with socialist tendencies were extremely critical of the not-so-romantic poverty of this neighbourhood. Such attitudes are powerfully presented in the writings of Herman Heijermans (1864-1924), one of Holland's greatest dramatists, famous for his stage plays presenting life in the raw. Heijermans did not share in the ideas of 'art for art's sake'. As he saw it, art had a social function. A socialist himself, he brought a sharply critical approach to all his work. He was no less critical of the Jewish milieu in which he had grown up and this can be seen in his books *Een jodenstreek?* (1892) (this can mean both a Jewish neighbourhood and, in a pejorative sense, a typically Jewish way of behaving…) and *Diamantstad* (Diamond City) (1898):

> It aroused faint, uncomfortable memories of another Jewish elementary school where he had learnt how to spell God in Hebrew letters – the Jewish commandments – where they felt frightened when the rabbi arrived on a visit, not daring to speak if one of the inspectors was standing in front of the class, one of those gentlemen-supervisors whose nice polite manner he now so thoroughly detested. How long ago would it have been? How long? Wasn't it as if everything had happened recently? Didn't he see himself sitting there, a shy awkward boy, too old for his age, with puffy face and rings under his eyes? Hadn't he too crawled out of one of those disgusting slum houses, its wood worm-eaten and soggy with rot, the plaster peeling off the walls, the window panes broken…It all came back to him – taking stale bread in a torn, dirty bag – drinking water from tin jars – sleeping in a narrow bed when you had fallen asleep in the classroom – the Jewish teaching – the Jewish – the commandments – the Ten Commandments – the everlasting Ten Commandments – sitting there like bedraggled parrots on a perch – hands to be kept on top of the table – on top – on top of the table — Then he remembered too how some of the boys already at a very young age would sit rubbing their willie under the table if the teacher couldn't see, then gently swaying and staring with glazed eyes would shudder rhythmically. There had been a boy like that sitting right in front of him. Time after time he would see the shaking back, the shuddering movement, the peculiar curve of the body towards the school bench, the eyes in fiery wide-open ecstasy as the boy looked up, the pale, bony face. They learnt it from each other. For those lads it seemed to be the one delight to be had in their world of filthy bricks and beams and roof tiles known as the Jewish Quarter… Yesterday was like today. The sewers in which humans lived, the rotten carcasses of houses from which some people earned rent, the whole silently decaying, shrieking monument of this capital city spawned children who were doomed to stay here – once a week kneaded into niceness by the gentlemen supervisors, by the rabbi.

The bitter realism of this picture of life in the Jewish quarter, which was all too often romanticized, hardly produced reactions of delight in many Jewish circles; indeed Heijermans's writings were strongly criticized and he was even accused of being anti-Semitic. After the 1901 Housing Act, Uilenburg was the first neighbourhood for which a slum-clearance plan was drawn up. A committee from the department of health declared many of the houses unfit for human habitation and so dilapidated that it wasn't worth renovating them. If possible the residents moved to new working-class neighbourhoods. The new Uilenburgerstraat was completely redeveloped and given some fine new buildings, notably the Public Baths, built in 1923. Under the German occu-

The impressive front of Boas Diamond Factory, today Gassan's: a monument of the Jewish diamond trade

pation in 1941 this was designated a specifically Jewish amenity. It was typical of the Nazi policy to isolate Jews from the rest of Dutch society, before deporting and exterminating them.

17 THE BOAS DIAMOND FACTORY, TODAY GASSAN'S

The back of the new buildings on Jodenbreestraat provides a splendid view onto the former diamond factory of the Boas brothers, which stretched along part of the canal called Uilenburgergracht. Today the factory is still the most impressive building on Uilenburg. When first opened, in 1879, it was the largest diamond-cutting factory in Europe, where about 10,000 carats of diamond were cut and polished each week. The factory building housed 357 diamond-polishing machines, a revolutionary phenomenon in the diamond industry of the day.

Boas and Van Moppes were the first jewellers to build their own factories. For centuries, diamond polishing had been a cottage industry, with women, generally speaking, working the polishing wheel. Like many forms of cottage industry, in the 19th century diamond polishing gradually shifted to become a factory job where the women driving the wheels were replaced by horses. The Diamond Cutting & Polishing Association built the first factory where the polishing wheels were steam-driven. This society was a form of cooperative of which almost all jewellers were member. The jewellers delivered the raw diamond, which was then cut and polished. They would rent a machine from the Diamond Cutting & Polishing Association.

The Boas brothers were the first who risked a solo venture. Encouraged by the bull market caused by the discovery of raw diamond in South Africa in what became known as the Cape Age, they bought

The Boas building and boilerhouse

up various plots of land between Uilenburgerstraat and the canal Houtkopersgracht, where they planned to build a factory. We may gauge the vitality of the diamond market in those days from the fact that apparently Boas recovered all his investments in the factory within a year. The Boas brothers bought the raw diamond themselves, polished it at their own cost and were also responsible for the sale of the cut diamonds. When towards the close of the 19th century the boom began to dwindle and business risks increased in the diamond trade, which was highly sensitive to the economic climate, Boas turned to renting out polishing wheels to freelance diamond workers. The Boas Diamond Factory, designed by architect J.W. Meijer, stands right in the middle of the Jewish quarter and is the largest surviving monument to Amsterdam's diamond industry. The vertical shaft at the centre of the building housed two steam-powered machines, which drove the polishing wheels elsewhere in the factory by means of moving belts. The building's many windows gave ample light, which was essential for the fine work of cutting and polishing the tiny pieces of diamond. The factory is not only interesting as an industrial landmark building, it is also memorable from a social point of view. It provided hundreds of

Jewish families with a staple income, earning enough to finally escape a proletarian existence. The significance of the factory in the Jewish neighbourhood was instanced in 1887 when Boas had a small synagogue, or house of prayer, built on the premises for the Society Agudas Beis Ja'akob (House of Jacob).

In the 1930s Depression the diamond trade, like so many others, collapsed. Other industries replaced diamond polishing in the large Boas factory, among them textile weaving, manufacture of stockings, and the production of bedroom slippers. During the occupation the Nazis attempted to get the diamond business on its feet again for their own profit. This failed and the business was wound up in 1944. Some of the Boas family managed to escape abroad in time but three of the founders' six children were killed in death camps. After the war the building was used as a warehouse for textiles. Early in the 1990s it was taken over by the Gassan firm, who restored the tradition of diamond cutting in a Jewish ambiance. Initially Samuel Gassan was a diamond dealer who worked on the Diamond Exchange. After the war he set up a diamond factory with one eye on the tourist trade. The Boas building, after thorough renovation, offers Gassan increased possibilities such as guided tours through the works. The former Chewre shul, which was very dilapidated, has been pulled down. Although Gassan's employs a number of diamond polishers, the emphasis lies on the sale of diamonds, especially to foreign tourists, who number about 300,000 annually. Guided tours lead visitors through the diamond polishing rooms where the process of production from raw diamond to scintillating brilliant is explained. The differences in quality that emerge during this process are made clear. In the reception hall you can see a plaque commemorating the first stone laid by Boas in 1878, and a bronze head of the founder of today's factory, Samuel Gassan (1910-1983).

18 UILENBURG SHUL

Walk on a little past the Boas Diamond Factory and you come to a high brick wall. Behind this is Uilenburg Shul, consecrated by the Ashkenazim in 1766 as their fifth Amsterdam synagogue. The first four synagogues, on today's Jonas Daniel Meijerplein, now form the Jewish Historical Museum. As early as 1724 there was a shul belonging to the society 'for the giving in marriage of young daughters' which was, however, not officially recognized. But after a number of lawsuits it was decided in favour of the Jewish community and they bought the shul, speedily replacing it with a fine new synagogue. It has two stories, with two ground-floor rooms.

It is not a shul for the wealthy, standing as it does at the heart of the working-class neighbourhood, and it has been home to a wide variety of activities. Weddings have been celebrated here, it has been an 'overflow'synagogue, it has served as a soup kitchen, and was used to hold sessions 'for impecunious eye-patients'. Here too poultry was slaughtered according to Jewish ritual laws. It last saw service as a synagogue for young people during World War II, after which it was completely looted. In 1954 the Amsterdam municipality bought the building to use as a workplace for the municipal department for the restoration of landmark buildings. Later, the synagogue was completely restored; the ground floor is still used as a workshop for historic restoration. Upstairs is the old synagogue with the women's gallery. Where the Aron Hakodesh, the Holy Ark, once stood is the text from the Psalm, written in sober lettering, *I have set the Eternal always before my eyes*. The National Restoration Foundation holds lectures and classes in the former shul. The hall may also be hired for cultural activities. Recently, it has been used increasingly by Jewish bodies and organizations, as well as private individuals.

Once a month a concert of works by Jewish composers is organized here by the Leo Smit Foundation. Leo Smit (1900-1943) was until recently completely unknown but is now reckoned to be one of the Netherlands' outstanding composers from the first half of the 20th century. The highly talented Leo Smit

The people's shul on the island Uilenburg, front courtyard closed

was already teaching at the music conservatory in Amsterdam at the age of 24. Later he spent a few years in Paris, where he came under the influence of French composers. In the 1930s the Concertgebouw Orchestra performed several works by Smit. With the German occupation of the Netherlands, Smit could only function within Jewish circles, for example with the New Jewish Chamber Orchestra. In March 1943 Leo Smit, his wife and father were deported to Auschwitz, where they were killed. His music was forgotten. Not until the 1990s was it rediscovered, thanks largely to the work of the Leo Smit Foundation, which brought out a CD in 2000 with his complete works. Furthermore, a biography of Leo Smit has been published in Dutch. In 1997 the former shul was re-consecrated by having a mezuzah placed at the entrance. Since then it has been used for religious services and meetings by Beit ha'Chidush, a progressive group who search for new answers to the age-old questions of Judaism and life. The original purpose of the building as a synagogue, a place of learning, has thus been partially restored.

19 SOPHIE ROSENTHAL KINDERGARTEN

The small brick building in the grounds of the municipal workplace was until the Second World War the house belonging to the Sophie Rosenthal Kindergarten. A plaque in the wall at the rear records that Robert Heinrich May and Frederik Martinus Cohen laid the first stone for the building on 15 June 1887. The building of the Kindergarden was financed by Sophie Rosenthal-May (1838-1921), widow of the banker George Rosenthal, and the kindergarten was named after this generous benefactress. Standing as it did right in the Jewish quarter, most of the children who attended the kindergarten came from Jewish families. Few of them survived the war and the school lost its function. After the war the school was for sometime in use as a chemical workplace until in 1956 it was decided to pull it down. Only the house survived. Nowadays it is used for storage space.

20 OFFICE OF THE JEWISH COUNCIL 'AID TO EMIGRANTS'

The Jewish Council had several offices in various parts of the city, including the present-day dwelling at number 92, Oudeschans. This was the centre for the section dealing with those 'emigrating' and those 'going' to concentration camps. Here such things were organized as warm clothing and necessary articles to take to the camps, including 'food hampers for the journey'. Such unbelievable phrases, which illustrate the indescribable cynicism of the Nazi system, were apparently intended to give the staff of the Jewish Council and the so-called emigrants the illusion that they were really being offered help, rather than being prepared for deportation and death.

21 DE PINTO HOUSE

The house built for the Jewish merchant family of De Pinto stands exactly at the point in Sint Antoniebreestraat where the street makes a slight kink. It is the sole building in this street that recalls its Jewish past. Before the war, Jews were living in almost every house on Sint Antoniebreestraat and the shopkeepers too were Jewish. With the deportations, the Starvation Winter of 1944-45 and the slum clearances of the 1950s and 60s, as well as the much-disputed building of the metro line, all the historic buildings have gone. Indeed, the De Pinto House almost went too, nearly pulled down to make room for a wide through-road. After stormy protests from the local residents the traffic plans were rejected and De Pinto House was saved. Since that time Sint Antoniebreestraat has been built full again, the houses following the former line of building fronts along the street. De Pinto House was acquired by the De Pinto Foundation who restored it thoroughly in 1975. It was later bought by the Amsterdam Fund for Landmark Buildings. It is presently used as a public library.

The 'Palace of the noble gentleman, Mr De Pinto' is one of the finest examples of the proverbial wealth of the Sephardi merchants, though few of them rivalled the De Pintos in affluence. Isaac de Pinto arrived in Holland from Antwerp in 1646, fleeing the Spanish Inquisition. Initially he and his family settled in Rotterdam, but soon, like the majority of Sephardi Jews, he moved to Amsterdam. There in 1651 he bought the house of Jan Janszoon Carel, one of the founders of the Dutch East India Company. In 1686 Isaac's son David Emanuel de Pinto radically rebuilt the house, giving it the present Italian-Renaissance inspired façade with its six symmetrical pillars and attractive wrought-iron tracery in front of the windows. Inside too the house is sumptuously decorated. The poor folk living in the Jewish Quarter had the saying, 'As rich as De Pinto'.

It was the son of David de Pinto and Lea Ximenes Belmonte, Isaac de Pinto (1717-1787), named after his grandfather, who earned the greatest fame. He was one of the governors not only of the Dutch East

De Pinto House, showing Isaac de Pinto's initials in the wrought-iron fencing

India Company, the VOC, but also of the West India Company, the WIC, and was a personal friend of the Dutch stadholder, Willem IV. As ambassador to the court in Paris he would take part in highly intellectual discussions, for instance with the French philosopher Voltaire. He gained himself an international reputation with trail-blazing contributions to economic questions and in particular for dealing with the financial policy in connection with the National Debt. He was one of the first 'economists' of Europe to propose that a nation's wealth depended not only on its agriculture but could be created by the circulation of money. He proposed the Dutch Republic as model for other European states. With his vast knowledge and many contacts in the non-Jewish world, De Pinto was also a leading figure in the Sephardi community, where he functioned as a parnas.

In the 19th century De Pinto House was used for offices and became sadly neglected. But because few architectural changes were made to it, it was possible to completely restore the house to its original state when it was renovated in 1977. Both the first phase of the building from 1602 under Jan Janszoon Carel as well as that under De Pinto from 1686 can be clearly distinguished inside the house. Especially attractive are the painted ceilings and the splendid marble mantelpiece. The pictures in the front part of the house are original old masters that have been restored; those in the back half of the house are reproductions.

22 THE LOCK-GATES SINT-ANTONIESLUIS

Looking northwards from the lock of Sint-Antoniesluis there is a panorama – unfortunately slightly diminished by the new buildings in view – across the waters of Oude Schans with the Montelban Tower in the background and Uilenburg to the right. The Montelban Tower is a remnant of the former fortifications dating from the early 16th century and was the landmark against the skyline for sailors approaching Amsterdam from the Zuyder Sea. This is why rabbi Moses Uri b. ha-Levi from the German port of Emden made a rendezvous with a group of Amsterdam Sephardi Jews at the Montelban Tower when in 1600 he arrived in the city. He was one of the first to openly live as a Jew in the Netherlands. Tradition has it that the very first synagogue services were held close by the Montelban Tower.

The Oude Schans and the Sint-Antoniesluis lock gates have always formed a kind of unofficial border to the Jewish Quarter. The neighbourhood was never one hundred percent Jewish and also Jews have always lived in districts outside the so-called Jewish quarter. Sometimes this annoyed the non-Jewish residents. Indeed, in 1750 the citizens of Sint-Antoniebreestraat petitioned the city burgomasters to establish a district (a ghetto in other words) where all the Jews could be sent to live:

The Jews, and chiefly the worst and poorest sort among them have for some time now been

Oudeschans and the Montelbaan Tower, from the St. Anthony Lock, with Gosler's House

spreading into the St Anthonys Sluys area where not only does their shabbiness cause the greatest inconvenience to the Christians who live near them but furthermore is highly detrimental to their trade and industries, their crafts and other means of existence... for the Jews have intruded with all kinds of wares and goods including old clothing and rags and patches.

The request was flatly turned down and the Jews of Amsterdam were never forced to live in what amounts to a ghetto. The Sint-Antoniesluis became a centre for a lively street market, particularly dealing in second-hand clothing. Many of these dealers adopted the family name of Sluis or Sluys. The attractively restored house at the lock gates, today a café, formerly called Gosler House, used to be an iron and metal business.

23 MONUMENT TO JACOB ISRAEL DE HAAN

Where Jodenbreestraat joins Sint Antoniesluis you will see a small column standing on a pedestal inscribed with some lines in praise of Amsterdam by the Dutch poet Jacob Israel de Haan (1881-1924). The memorial column was placed here to commemorate 'the spot where the large-scale slum clearances played havoc with the historic shape of the city.' After Jodenbreestraat and the Sint-Antoniesluis had been widened the plan was also to make Sint Antoniesbreestraat broader. Violent protest from the local residents managed to prevent this. Nowadays in the summer time pavement cafés adorn the wide sidewalk of Sint Anthoniesluis.

Jacob Israel de Haan was a complicated character who in many ways reflects the developments taking place within the Jewish community during the early decades of the 20th century. He was born in Smilde, son of a hazzan, or cantor. Like his sister, the famous Dutch writer Carry van Bruggen, his literary talents appeared at an early age. A reclusive figure, Jacob went to live in the neighbourhood of south Amsterdam known as The Pipe. He worked as a schoolteacher, journalist and later as a lawyer and private teacher. Brought up in an Orthodox Jewish family, Jacob grew increasingly alienated from this milieu and became attracted by socialist ideas. His novel *Pijpelijntjes* (the title means something like *Lines from The Pipe* – with a suggestion of oral sex) published in 1904 caused quite a commotion. Because of its direct homosexual revelations the book was withdrawn and Jacob Israel de Haan was dismissed from his job as journalist for the left-wing paper *Het Volk*. Later he once more embraced Judaism and set out for Israel as a convinced Zionist. There he was inspired to write intense poetry, filled with memories of his childhood and religious symbolism. The tension between his religious convictions and his homosexuality continued, and he wrote in Jerusalem:

In Amsterdam it was my holy city.
Here it's a place of secret alleyways.
A passionate people, those seductive boys.
I've always worshipped beauty above holiness.

Finally De Haan also became disillusioned with Zionism; he wrote the lines which are now inscribed on the pillar in Amsterdam:

In Amsterdam he'd often say 'Jerusalem',
Went to that city as a driven man,
Now murmurs softly in low tones,
'Amsterdam, Amsterdam'.

In 1924, on the point of returning to the Netherlands, Jacob Israël de Haan was assassinated by Jewish activists who apparently felt threatened by his ideas.

The Jacob Israel de Haan monument in front of the Rembrandt House, Jodenbreestraat (Jews Broad Street)

24 THE REMBRANDT HOUSE

The Dutch artist Rembrandt van Rijn (1606-1669) lived at the very heart of the Jewish quarter from 1639 to 1660. He owned a house on Breestraat (Broad Street), at that time quite a smart street which gradually gained a more and more Jewish flavour and came to be called Jews Broad Street, or Jodenbreestraat. Today Rembrandt's home is a museum where many of his etchings and some paintings by him and by his contemporaries may be admired. The house was built in 1606. When Rembrandt bought it he was already an established artist receiving important commissions. Later, however, he was to land in deep financial difficulties and was forced to sell the house along with the impressive collection of art that he had built up. In the 19th century a wholesale dealer in watches, rebbe Izak Aron Spitz (1845-1916) also had a small synagogue, a shtiebel, on the upper floor of the Rembrandt House where he performed and tried to keep alive the mystical rites of the Lubavich Hasidim. The building was bought by the Amsterdam municipality in 1906 who turned it into a museum. In the 1990s the museum was extended with a modern wing and Rembrandt's home and studio were restored to their 17th-century state. Most of the 280 etchings that Rembrandt made can be seen in his house. They show clearly that his work was profoundly influenced by the Jewish neighbourhood in which he lived. A non-Jew, Rembrandt received commissions to paint their portraits from certain well-to-do Jews. One such was his friend Ephraim Bueno, a well-known Sephardi physician and also the patron of Manasseh ben Israel. Rabbi Manasseh ben Israel lived across the road from Rembrandt and commissioned him to make four etchings to illustrate his learned book *Piedra gloriosa*, a mystical treatise in Spanish dealing with the coming of the Messiah. The etching titled *The Jewish Bride* is thought to show the daughter of Ephraim Bueno. Rembrandt's Jewish neighbours are also pictured in the many Jewish and biblical scenes that he made, for instance the very fine work titled *Jews in the Synagogue*. Evidently, Rembrandt would often use an anonymous, often Jewish, neighbour to pose for him.

25 WATERLOOPLEIN

Waterlooplein was created when the two canals Houtgracht and Leprozengracht were filled in and what had been the island of Vlooyenburg was enclosed. It is now impossible to relocate this former island, since the building of the Town Hall cum Opera House has completely changed the look of this part of the city. Several centuries ago Vlooyenburg was a marshy plot that flooded continually (hence its name). Building began on Vlooyenburg in 1602. Two roads at rightangles to each other, Korte and Lange Houtstraat partitioned the island in four equal blocks. The first Sephardi Jews arrived in Amsterdam about this time and the neighbourhood seemed the obvious place to settle. Between the shipbuilding yards and the timber depots they could practise their religion unobserved. Early in the 17th century the first secret synagogue stood here and in 1639 the first open Sephardi synagogue was built on the Houtgrachtcanal.

The mid-17th century saw the arrival of large numbers of Jews from Germany, and Vlooyenburg became the home of predominantly poor Jews. The poverty-stricken nature of the place increased when towards the end of the 17th century the Jews who could afford it moved into houses on the new canals east of the river Amstel. Together with Uilenburg

Market stalls on Waterlooplein

Waterlooplein showing the market; left the Town Hall, right Moses and Aaron Church

and Marken, Vlooyenburg became the nub of the Jewish Quarter, characterized by its poverty but also by its colourful street life. A fish market was held on Houtgracht while beside Moses and Aaron Church there was a vegetable market and a hay market on Leprozengracht. Most of the Jewish stallholders traditionally worked on Jodenbreestraat, but according to the city council they were a menace to traffic. So it was decided to move the street market to the new square that would be created when the Hout- and Leprozen canals were filled in. This took place in 1882 but the stallholders resisted the move for some time, because they said the new square was too windy. In fact, it wasn't. The Waterlooplein market developed into a cheery, folksy place typical of the Jewish Quarter although always retaining its stamp of poverty. The Dutch poet A. van Collem (1858-1933) in his poem 'The Jewish Quarter', described it as follows:

Barrow-boy prophets live in these streets
Prophetesses rock the carts to and fro, ...
passionate local affairs – Eastern bazaar –
a sickly smell – sweetish, the wind of chatter
from old women, worn thin with laughter;
between the tangled market stalls
that hide the view of hanging skins and rubbish
between the whisperings of those who, unseeing
look for a client who will maybe come...
they pass their days, dawn-fire and fall of dusk
And keep proclaiming they're the Chosen Folk.

In 1924 a good 90 percent of the inhabitants around Zwanenburgwal were Jewish. In the decades before the Second World War Vlooyenburg stood on the list of nominations for the next slum clearance, after Uilenburg and Marken. This never happened. The war intervened and did the work instead. Almost all the residents were deported and killed. In the Starvation Winter (1944-45) their houses were plundered and partly pulled down. Almost all the Jewish stallholders were killed in Nazi death camps. The street market continued after the war but today there are very few Jewish stallholders. The colour and the life seem to have drained away.

In April 2002 the King Solomon Restaurant opened on Waterlooplein. It has a kosher food licence from a Sephardi rabbi. This has led to a dispute with the Ashkenazi community because they weren't recognized in the rabbinical licence. In order to obtain the licence, everything metal in the kitchen was heated above a certain temperature, the cutlery was boiled in a kosher pan and all the ceramic dishes were immersed in the mikweh of the Sephardi community. The restaurant only uses meat from a kosher butcher and is inspected by a rabbi to ensure that all the dietary laws of kashrut are strictly observed.

26 SPINOZA

For many centuries the first synagogue of the Sephardi community of Amsterdam, built in 1639, stood on the eastern side of today's Waterlooplein. It was here that the world famous philosopher Baruch d'Espinosa, or Bento de Spinoza, was excommunicated from the Jewish community. In his day he was a highly controversial figure, not least for his supposed atheism. In reality, Spinoza's thinking transcends questions of theism and atheism. Spinoza was born on 24 November 1632 in Amsterdam, the son of Portuguese crypto-Jews or Marranos, a merchant family who had fled the Inquisition in Portugal. Once in Amsterdam, the family rediscovered their Jewish identity. Baruch's father became a prominent member of the young Sephardi congregation in Amsterdam, and as parnas was one of the leaders of the community of Beth Jacob. Baruch attended the Talmud Torah school. There he changed his name to Bento, later adopting the Latin form of Benedictus. After his father's death he and his brother Gabriel took over the family trading business as Bento y Gabriël de Spinoza. Thanks partly to his many contacts through trade, the young Spinoza already had many acquain-

tances among Protestant Christians and freethinkers. He made it no secret that he believed many Jewish religious laws to be arbitrary, while he declared certain Jewish dogmas to be absolutely ridiculous. His appreciation of the Dutch administration of justice also provoked bad feeling among the Sephardim. In the end his self-assured pronouncements alienated him from the Sephardi community. When he was 25 years old they excommunicated him:

The chiefs of the council make known to you that having long known of the evil acts and opinions of Baruch de Spinoza, they have endeavoured by various means and promises to turn him from his evil ways. Not being able to find any remedy, but on the contrary receiving every day more information about the abominable heresies practised and taught by him, and about the monstrous acts committed by him, having this from many trustworthy witnesses who have deposed and borne witness on all this in the presence of said Spinoza, who has been convicted; all this having been examined in the presence of the rabbis, the council decided, with the advice of the rabbis, that the said Spinoza should be excommunicated and cut off from the Nation of Israel, which they now do with the following curse:

According to the decision of the angels and the judgment of holy men we ban, excommunicate, anathematize and curse Baruch de Spinoza, with the assent of Holy God, blessed be He, with the assent of this entire holy congregation, in accordance with the holy Book of Law containing the 613 prescriptions which are written therein; with the curse whereby Joshua cursed the city of Jericho, with the curse whereby Elijah cursed the young men and with all the curses that are written in the Book of Law, etcetera.

Spinoza accepted the excommunication, or *herem*, and the separation from his family, including his brother Gabriel:

Seeing that is what they wish, I gladly tread the path that lies open before me, with the consolation that my departure is more full of innocence than was the exodus of the Jews of old from the land of Egypt. Although being able to support myself in life is no more certain than it is for them, I deprive no one of anything and whatever injustice has been done to me, I can rest assured in the fact that no one can reproach me with anything.

He left Amsterdam a few years later and went to live in the Dutch village of Rijnsburg, later moving to The Hague. Supported by friends, the sober-living Spinoza devoted himself entirely to developing his philosophical ideas, becoming famous throughout Europe and corresponding with scholars from many countries. His philosophy is a blend of traditional Jewish and rational theories, which he united in his own system. He began from the assumption that everything is explicable, and has a cause. He reduced all substances to one all-embracing substance, the eternal, perfect Being, that can also be called God and that transcends all human qualities in an eternal essence.

Spinoza supported freedom of religious thought and considered the state primarily as a body existing to protect people and offer them hope. As he saw it, the Church was subordinate to the law of the state. These ideas were very similar to those of the De Witt brothers, Johan and Cornelis, prominent political figures in the Dutch Republic. After their downfall and murder in 1672 much of Spinoza's writing was banned in the Netherlands.

Spinoza died in The Hague on 21 February 1677. His grave in The Hague's Nieuwe Kerk was later cleared away so that his earthly remains have been lost. After his death friends published his most important writing, the Ethics. It immediately roused great controversy and in the very same year the States-General of the Dutch Republic banned it. Not until the 18th century did Spinoza's star begin to rise, when with the spread of rationalism and the Enlightenment, his ideas found wide favour. Since that time he is generally considered to be a major thinker in the history of philosophy.

27 THE TOWN HALL

After years of debate the Amsterdam municipality designated the run-down neighbourhood of Vlooyenburg as the location for the new Town Hall cum Opera House complex. It has of course no specifically Jewish history. However, from the end of the 19th century onwards Jews have played a significant role in the municipal government of Amsterdam. Earlier on, under the Dutch Republic, Jews were not part of the wealthy ruling class, called the regents, that dominated the city. Not until the rise of liberal and socialist political parties in the second half of the 19th century did the Jews gain political emancipation. Members of the integrated Jewish elite, such as A.C. Wertheim (1832-1897), tended on the whole to join liberal political groups, while the Jewish proletariat was very active in the Dutch socialist party, the SDAP (Social-Democratic Labour Party) and later in the Dutch Communist Party, the CPN. In the 19th century the Jews, unlike other religious groups, did not form their own political pillar. Presumably this was partly due to their small numbers, but the chief cause lay in the fact that Orthodox Judaism continued to resist integration and (especially) assimilation into Dutch society. The elite educated class of Jews, on the other hand, secularized and merged into the Dutch middle class. As a result, the working-class Jew became alienated from both the Orthodox religious leaders and the educated elite and sought emancipation within the socialist movement.

Before the Second World War many Jews were members of Amsterdam city council either as members of the socialist party or other left-wing parties. Indeed, some were appointed alderman. The first to become a city councillor was Henri Polak (1868-1943) in 1902, soon followed by influential figures from the Jewish Quarter such as David Wijnkoop (1876-1941) and A.B. Kleerekoper (1880-1943). In 1921 the advocate of Socialist-Zionism, Sam de Wolff (1868-1960) was city councillor for only one day because immediately after the elections he was so disillusioned by his colleagues' betrayal of the voters that he stormed out of the council chamber

Monument to Jewish Resistance in World War II

in a rage. In the early 1930s four out of Amsterdam's six aldermen were Jews. Besides the Liberal E.J. Abrahams, there were the prominent leaders of the Social-Democrats, Emanuel Boekman (1889-1940), Monne de Miranda (1875-1943) and Eduard Polak (1880-1962). One of the most remarkable Jewish socialists was Ben Sajet (1887-1986). Growing up in the old Jewish quarter, he became aware at a very early age of the struggle against class injustice and saw how the poor and vulnerable were exploited by the rich. Later, working as a doctor in charge of the TB sanatorium *Zonnestraal* (meaning ray of sunlight) just outside Hilversum – incidentally founded and subsidized by the *Koperen Stelen Fonds*, a charity established by the predominantly Jewish diamond workers – Sajet managed to achieve considerable improvement in the general health of the ordinary people of Amsterdam. He was city councillor for the Social-

Democrats from 1923 and later also councillor for the Province of North Holland. Writing his autobiography, titled *Een leven lang* (A Lifetime), he recalled how socialism tied in with his experience of Judaism:

I think about it like this: there was, I suppose, something fundamentally compassionate in the things I learnt from Judaism and especially in the way it was practised in our family, that found a resonance for me in the caring nature of the socialist movement...so if I think about Judaism, that's where I find the source. You'd learnt the Ten Commandments ... you shall not do anything that's evil.

The commandment to 'love your neighbour as yourself' is commonly thought to be the cornerstone of Christianity but of course it's in the Torah. Only it's not there in so many words, I learnt that from Sam de Wolff. The Hebrew says, 'Ve ahavta et-reicha kamocha'... and if you translate that literally it means, 'love the person next to you [because] he is just the same as you are.' Now that's something quite different, I think it's also far more powerful than if you say, 'love your neighbour, in the same way that you love yourself.' In that case, you begin with the assumption that you love yourself and then you should love 'the other' in the same way. But if you say, 'love the person next to you because they are like you are,' well – that's solidarity.

These developments were brought abruptly to an end by World War II. Shortly after the outbreak of war, Emanuel Boekman committed suicide. Fortunately, he did not live to see the mayor and aldermen and town council of Amsterdam being placed under the supervision of the Nazi Hans Böhmcker, nor how first the communists were dismissed, swiftly followed by the Jewish council members, then all Jewish civil servants throughout the Netherlands; nor how the remaining council members accepted the proposal of mayor and aldermen to deprive the councillors who had been dismissed of their free entrance ticket for performances at the city's theatre, the Stadsschouwburg; nor how shortly after the February Strike of 1941 the whole lot (mayor, aldermen, city councillors) were fired and Amsterdam acquired a Dutch Nazi mayor in the person of E.J. Voûte, and finally how Jewish ex-councillors such as Alderman De Miranda, were arrested and later killed.

After the war the Jewish contribution to Amsterdam city government would never again be so great. Few of those who had been active in prewar years survived. Two of those who did return were Ben Sajet, who had escaped in time to England, and the lawyer Van der Velde who was a member of the Dutch Communist Party and became an alderman. Another active communist, Ben Polak, who did a lot in the Resistance and managed to escape from the Hollandsche Schouwburg, became city councillor for the Communist Party until 1948. Since 1970 almost every mayor of Amsterdam has had a Jewish background and been a member of the Dutch Labour Party. The mayors were successively: Ivo Samkalden, Wim Polak, Ed van Thijn and after a brief interlude with Schelto Patijn as mayor, the present incumbent, Job Cohen. Several conference rooms in the Town Hall have been named in memory of prominent Jewish councillors, such as Ben Sajet, Alida de Jong and Emanuel Boekman. The latter was inaugurated by his granddaughter Claire.

28 THE MONUMENT TO JEWISH RESISTANCE

At the corner where the Amstel meets Zwanenburgwal stands a striking memorial, set up at the initiative of the Committee for the Jewish Resistance 1940–1945. It commemorates the men and women of the Jewish Resistance who were killed in the fight against Nazi terrorism. It is a slab of polished black granite, standing in stark contrast to the white marble of the Opera House. Some words from the prophet Jeremiah are engraved on the side in Hebrew and Dutch: 'Were my eyes a fountain of tears I would weep day and night for the fallen defenders of my beloved people.'

The two stone tablets symbolize the Jewish people.

Above all, the monument is intended to make the statement that the Jewish people didn't simply let themselves be herded off to the death camps without raising a whisper of protest. Dutch Jews, among them Walter Süskind, Gerhard Badrian, Eduard Veterman and Leo Frijda were active in resisting the Nazis. Although there is of course a fine line when it comes to distinguishing between active and passive resistance, the figures would seem to suggest that there was a relatively larger proportion of Jewish resistance fighters than there was among non-Jews. At the very least we may conclude that the Dutch Jews were no more passive than their all-Dutch counterparts.

An annual memorial is held at the monument on 9 November, recalling The Night of Broken Glass, formerly known as *Kristallnacht,* when throughout Germany in 1938 there was a massive smash-up of Jewish property, shops, homes and synagogues. This was instigated by the Nazis and is generally taken to be a turning point in the systematic persecution of Jews in Germany.

29 MONUMENT FOR THE ORPHAN BOYS' HOME

The artist Otto Treumann (1919-2001) designed a memorial for the place where once the Orphan Boys' Home Megadle Jethomien stood on the Amstel side of the new Opera House. It is a line of ceramic tiles set in the paved ground, outlining the shape of the boys' home. A text inscribed in the white stone tells how the orphans' home was founded in 1738 and stood on this spot between 1865 and 1943, when it was raided by the German SS in March of that year. All hundred boys and three carers were transported to Sobibor death camp. Two of the boys managed to jump from the train and escape. The rest were killed in Sobibor.

THE JEWISH CANALS

Almost as soon as the new canals lying east of the river Amstel were built, Jewish families went to live there and before long they were commonly known as 'the Jewish canals'. This canal section was created when the city of Amsterdam was extended in the 17th century. The extension started with the inner ring of canals beginning at Leidsegracht near the city centre. The canals were extended to the other side of the river Amstel and through to the islands of Kattenburg, Wittenburg and Oostenburg. Before long the canals on the west side of the Amstel were lined with houses and today these are still among the finest and most elegant buildings in Amsterdam. Gradually, however, the Dutch economy slumped and consequently the canals east of the Amstel became less grand. Also, large plots of land were donated to charitable bodies and nursing homes, and a town park emerged, known as the 'Plantage'.

The more well-to-do Jews snatched at the chance to move from the old Jewish Quarter, which was fast becoming run down. So it was that the wealthy Sephardim settled along the new 'Jewish canals' east of the Amstel. Soon the poorer Sephardim followed in their wake, settling in houses lining the narrow side streets between the canals, in particular in Nieuwe or Jodenkerkstraat. Most of the Ashkenazi Jews, generally poor as church mice, were doomed to stay in the old Jewish Quarter. In this way the Jewish quarter as a whole was considerably enlarged, and came to house distinct social groups within its confines. Writing in around 1870, Julius van Bergen vividly describes in his account *Amsterdam bij dag en nacht* (Amsterdam by day and night) the contrast between the poverty-stricken Jewish neighbourhood and the well-to-do Jewish canals:

> But let us say farewell to the plebs of Palestine (found in the alleyways off Jodenbreestraat and on Marken, where the authentic examples of the Palestinian working class live, breed and die) and visit the aristocracy of the modern Amsterdam's Jerusalem, who reside on the Jewish canals. What a world of contrast between these elegant attractive houses and the wretched hovels of Marken. There you see dust and dirt and mire, the depths of poverty – here all is neat and clean, varnished doors agleam, windows whose panes mirror a sparkling outside, while indoors all is luxurious, elegant and beautiful. These are the homes – just as on Herengracht and Keizersgracht canals – of the capitalist barons and co-backers of loans, who ride in glittering coaches and maintain a bevy of servants. The ancestors of many of them came from the banks of the Tagus or the Guadalquivir, the Douro or the Minho to the borders of the river Amstel, escaping religious persecution so that they could practise their own religion undisturbed in the hospitable and tolerant Netherlands. Their Spanish and Portuguese names witness to

> their origins. As upright citizens and generous patrons and sponsors they deserve our praise.

This situation remained virtually unchanged for two centuries. With the industrial developments of the 1860s the city once more needed to expand. This sizeable extension created large working-class districts beyond the outer ring canal, called the Singelgracht. Although quite a few Jews moved out to these new neighbourhoods the Jewish canals retained a predominately Jewish population and many Jewish establishments. All this ended in the Second World War. The Jewish character of the neighbourhood is almost entirely gone. Today, no one ever refers to the Jewish canals or Jews Church Street, although there is much that recalls the centuries of Jewish presence here, as well as memories of their destruction.

1 WALTER SÜSKIND BRIDGE

The drawbridge across Nieuwe Herengracht is one of the most attractive of its kind in Amsterdam. After the war it was given the name of a German Jew, Walter Süskind (1906-1945), who during the German occupation worked at the children's crèche across the road from the Hollandsche Schouwburg. The crèche acted as a reception centre for Jewish children whose parents were deported. Together with Felix Halverstad and Bert de Vries, Walter Süskind managed to smuggle out many children and so save their lives. Walter Süskind himself was finally arrested and taken to Auschwitz where he was killed.

2 PORTUGUESE ISRAELITE OLD MEN'S HOME

At number 33, Nieuwe Herengracht a restored wall plaque with brilliant colours announces in Hebrew and Dutch: 'Heaven looks favourably upon those who support and nourish the aged, and gives them blessing and protection.' In 1794 the Mishenet

משענת זקנים

DES HEMELS GUNST BESTRAALT EN ZEGEND EN BEHOED
DIE DE OU E BEJAARDE LIE STAAG ONDERHOUD EN VOED

Attractive wall plaques, former Portuguese Israelite Old Men's Home

Zekenim Society (Support of the Elderly) was founded on these premises, which had been donated to house old men from the Jewish Portuguese community. Dating to so early a period, it is one of the oldest Jewish nursing homes. A minimum of ten old men were cared for in the home, in order to compose a minyan, the quorum of ten male adults aged thirteen years or older, necessary to conduct religious services. On the second storey a small house shul was constructed by forming a square opening in the ceiling and supporting the gallery that was so produced on six wooden pillars. In the garden at the back of the house a sukkah, or tabernacle, was constructed. The tabernacle is used during the Feast of Tabernacles, or Booths, when Jews spend some time under the open sky. It recalls the temporary booths that the Jews built when they were trekking through the desert from Egypt towards the Promised Land. The roof should be made from branches and suchlike, so that the people inside the sukkah can look right up to the sky. This symbolizes people's dependence upon the protection of God. In the rainy Netherlands this prescription is generally followed by constructing a roof that can be opened at times. Because the Feast of Tabernacles is an autumn festival, celebrated when the last harvest is being gathered in, it has become a festival of thanksgiving for the fruits of the earth. During the war this house was emptied of its inhabitants, who were all killed. Later, a students' society was housed here and the place was used for student accommodation. The wall plaque, as well as the sukkah and the house shul, can still be clearly seen.

Wooden pillars recall the house shul in the former Old Men's Home

3   HOME OF LOPEZ SUASSO

The building at number 43, Nieuwe Herengracht is one of many that were plundered during World War II. It was probably here that the breakaway group of enlightened Jews called Adath Jeshurun (Community of Israel) met in 1796, before they received their own synagogue on Rapenburgerstraat. The house once belonged to the immensely wealthy Lopez Suassos. As early as the mid-17th century members of the Lopez Suasso family had settled in Amsterdam. Together with the De Pintos, Pereiras and Belmontes they belonged to the Sephardi elite of the city and lived like other Western European aristocrats. One of the habits of the rich was to patronize the arts and to collect art treasures. In the 19th century Augustus Lopez Suasso was one of the most important art collectors of the Netherlands. A wall plaque commemorates the house renovations he carried out in 1882. After his death in 1890 his widow donated his large art collection to the Amsterdam municipality. This collection forms the nucleus of today's Stedelijk (Municipal) Museum.

4   HOME OF ISAAC DA COSTA

The well-known writer and poet Isaac da Costa (1798-1860) grew up in the house at number 45, Nieuwe Herengracht. He and his wife Hanna Belmonte caused great consternation when they converted to Christianity and became members of the Dutch Reformed church in 1822. Across the centuries there have always been Jews who converted to Christianity – frequently under compulsion. In the Netherlands it was rare. After the French Period at the turn of the 18th century, however, serious proselytising campaigns were organized under the aegis of the Protestant Reformed 'Reveil' movement, which greatly perturbed the Jewish community. It seems that the chilly cerebral nature of

The popular name for Nieuwe Herengracht was 'Jews' Gentlemen's Canal'

Dutch Judaism largely contributed to Isaac da Costa's decision to convert. He did not consider his turning to Christianity as a rejection of Judaism, and was proud of his Sephardi background. He idealized ancient Israel and considered the Old Testament as the basis of his faith, regarding his conversion to Christianity as a step towards the fulfilment of the promises in Judaism. Like the members of the Reveil movement, Isaac da Costa opposed the liberal ideas spreading through church and society as a result of the Enlightenment and the French Revolution. He wrote:

O rebellious of the earth
How paltry is the tolerance you reveal!
This has no value for a Jewish heart
That waits for salvation of another sort.

Isaac da Costa is one of the major voices of the Reveil movement. As poet and writer he was to become one of the leading figures of 19th-century Holland. After Isaac da Costa almost everyone who

lived in the house has been Jewish. Famous inhabitants were father Sem Premsela (1869-1936) and son Meijer Jacob Premsela (1904-1971), both physicians and thus closely involved in the welfare of the Jews living in the neighbourhood.

5 HOME OF NUNEZ DA COSTA
Number 47, Nieuwe Herengracht is the finest house in the stretch of canal between the Amstel and Weesperstraat. It was the home of Moses Curiel, alias Hieronymus Nunez da Costa (1620-1697). In the early 17th century his father was a prominent member of the Sephardi community in Hamburg as well as being ambassador of the king of Portugal. In 1642 Nunez da Costa set out for Amsterdam because the city was rapidly gaining importance as an international trading centre. He was one of the first Jews to settle on Nieuwe Herengracht, east of the river Amstel.

In 1645 Nunez da Costa, as supporter of Portuguese independence, was appointed by the king of Portugal as agent for the crown; among his perks was exemption from paying taxes. He was later raised to the nobility. His activities as a merchant occupied him throughout his life; he traded mainly in diamonds but also dealt in figs, tobacco and sugar. In this Nunez da Costa provides a good example of the contribution made by Sephardi merchants to the expansion of Dutch trade in the Republic's Golden Age.

In his elegant house Nunez da Costa, famed for his sophistication and erudition, was host to many diplomats and aristocrats. He was a personal friend of the stadholder Willem III (later king William III of England), who was a frequent guest at the house on Nieuwe Herengracht. It was partly thanks to his generous financial contribution that Amsterdam's splendid Portuguese synagogue could be built. Indeed, he gave the rosewood from which the Ark is made.

From the age of 45 until his death, Nunez da Costa was parnas, or leader, of the Portuguese Jewish congregation in Amsterdam. His sons Duarte (Aron) and Alexander (Selomoh) also held this post for many years. During the First World War the house was used by Hasidic refugees from Germany. Today's building was restored in the 1990s after it had been pulled down to make room for Amsterdam's metro line.

6 HOME OF VAN LIER

The house at number 51, Nieuwe Herengracht has also mainly been home to Jewish families though the years. According to its foundation stone on the façade the present house was begun in 1851; the stone was laid by 12-year-old Ruben Isaac van Lier. Several generations of this family were active in the Jewish community, including being director of the funeral society Agudas

Weesperstraat – changed beyond recognition

Reingim. This building was also pulled down when Amsterdam's metro was being constructed, and rebuilt in the 1990s.

7 WEESPERSTRAAT

There is nothing on today's Weesperstraat with its massive building blocks and four-lane throughway to remind you that it was once a friendly shopping street, home to many Jewish shops and businesses. When the Second World War was over it was decided to locate a traffic thoroughfare on the site of the badly run-down Weesperstraat. This arterial road would link up with Jodenbreestraat and Sint Antoniesbreestraat. Later on, part of the city's metro would lead underneath this area. Not until the 1990s did the street return to normal. Plans have now almost been finalized to restore a sense of unity to the jigsaw pieces of Weesperstraat, as far as that's possible.

A few monuments have escaped the noose, and these still testify to the Jewish history of the street. All the bridges crossing the canals are named after prominent Jewish citizens. The bridge over Nieuwe Herengracht bears the name of A.M. Vaz Dias (1881-1963), founder of the press agency of the same name and for many years secretary of Amsterdam's Sephardi congregation. Across Nieuwe Keizersgracht is a bridge called after L.H. Sarlouis, who from 1936 was chief rabbi of Amsterdam. During the war he continued to encourage and support the Jews, until he was himself deported and killed.

8 MEMORIAL OF JEWISH GRATITUDE

In a small park off the sidewalk of Weesperstraat you will find the Memorial of Jewish Gratitude The first war memorial to be set up in Amsterdam, it

Memorial of to Jewish Gratitude

was made in 1947 by the Jewish sculptor Johan G. Wertheim (1898-1977), a survivor of the camps at Westerbork in the Netherlands and Theresienstadt in the former Czechoslovakia. In five relief carvings Wertheim has expressed the involvement of the Dutch people with the Jewish victims of the Nazi reign of terror:

Accepting the will of God
United with you in resistance
Protected by your love
Strengthened by your defiance
Mourning with you

The theme of protection is consciously given central place because the sculptor felt it to be the highest expression of human caring. Also, Christian and Jewish ethical ideas are represented, to show their close connection.

The memorial was presented by the Jewish community as a mark of gratitude, this having being suggested by 'the powers that be' as an appropriate gesture. In the Netherlands immediately after the war many people extolled the courage of the Dutch Resistance movement; the time was not ripe for a critical assessment. As the years passed more came to light about Dutch collaboration with the Nazis and how in fact the resistance had been very small-scale. The protection that was sometimes offered to the Jews needs to be seen beside the fact that about 80 percent of the Jews in the Netherlands were killed in the war. After Poland, this is the second highest percentage in all of Europe.

9 ROSENTHAL-MAY NURSES' HOME

There were quite a few Jewish establishments on Nieuwe Keizersgracht, including the Jewish Benevolent Fund at number 61, that advanced money to street traders. There was a secret synagogue at number 33 where services were held from September 1944 to the end of the war.

The most important building on Nieuwe Keizersgracht was the Dutch Israelite Hospital. After the war it was no longer needed and was pulled down. Apart from the former mortuary on Nieuwe Kerkstraat all that remains of the hospital is the Rosenthal-May Nurses' Home at number 116, Nieuwe Keizersgracht. The Dutch Israelite Hospital (dating from 1885) was built when the space on Rapenburgerplein had become far too cramped. The nurses' home, with its attractive façade, was designed by Harry Elte (1880-1944), also the architect of the Jacob Obrecht synagogue in South Amsterdam. The building dates from 1915 and was subsidized by the Rosenthal May Fund, set up by the widow of the banker George Rosenthal. Following the dismantlement of the hospital the building was presented to the Dutch Israelite Institute for Social Work. Today it provides shelter to around forty elderly Jews.

10 HEAD OFFICE OF THE JEWISH COUNCIL

During the war the New or Jews Keizersgracht earned itself yet another name: it became known as the Martyrs Canal. Behind the historic façade of number 58, where once the wealthy merchant Sem Jitta lived, the Jewish Council carried out its work during the war years. Whenever the Germans occupied territory they established a *Judenrat*, a Jewish Council led by respected members of local Jewry. The Jewish Council for Amsterdam was set up on 25 October 1941, during a meeting between professor Cohen, the German Böhmcker, *Beauftragte* (personal representative) for Amsterdam, and Lages, chief of the German SP, or security police. The task of the Council was to implement orders given by the German occupiers. This gave the impression that the Jews were still in control. The job description of the Department of Evacuation ran as follows:

'The provision of transport and the lodging of evacuees... Help in the widest sense of the word for all those who have to leave their homes' while the Department of Assignment had the task of 'carrying out all the activities connected with the individual house moves recommended by the German authorities...'

Head Office of the Jewish Council

In this way the Germans managed to counteract to a large extent any opposition to their anti-Jewish measures; they also manipulated the Jews into working for their own ultimate destruction.

The Jewish Council had two chairmen, Abraham Asscher (1880-1950), chair of the council of the Dutch Israelite Chief Synagogue, and Professor David Cohen (1882-1967). The organization involved around 17,000 (Jewish) employees who hoped through this work to escape their own fate. In his book *Kroniek der Jodenvervolging* (Chronicle of the Persecution of the Jews) published in English in 1956, the famous Dutch writer Abel J. Herzberg (1893-1989) says the following:

> *The Jewish council came to represent the automatism of misery. It forced upwards from below and tipped what was on top back underneath again. People organized, and people organized superbly. But what in fact did they organize? Once someone remarked in the cultural committee: 'You organizers think that coffee gets sweet because you stir it. Wrong. You have to add sugar. Why are you doing all this? What's the spiritual, or the ethical purpose of it? You're organizing a vacuum!' Accountants and efficiency-engineers constructed brilliant systems and the technicians made blueprints of these systems and the errand-boys delivered the blueprints to the various departments ... etcetera, etcetera, back and forth and the whole caboodle was in fact nothing more than a cover for that one question, 'deportation or not?' That was the soul of the matter. And every time the Jewish Council faced the question: 'disband the organization or continue?' the question would travel up and down all the staircases in the hierarchy, up and down. That was part of its automatism and that wouldn't allow it to die until the Germans punched a needle in its stomach and then everything imploded.*

When the Jewish Council was set up, not a word was whispered about deportation – but this soon came. Then the Council became a kind of life buoy, which could provide the official stamps necessary to avoid deportation. The term used was *Bis auf weiteres* – until further notice. The Jewish Council formed the supreme manifestation of an illusion – up until the time when the Council received orders to select its own staff for deportation. These orders were also carried out. Very few who worked for the Jewish Council survived the war.

After the war the chairmen of the Council defended their actions by arguing that they prevented worse from happening. Clearly, they were placed with their backs against the wall – but sometimes it's impossible to find a compromise between good and evil without in fact becoming a collaborator. An occupying force that permitted no compromises did not grant any room to manoeuvre. In its attempt to 'prevent worse' the Jewish Council actually succeeded in having 80 percent of the Jews of Holland killed. The (rare) example of the Dutch city of Enschede, where the local Jewish leaders frustrated the German regulations as much as possible so that at least 40 percent of the Jews of Enschede survived the war, shows that determined opposition could produce results. The leaders of the Jewish Council were not brought to trial. But a Jewish Council of Honour condemned their actions as being utterly reprehensible.

11 SOCIETY FOR KNOWLEDGE AND PIETY

The attractive canal house at number 54, Keizersgracht housed the Society for Knowledge and Piety. During the 19th century, Jewish education had greatly declined particularly because the 1857 Education Act abolished subsidies for independent schools. After the Education Act of 1889 stated that private elementary schools might – once again – receive a limited form of subsidy, more Jewish schools were founded. In 1895 Herman Elte (died 1925) established the Society for Knowledge and Piety which had as its aim: 'To found and maintain schools in which elementary teaching, that is a basic nucleus and a more expanded version, together with Jewish Religious Education according to traditional underlying principles, may be given.' Only with the constitutional reforms of 1917 and the Education Act that resulted from them in 1920, would private education – including Jewish – receive the same financial treatment as public schooling. After that Jewish education, to a certain extent, perked up.

Initially the Jewish School for Knowledge and Piety was also housed on Keizersgracht. Soon they also took over a school on Nieuwe Achtergracht, founded in 1874 by Herman Elte and called after him. In the 1920s this school moved to Van Ostadestraat in Amsterdam's *Pijp* (Pipe) neighbourhood. After 1929 the Society also ran Palache School on Lepelkruisstraat. Two years previously the school for Jewish Expanded Elementary Education (in Dutch, JULO) had opened on Weteringschans and one year after that a Jewish secondary school (Dutch, HBS) opened on Nieuwe Herengracht, and in 1938 moved to Stadstimmertuin. After the war the Society for Knowledge and Piety was absorbed into Jewish Private Education.

12 BOAS DIAMONDS

The diamond business of Boas now dominating Uilenburg started off at number 16, Nieuwe Keizersgracht. The three brothers Israel, Marcus and Hartog Boas were the children of Juda Boas the cobbler and Betje Groenteman. Israel and Marcus went to Paris at an early age where they learnt all about the diamond trade. The brothers started their own diamond business in about 1870. Israel and Marcus bought the rough diamond in London and sold the cut and polished gems in Paris. Hartog Boas lived and worked on Nieuwe Keizersgracht. He organized the diamond polishing in the period when this was still a cottage industry. However, not long after the start of their business, large quantities of raw diamond were discovered in South Africa, leading to a boom in the diamond trade. There was a huge demand for diamond cutters and polishers. The Boas brothers decided to build a large factory on Uilenburg, which would not only increase their

production capacity but also mean that they had the entire process under their control.

In 1894 Hartog Boas died from tuberculosis, leaving behind a young family with six children. His two brothers remained childless in Paris. The huge diamond factory was then run by a business agent.

13 PORTUGUESE ISRAELITE OLD WOMEN'S HOME

In the unpretentious canal house at number 53, Amstel on the corner with Nieuwe Keizersgracht, stood the Old Women's Home of the Portuguese Israelite congregation. After the Portuguese Israelite Home for Old Men moved to Nieuwe Herengracht in 1794, the Sephardi elderly women were given a separate house. They were lodged in a home on Weesperstraat that had been founded in 1749. Then in 1887 came a Home for Sephardi old couples. As well as caring for unmarried old women, the Old Women's Home also nursed the elderly and infirm. The home did not survive the war. The premises have become dwellings.

14 NIEUWE KERKSTRAAT

This street, like the Jewish canals, had a nickname too and was popularly known as Jews' Church Street. In turn, Jews would often refer to 'Christians' Church Street', meaning the section of the long Kerkstraat on the other side of the Magere Bridge (the attractive wooden drawbridge often called the Skinny Bridge) across the Amstel. From its beginnings, at the end of the 17th century, it was a humble street between the fashionable new canals. It was chiefly poor Sephardim who settled there, which explains why this section of the long Kerkstraat was often known as 'Portuguese Church Street'. Many of its buildings recall a Jewish past. The two bothers Israel (1872-1932) and Emanuel Querido (1871-1943) lived here. Both became well-known authors. Emanuel is also famous as the founder of the still-flourishing publishing house of Querido. Under the pen-name of Joost Mendes he wrote the ten-volume cycle of novels *Het geslacht der Santeljano's* (The Santeljano Saga) in which he describes the typical Jewish milieu of Amsterdam:

> Many Jews lived in that big, little-Dutch town there on the river Dort. And because they were always milling hither and thither, it looked as if there were even more of them than there actually were. They dominated the entire street trade. They were the trumpeting, reverberating operatic voices, the powerful heavily puffing hawkers who could unexpectedly erupt into a street; who banished the civilized peace and quiet of the quayside with their cries of longing resounding warm and passionate against the walls ... They were the most strikingly individual group among the Jewish population of Dortendam: the type of toiling Jew, whose days are filled with endless drudgery, and who lets loose all the pent-up pain and suffering, all the hate and ignominy he has put up with because of his race, in his enormous reverberating street cry.

Today the office blocks along Weesperstraat divide the New or Jews Church Street (Kerkstraat) in two. The section east of Weesperstraat was the most run-down, inhabited largely by Ashkenazi Jews.

15 CHEWRE SHUL

In the 19th century various societies were founded in Jewish Amsterdam that established their own shuls. Initially this met with violent opposition from rabbis and parnasim of the Jewish congregations but they were unable to stem this spontaneous expression of a more personal and intimate way of worship. One of the oldest such societies was *Neir Mitswoh Wetouro Our* (meaning, The Law is like a lamp, and Torah is like a burning flame). As early as 1841 there is already mention of services being held at 26, Jews Church Street. The shul there was one of the most vital and popular chewre shuls in Amsterdam. In 1879 it was considerably enlarged and on 28 October 1913 a new building was dedicated at numbers10-14. The architect was Harry Elte (1880-1944), who also designed the

Nunes House and *Neir Mitswoh Wetouro Our*

imposing synagogue on Jacob Obrechtstraat in 1927. The shul on Jews Church Street seated 192 men and 36 women and had an Ark framed in black marble.

The shul was completely looted in the war. All that remains today to show the building's original purpose is the structure of the outer walls: the first floor recalls the women's gallery that was once there. The premises at number 26 is presently a garage.

16 HOME OF FERNANDES NUNEZ

A plaque on the façade of number 16, Nieuwe Kerkstraat, the building beside the former shul, announces that this was formerly the Fernandes Nunez House. It was a small courtyard built for poor Sephardi women. In his will Joseph Fernandes Nunez stated that after his death a foun-

Front of Fernandes Nunes House

Keizersgracht were laid out. The somewhat cynical saying went: 'In on the Emperor Canal, out on Church Street.' Like the hospital, the mortuary was no longer used after the war.

18 PORTUGUESE ISRAELITE RELIGIOUS SCHOOL

The Portuguese Israelite Religious School was located at number 141, Nieuwe Kerkstraat. The school provided additional lessons in religion for about 150 Jewish children who attended Dutch state schools. At the end of the 1920s the school was closed, and a tobacco store came in its place, which in turn closed down in the war. The Germans ordered the former school to be used only for Jewish children. This time it was compulsory, not extra lessons. The murals on the building's ground floor still show cheerful gnomes, cats and swans. In 1943 the children were taken out of the building and later killed. It was never used again as a school. A plumber's firm has worked there since 1980.

19 SAILORS' SHUL

Before the war the house at number 147, Nieuwe Kerkstraat was known as the Sailors' Shul, belonging to the society for Song and Prayer, 'Rino oe-Tefillo'. The society dates from1878. After 1888 the society held services at number 10, Waterlooplein. There is no record explaining why the three-storey shul building was exchanged in 1896 for the much more cramped quarters on Nieuwe Kerk-straat. In any case, the shul didn't have a women's gallery. The women sat on a low platform at the back. Nor is it clear where the nickname 'sailors' shul' comes from. Quite possibly a number of Jews, in order to escape grinding poverty, signed on as sailors and had their shul on Jodenkerkstraat. Again, it is possible that morning services in the shul were attended by Jewish merchants from Rotterdam who had sailed into the city on barges, and tied up alongside the quay beside the 'Skinny' Bridge. The Sailors' Shul remained in use until 1943.

dation should be set up for the benefit of these poor women. In the façade a restored plaque reads in Hebrew and Dutch: 'And the Lord was with Joseph, and he prospered.' These words from the book of Genesis emphasize Nunez's action as being a deed of charity, or zedakah, which is one of the obligations laid upon Jews who themselves are prosperous. Through the centuries the majority of Jewish congregations have survived because of this religiously-based solidarity.

17 THE MORTUARY

Although its façade has been fundamental-ly rebuilt and the sculptural decorations have disap-peared, the former mortuary, or house of ablution, at number 127 can still be recognized. The mortu-ary was the place where patients who had died in the Dutch Israelite Hospital on Nieuwe

20 RUSSIAN SHUL

When from the 1880s onwards there were widespread pogroms throughout eastern Europe, thousands of Jews fled westwards. They would often pass through Amsterdam, hopefully on their way to America, but many in fact remained in Mokum. In 1884 they founded the Nidchei Yisroeil Yechaneis Society (from Psalm 147:2 'The Lord gathers together the exiles of Israel') and in 1889 set up a shul at 149, Nieuwe Kerkstraat. The society was started by Misnagdim, opposers of the Hasidic movement which began among Jews in eastern Europe. The Hasidim emphasize the emotional aspects of religious experience in contrast to the more intellectual approach of the Misnagdim. In Amsterdam this century old opposition faded away. Hasidic jews also attended the Russian Shul and even hold services for themselves. The unique atmosphere inside the Russian shul has been vividly captured by the Dutch writer Abel J. Herzberg in his book *Brieven aan mijn kleinzoon* (Letters to My Grandson) published in 1964:

> *They did not have trained voices and their musical talents left much to be desired, their singing didn't do justice to the ancient melodies, but it was full of warmth and sensitivity. What it lacked in beauty of detail, it won in sincerity. It was all sincere and genuine. The sense of order and decorum, which is so valued in many Western synagogues, was almost completely absent. All that mattered was the spontaneity and warmth … especially … in the Kerkstraat shul, where the religious outpourings appeared unrestrained and almost wild. People prayed with fervent passion, for to be restrained was considered cold and intellectual. …So it was that, especially in the early days, various customs kept the newcomers at a distance from those who were already settled in Amsterdam. And the natural suspicion that always greets a stranger only increased the gulf. He, in turn, was unable to project himself into the mind of another. … So little by little a separate Russian-Jewish milieu developed in this city.*

Initially the Russian shul was housed in a living room

Star of David on façade of Russian shul

but after the renovations of 1910 a shul with women's gallery was created on the ground floor, by removing the first floor. As well as holding religious services the society cared for the needy. The Russian shul did not survive the war. It stood empty for several decades after the war but was then carefully restored. The small intimate shul with its beautiful Star of David set in the façade was reopened by Nidchei Yisroeil Yechaneis in 1987. Recently the numbers attending have increased sharply, partly because of the arrival of Russian and eastern European Jews after the fall of Communism. This vigorous congregation extended the synagogue in the late 1990s – despite protests from the neighbourhood who didn't want the historic inner courtyard changed – and built a ritual bath, or mikveh.

in the war years, in her poem titled 'Geography':

She had a poor grade for Geography
on that last day.
But a week later knew
exactly where Treblinka lay –
briefly.

22 ARTISANS' SOCIETY OF FRIENDS

Numbers 140 to 144 Nieuwe Achtergracht have commemorative tiles set into the façade. This building, now converted into apartments, once housed the Artisans' Society of Friends founded in 1869 as a society for Jewish workers. They provided small scholarships to children from the poorest Jewish families, paying to train them in one of the handwork skills so that later they might earn a living. Excluded from the Dutch guilds of craftspeople for centuries, Jews – despite the emancipation of the Napoleonic period – had little tradition of working as skilled craftsmen. Shortly after its foundation, the society also began providing needy families with help in times of sickness or death. They also organized lectures and set up a library, with the aim of improving general knowledge.

As the 19th century progressed, this initially Jewish society became increasingly influenced by socialist ideas. In 1895 they founded the General Amsterdam Society for Health Care and Midwifery called *Ziekenzorg* (meaning Health Care), which was one of the first bodies to offer reliable health insurance. Helping the sick is one of the chief forms of zedakah, a word encompassing many types of charity. From the beginning of the 19th century care for the sick had been the task of the Dutch Israelite Paupers Board, linked directly with the Jewish congregation. When such organizations began to be funded by central government, and particularly with the development in the Netherlands of a system of health care organized by socialist groups, the Jewish working class was at last able to free itself of dependence on charity. The Jewish proletariat of Amsterdam, largely socialist in outlook, joined the

Former office of Artisans' Friendly Society

21 PALACHE SCHOOL

The redbrick building of the former Palache School stands on Lepelkruisstraat. It was under the aegis of the Society for Knowledge and Piety that supervised several schools. One of the Jewish schools to be founded shortly after the 1920 Education Act, Palache School provided elementary education and was subsidized by the Dutch government on the same footing as Dutch public schools. The school, named after a great supporter of Jewish education, rabbi Juda Palache (1858-1920), opened in 1929 and was, together with the Herman Elte School and the Talmud Torah, one of Amsterdam's three prewar Jewish elementary schools. In the course of the war most of the children were deported and met their deaths in extermination camps.

The Dutch poet Ida Vos, herself a survivor of the war, gives a poignant comment on Jewish schools

general health care organization, Ziekenzorg, almost en masse. In 1925 there were 52,000 members of the Ziekenzorg, most of them Jewish. Another major activity of the Artisans' Society of Friends was to make affordable accommodation available, in particular through the housing association *Handwerkers Vriendenkring*. This was established after the 1901 Act made it possible for the city council to clean up slum districts. Housing associations organized good and affordable dwellings for their members. The *Bouwfonds Handwerkers Vriendenkring* was the first housing association to implement the new law after the clearance of Uilenburg in 1917 and in 1926. The general nature of the health service Ziekenzorg and the housing association *Handwerkers Vriendenkring* illustrate how the Jewish proletariat gained its emancipation almost entirely within a socialist milieu.

23 DR MEYER DE HOND BRIDGE

The bridge over Nieuwe Achtergracht is called after Dr Meyer de Hond (1882-1943), a colourful but controversial figure in the Jewish community. He was rabbi of the Touro Our Society (The Law is a light) but the chief rabbi Dünner refused to recognize him as a rabbi, even after he'd completed his studies in Berlin. Not until the deportations did the (then) chief rabbi Sarlouis confer upon him the honorary title of *Morénoe* (our teacher).

Meyer de Hond was a true rabbi of the people, with an almost Messianic influence over his many followers. He was active in many fields, such as labour organization, the theatre, the press (papers such as *Betsalel* and *Lebanon)* and especially in initiating the building of the *Joodse Invalide* health centre. He was opposed to social reform in any shape, either socialist or Zionist. He glorified the traditional Jewish way of life, of people like the barrow boys, which he described in his well-known writing titled *Ghetto-kiekjes* (Ghetto Snapshots):

> I can tell by his street cries that he is one of my people. Ah, you find them everywhere, the small folk, the street peddlers. … Wherever you find people, they'll come with their barrows. And if somewhere a street urchin taunts 'Dirty Jew' chucking an orange peel at him, or some men with 'adult' intelligence jeeringly imitate his street cry, mockingly copying the ghetto burr, experience has taught him to shamble on and swallow his outrage. They feel, in fact, that people are waiting for 'the pears-Jew' and looking out the window until the 'vegetables-Jew' appears. Anti-Semitism doesn't hide in streets and barrows, nor in yelling out a racist slogan. Instead, it lurks in well-polished, civilized, elegantly stylized conversation.

Such opinions brought the people's rabbi into conflict with socialists and trades-union supporters such as Henri Polak. The Zionists also poured scorn on his idealization of the impoverished ghetto life. When Meyer de Hond described the street vendors' life as idyllic, especially when he saw children helping their fathers push the barrows, he once heard the dry retort from a hawker that 'he'd rather tip the barrow with its contents into the canal'. In the 1930s Meyer de Hond sought refuge in a pious attitude, typical of which is his pronouncement that 'the shul is our air-raid shelter and the tefillin (phylacteries) our anti-aircraft guns.' On 20 July 1943 rebbe Meyer de Hond was deported to Poland where he was killed.

24 THE JOODSE INVALIDE

The new building the *Joodse Invalide* on the corner of Nieuwe Achtergracht and Weesperplein was completed in 1937 at a time when fascism and National-Socialism were steadily gaining in power. The new building was realized by large-scale collections. There were radio campaigns and famous performers staged charity concerts and nationwide lotteries were held.

Traditionally, disabled Jews were dependent on charity and the poorhouse. In 1911 rabbi Meyer de Hond proposed setting up the society called *De Joodse Invalide*, which had its headquarters at 70,

The *Joodse Invalide* building, a pinnacle of modern Dutch architecture

Nieuwe Keizersgracht. This house, now no more, was followed in 1925 by a nursing home at 98, Nieuwe Achtergracht. Space shortage finally urged on the decision to build the new block on the corner of Weesperplein. The building is one of the pinnacles of Amsterdam's modern architecture. Designer J.F. Staal (1879-1940) used materials fashionable in the *Neue Sachlichkeit* (New Objectivity) movement of the time, such as glass and glazed brick, but also employed the plastic shapes popular with the Amsterdam School. The brick walls as they move upwards blend into glass and there are highly decorative arched roofs over the balconies.

The attractive building was not used for very long for its original purpose. On 1 March 1943 the Nazis entered the hospital and emptied it of all the patients and staff who were present. About one quarter of the patients and a large number of the staff had managed to go underground at the

eleventh hour, having been warned by members of the Jewish Council of the planned eviction. Despite this, just before the Germans arrived a phone call came from Asscher, chairman of the Jewish Council, saying there was nothing to worry about. Those who were still in the Joodse Invalide were all prepared for departure – they had clothes, backpacks, toiletries, bag and baggage ready to go. Everyone in the building was taken, including the elderly, partially mobile, blind, or sick. The Nazis, disappointed perhaps that so many of the staff had escaped, looted and damaged the building.

After the war the Joodse Invalide revived and now part of it houses the nursing home Bet Shalom, where there are still about sixty Jewish patients. On the façade is a sober memorial plaque designed by Lepkas Stouthamer. It commemorates those who were deported and killed and bears the words (in Dutch): *The State of Israel was forged from the iron*

The former Diamond Exchange with its elegant dome

of their chains. It expresses the conviction, so strong in the first decades after the Second World War, that such great suffering could only be given a meaning through the State of Israel. The people whose lives were plucked from them never realized that their death would gain this meaning.

25 THE DIAMOND EXCHANGE

A flourishing trade in diamonds followed in the wake of the diamond cutting and polishing business in Amsterdam. The diamond business was not regulated by the Dutch guilds, which allowed the Jews to find a niche where they could work. Traditionally, this was an area where Jews predominated and in the 'Cape Age' of the 1870s, large trading houses were established. The trading, a somewhat ad hoc business, initially took place in Amsterdam cafes on the central Rembrandt Square.

When this flourishing trade expanded into more and more cafes it seems that a Wild West atmosphere sometimes gained the upper hand. At one time Café Rembrandt had to be closed. In 1889 a committee of diamond dealers decided to build a centre especially for diamond trading. Although conflicts in dealing in the cafes continued for several years, the diamond dealers managed to draw up rules for trading. Indeed, a Diamond Exchange was established and in 1911 moved into its own premises on Weesperplein, on the corner with Nieuwe Achtergracht.

The remarkable Diamond Exchange building by architect G. van Arkel (1858-1918) is designed in sober Art Nouveau style. It has a striking clock tower, which once rose high above the surrounding buildings. The Exchange became the symbol of Amsterdam's flourishing diamond trade, which dominated the European market. The Exchange maintained a neutral position in the conflicts that regularly arose between the diamond bosses and the workers, who had formed the trade union ANDB (General Dutch Diamond Workers Union). Thus the Jewish socialist politician, Henri Polak, was able to speak the following words of praise for the Diamond Exchange:

> Today the Exchange has its own attractive, spacious building bordered by canal and open square…This advance in architectural space reflects the advance of the Exchange in a commercial sense. After all, the Exchange has been so far disparaged and looked down upon by the powerful and mighty as if it were insignificant; but it has slowly been growing into an item that is not to be ignored. It has become, in a manner of speaking, the mother organization in the diamond industry, parent of many associations of dealers, agents and brokers. What it has to say counts with both the municipal and national government. No longer is it merely the retailers who shelter under the Exchange's wings; nor does it chiefly deal, as formerly, in by-products…No, major business deals are now carried out within its walls and under its approving gaze. The Exchange has become a centre of vital activity. It is now impossible to imagine our diamond world without it: it has become the very hub of our activity.

The Diamond Exchange has always occupied a central position in the Jewish life of the Weesperstraat neighbourhood. Almost every family had direct or indirect connections with the diamond trade or industry. On 13 February 1941 there were around 5,000 Jews listening to a speech held by Abraham Asscher, newly-appointed chair of Amsterdam's Jewish Council. On the orders of the German occupiers Asscher called upon those present to surrender any firearms, knives or other weapons. But since the Jews were in no way prepared for the conflict that would shortly come, they had no cache. No booty for the Nazis. Four years further on, with the murder of most of the Dutch Jews, the diamond trade suffered a huge blow. After the war the Exchange functioned on a limited scale for some

time. However, the city of Antwerp in Belgium where there had been comparatively few Jewish victims of the war, had taken over Amsterdam's dominant pre-war position. Today Amsterdam deals chiefly in diamonds for tourists. Following a renovation which divided the splendid auction hall into two, the Diamond Exchange was taken over by the Amsterdam municipality.

26 JEWISH HIGH SCHOOLS

An unobtrusive name-plate on the façade tells the reader that number 2, Stadstimmertuin was formerly the Jewish Maimonides High School. Jewish education declined in the 19th century but later measures, in particular the 1920 Education Act, granting financial equality to all private schooling, helped Jewish education get on its feet again. In 1928 an Orthodox Jewish secondary school (Dutch HBS) opened on Herengracht, moving ten years later to Stadstimmertuin. Across the road at number 1, Stadstimmertuin a Jewish High School was opened on the orders of the occupying forces in September 1941. All Jewish pupils at Amsterdam high schools such as the famous Barlaeus, Vossius and Montessori schools were expelled and sent to the Jewish high school. Among them was Anne Frank, until her family went into hiding. So for a short time the Orthodox Jewish children, whose families had chosen for them to have a religious

Jewish high school used during World War II, opposite another type of Jewish high school

Nameplate recalling the former Jewish high school 'Maimonides Lyceum'

education, went to school in Stadstimmertuin. They would find themselves together with children from Liberal Jewish families or even secular Jewish homes – all forced by the Nazis to attend a school for Jews only.

All the teachers were also Jewish, among them Jaap Meijer (1912-1993) and the historian Jacques Presser (1899-1970). In his monumental life-work *De Ondergang* (Ashes in the Wind: the destruction of Dutch Jewry) Presser describes the Jewish high school (Dutch HBS) as follows:

> *A school like any other, some pupils arriving late, some disobedient children, punishments, absenteeism … At this point the writer hesitates a moment, since absentees at this school were a very rare phenomenon. If there were 'disturbances' in the city there would be noticeable gaps in the classrooms; but that wasn't the only thing. The writer will never forget the gesture (it*

was scarcely ever more than that) with which the class followed his glance (it was scarcely ever more that that) towards an empty place; sometimes it was a small flick of the hand, meaning gone underground; sometimes it was a clenched fist, meaning arrested; pantomime lasting a couple of seconds, performed many times. Class 2b, which had 28 pupils when school term began in autumn 1942 had dwindled by mid-May 1943 to a mere four, who huddled together in a couple of desks forming the entire class and provided a small group of teachers with the stamp: 'indispensable'.

The teacher and composer Sem Dresden (1881-1957) also narrates how the schools carried on maintaining the everyday routine as far as possible:

> *After July 1942 the schools literally became absurdity itself. … People hung on … there was only one thing the school could do and that was to persevere…the school wasn't closed down, the school literally bled to death.*

After the war the Jewish High School picked up the broken pieces. It followed the Dutch high school system and became a kind of comprehensive with several ability streams. At the end of the 1950s the school was named after the great Jewish scholar Maimonides, who in 12th-century Córdoba contributed to the flowering of the Jewish intellectual community in that Moorish city.

In the decimated postwar Jewish Amsterdam the Maimonides High School in Stadstimmertuin faced growing difficulties because of a steady decline in pupil numbers. In 1973 the school moved to the Amsterdam suburb of Buitenveldert. Besides the name on the façade, a black marble memorial plaque in the entrance hall commemorating the fall of the Temple in Jerusalem, serves to recall the school's former Jewish tradition. The high school across the road, used during the war, has a contorted Star of David above the main entrance and the dates 1941-1943. Beside the door a simple plastic plaque records the 400 schoolchildren who never returned.

The dignified Amstel Hotel, an initiative of Dr Samuel Sarphati

27 THE AMSTEL HOTEL

The Amstel Hotel was one of Samuel Sarphati's dreams. He had high-flying plans for extending the city of Amsterdam. Beginning in around 1860 there was slow but steady urban industrial growth, creating a demand for housing and other municipal amenities. Sarphati was the first to have ideas about how to use the space that became available after the old city defence buildings were pulled down. He planned a spacious boulevard, lined with homes for the well-to-do. There would be recreational areas and large, imposing buildings. Undoubtedly the most famous of these was the *Paleis voor Volksvlijt*, a crystal palace dedicated to the industriousness of the people, unfortunately totally destroyed by fire in 1929. Today the Bank of the Netherlands stands on the site. The Amstel Hotel designed by C. Outshoorn (1812-1875) was a monumental building – although what we see today is only one wing of the original design that Sarphati conceived. The splendid building is one of Amsterdam's major hotels. Sarphati himself didn't live to see his dream realized – he died before building was completed and thus it may be considered his legacy to the city. The road running alongside the hotel is called Sarphati Street after the energetic planner. His dream was of a boulevard comprising this street and the impressive Hogesluis Bridge across the river, which in its elegance and charm would rival Paris or Vienna.

28 LIPPMAN ROSENTHAL BANK

In May 1941 the Germans ordered all Jewish financial assets to be placed in one bank. In order to ensure that the money would be available when the *Endsieg* (the final victory of National-Socialism) took place, the Germans selected a small Jewish bank with a good reputation: Lippman Rosenthal. Meanwhile this bank had been given a *Verwalter*, or administrator, who was ordered to privatize the branch at number 47, Sarphatistraat. In

August 1941 all cash, cheques, securities, balances and deposits belonging to Jews had to be placed at Lippman Rosenthal's. Soon after, all Jewish assets were expropriated and the possessions of Jews who had been deported were also deposited 'for safe-keeping' in the bank. Furthermore, the bank financed the system of Jewish education imposed by the Nazis, and acted as a depository for art objects, jewellery and (art) collections and all Jewish life insurance policies. It is estimated that Lippman Rosenthal 'administered' the equivalent of between 140 and 180 million euros of the day, of Jewish assets. The Nazis used this to finance the German administrative machine, to pay the Jewish Council, and to cover the cost of the concentration camps in Westerbork and Vught. To cap it all, these assets were used to pay the rewards to those who betrayed Jews who had gone into hiding – in short, blood money. As the historian Presser described it, Lippman Rosenthal's bank on Sarphatistraat was:

> A den of robbers, a front for looting or 'plunder façade'. In the expropriation of the Jewish entrepreneur, shopkeeper, businessman … lay a splendid territory where the Aryan folk … could expand their activities and achieve the destruction of the Judeo-plutocratic-capitalist communist parasites, these sub-human vermin or *Untermenschen*, by means of German efficiency, not to mention German cleverness. …Those who had occasion to deal with these ladies and gentlemen received the impression that large amounts of the Jewish money that was flowing in purely along permissible routes somehow seemed to stick to the people who had dug it out of Jewish pockets. A number of them, both Germans and Dutch, loyal to their Führer, others, especially the less highly educated Dutch personnel acting in a kind of political innocence which it is no longer possible to judge. Nazis or not, each one of them had their role in the relentless onward-rolling mechanism for the systematic plundering of the Jews; every bank entry, every message, every letter pushed the process a little further until the vic-

tims, stripped naked, entered the gas chambers. After the war the Dutch government set up a body for the liquidation of the *Vermogensverwaltung Sarphatistraat* (LVVS), whose task was to distribute the assets of the Lippman Rosenthal bank (LiRo). The LVVS, using the LiRo archive, compiled a collective account into which all Jewish assets were deposited, sorted out and documented. It provided an efficient overview of incomes including those from the sale of property during the war and expenses of various kinds. The archive was then presented to the organization for Jewish Social Work whose task was to deal with requests for compensation.

It was to take many years before the question of restitution of property or compensation in a more general sense was adequately addressed. Although individual banks and insurance companies and also the State of the Netherlands honoured their commitments in individual cases, an incalculable capital has never been returned; the survivors or next-of-kin cannot be traced.

In the course of the 1990s a number of revelations gave rise to heated discussions. Indeed, this formed part of an international development in which Jewish organizations were gaining the courage to state their historical and moral claims for compensation. The news that Jewish property such as rings, earrings, fountain pens and watches was sold amongst themselves for minimal prices by staff of the Financial Agency, caused quite a commotion. They had been entrusted with the items pending the owners' rehabilitation. More disclosures followed. It appeared that some banks had entered the invoices into their books for millions of accounts when they presumed the account owner or legal legatee was untraceable. Formally seen, this is not a legal offence but clearly there had been no thought of restitution to the Jewish community or of donation to a worthy cause. It appeared that the national government had destroyed large portions of the LiRo archive, simply part of routine procedure, without giving a second thought to the emotional and historical value of the archive. Remaining assets from LiRo were transferred to the state treasury in 1992. Quite by chance, part of the LiRo archive was found; it was the section where smaller accounts were registered, including businesses that were sold during the war, with the full name of the purchaser. Then it was the turn of the insurance companies, because they retained dormant policies that had never been paid out, and the Stock Exchange also came under fire because they had collaborated in trading in stolen Jewish stocks and shares.

Finally, two committees attempted to gather as many facts as possible and bring them into the open. The Scholten Committee researched the financial assets, particularly shares and bank accounts. The Van Kemenade Committee examined in a more general manner Jewish assets and bank accounts after the war. As a result almost all the bodies involved have offered their apologies and sincere regrets. On behalf of the Dutch government, the then premier Wim Kok expressed his genuine concern. The government, banks, insurance companies and the Stock Market Association all paid out substantial sums to the Jewish community. This is turn led to impassioned discussions as to whether such payments should be seen as rehabilitation, in other words, as actual compensation for injury, or as a moral gesture, and to what extent individual claims should be paid from these sums – or should the money be used for communal Jewish purposes. In the end, the Central Jewish Consultancy was put in charge of making the payments. As far as possible they try to honour individual claims; the remaining money will be used for the Dutch-Jewish community.

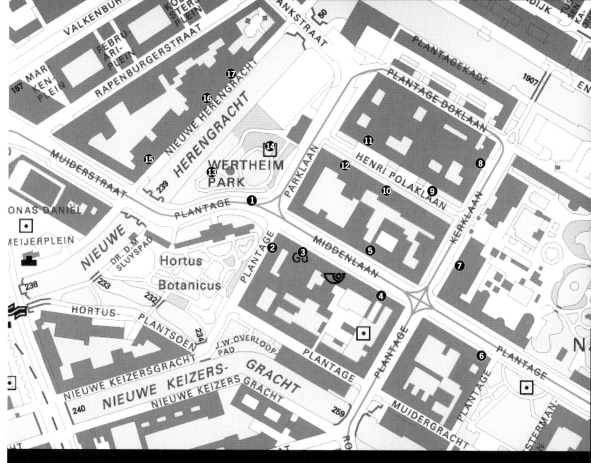

THE PLANTAGE NEIGHBOURHOOD

The neighbourhood of the Plantage emerged as a result of the large-scale city extensions begun in 1662. With the stagnating economy of the 18th century, parts of this new extension of Amsterdam remained undeveloped, especially the area north of Muidergracht. Here, right beside the Jewish quarter, came a city park, a recreational area, called the Plantage. With the industrial growth that started in the 1860s, the population expanded and open spaces in the city were soon used for housing. The Plantage district became home to the more well-to-do, many of them Jews. It was an elegant neighbourhood with fine wide streets. The fast-growing proletariat overflowed into new working-class districts outside the ring of inner canals. The Plantage retained its recreational character with the zoo, Artis, and several theatres including Frascati, later the Rika Hopper theatre, the Artis Theatre, to become the Hollandsche Schouwburg, and Plancius. The neighbourhood is still there, but its largely Jewish nature was destroyed during the Second World War and today the Hollandsche Schouwburg, in particular, remains as a sombre memorial to a Jewish past.

1 PLANTAGE MIDDENLAAN

Since its creation in the second half of the 19th century the elegant street Plantage Middenlaan has always formed a sharp contrast to the run-down Jewish quarter. In 1925 roughly half the residents of this salubrious street were wealthy Jews. The Jewish writer, Carry van Bruggen (1881-1932) recalls in her story *Four Seasons* how foreign the Plantage district felt to those who came from the Jewish Quarter:

...but across the bridge all that old familiarity ended. The wide avenue has a refined elegance, lacking the hustle and bustle of a shopping street. ... And in all those large grand houses with their shining doors framed in deep porches and their gleaming windows there lived people who knew about the Feast of Tabernacles. Oh, just let them say at school that you can't have rich Jews ...

Carry van Bruggen was the daughter of a cantor, or hazzan, and the sister of the writer Jacob Israel de Haan. In her work she comes to terms with her childhood and adopts a critical attitude towards Judaism particularly in the book *The Little Jew*. On the other hand, she describes her past with enormous affection, giving a warm picture of the intimate world of the Jewish family and community, as in *The House on the Canal*. Like her brother's, Carry van Bruggen's life had a tragic end. At the age of fifty-one, following a nervous breakdown, she committed suicide. There were several Jewish special homes on Plantage Middenlaan, including the Portuguese Israelite Boy's home Abi Yetomim (Father of the Orphans), housed in number 80 since 1930, and Zichron Ja'akov, for a while at number 10 before moving to Henri Polaklaan.

2 BEIS JISROEIL

The premises at number 9, Plantage Parklaan is sometimes called Hugo de Vries House, after the Nobel Prize winner who lived there from 1884 to 1916. From 1919 the Jewish society Beis Jisroeil (House of Israel) has used the building. Beis Jisroeil was founded in the previous year on the initiative of rabbi Abraham Asscher (1884-1926), who was later chief rabbi of Groningen, a city in the north of the Netherlands. He saw it as important that Jewish youth had a place where they could meet for social activities. Officially the aim of the society was 'to elevate and develop the Jewish population of Amsterdam.' Although members of the older generation would also come to the talks, which were of a non-intellectual nature, and were involved in offering 'practical tips for everyday living', the emphasis lay on activities for young people. It became a thoroughly Jewish 'at home' centre, where sometimes more than a thousand visitors would drop in during one week. Religious services were also regularly held there.

Shortly before the Second World War the Liberal Jewish congregation held its services in Beis Jisroeil. The house was closed down at the end of 1941 and a department of the Jewish Council moved in, including the 'Psychiatric Consultation Bureau'. The German occupier had given this bureau the task 'of giving advice to those who, due to the circumstances of the time, were undergoing psychiatric problems.' After the war the Jewish community of Amsterdam used the Hugo de Vries House as offices until 1970; a plaque in the façade records this in both Dutch and Hebrew.

3 RIKA HOPPER THEATRE

In 1879 Frascati Theatre was officially opened at number 8, Plantage Middenlaan by Gustave Prot. Until 1912 Prot, and later his son, ran the theatre – in the face of cut-throat competition from the many other local theatres. In 1927 Frascati was taken over by the husband of Rika Hopper, who re-named the theatre after his wife. The façade in Art-Deco style dates from that period. Although having a Jewish atmosphere about it, the theatre was not Jewish in a strict sense. This changed in World War II when the Germans ordered it to become strictly Jewish, running such programmes as 'Laugh Sanatorium'. The company that played there, consisting largely of German-Jewish refugees, was called *Der Prominenten*. Even Aus der Fünten, the German head of the *Zentralstelle für Jüdische Auswanderung* in charge of Jewish deportations, apparently enjoyed the German-Jewish cabaret, and could be found seated in the audience among the Jews who hadn't yet been sent on transport.

Like the actors and the audiences, the theatre didn't survive the war. For many years after the war it lived on as the Desmet cinema, closing in 2000.

4 THE HOLLANDSCHE SCHOUWBURG

On 14 October 1942 the German occupier declared the Hollandsche Schouwburg (meaning Dutch Theatre) to be the place where Jews would be rounded up before being deported. It has thus come to symbolize the destruction of most of the Amsterdam Jews.

In 1892 the Artis Theatre was opened, soon renamed Hollandsche Schouwburg. Its position in the Plantage, where many Jews lived, meant that it became closely associated with the Jewish community. Plays by the Jewish writer Herman Heijermans (1864-1925) were often premièred in the Hollandsche Schouwburg. The famous cabaretier Louis Davids (1883-1939) often performed here to a packed house. During World War II the building was called the Jewish Theatre; after September 1941 only Jewish performers were allowed to appear on stage here, to an audience consisting only of Jews.

As early as summer 1942 the Germans had decided to set up a deportation centre. Initially they had their eye on the Portuguese Synagogue, but rejected this building because it had no electric lighting. The Hollandsche Schouwburg, or Jewish Theatre, was most suitable. It could seat 900 people, the coffee lounges could easily be converted into a canteen, and it was no problem to guard the entrances

Solemn memorial place, the Hollandse Schouwburg, place of departure in World War II

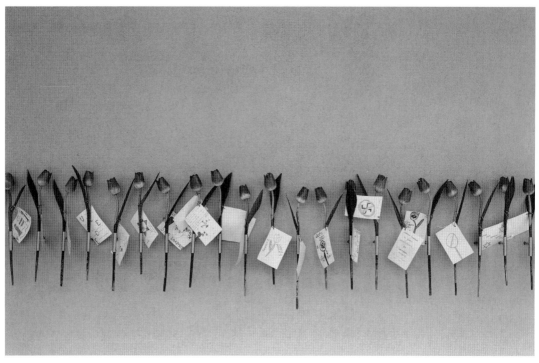
Monument inside the Hollandse Schouwburg

and exits. Twice a week, on average, large numbers of Jews, generally between three and four hundred of them, would be brought to the Hollandsche Schouwburg. The length of stay varied from a few hours to a few days, sometimes to a week. On arrival people were registered by staff of the Jewish Council. They would also type out the names of those who were deported. The lists were checked by only three members of the Waffen SS, supplemented by staff from Lippman Rosenthal Bank who ensured that all the possessions of the Jews were properly inventoried. Later on, quite a few members of the Jewish *Ordedienst* (a kind of police force) from Westerbork concentration camp were also called in, especially to control people trying to escape and bring them back to the Jewish Theatre. The poet Ida Vos describes this:

An actor straddle-legged across the stage
his text consists of names
names of victims who were brought here.
Each name resounds, sends shocks

of powerless pain
because the one who owns this name
must be an actor too

The Jews were taken by tram to the train station and thence transported to Westerbork camp. The tram and train fares were charged to the Lippman Rosenthal Bank, and paid for by the money the bank had in 'safe-keeping' for the departed Jews. On Sundays the Municipal Transport Company charged double for a ticket.

By the end of 1943 things had grown quiet in the Hollandsche Schouwburg. Amsterdam was to a large extent *Judenrein* (clean of Jews). The building was sold to a firm producing meat products and after the war plans were mooted to turn it into a kind of nightclub. However, this encountered much opposition and after a great deal of string-pulling the foundation for the Hollandsche Schouwburg acquired the building and presented it to the municipality on condition that it never again be used as a place of public entertainment. Years were to pass and the building was to grow ever more dilapidated. Clearly, it took a long time before Dutch society could face up to the appalling reality of the war years. Finally, in 1962 it was decided that the Hollandsche Schouwburg, by then in ruins, should survive as a place of memorial. The façade still stands, fronting an empty space, a quiet inner courtyard with a gallery on either side. A simple obelisk rises to form a Star of David. Behind it, the text reads 'In memory of those who were taken from this place, 5700-5705 (1940-1945).' Beside the entrance on the left a special area has been created with an eternal flame set in the floor. On the wall are the 6,700 family names of the 104,000 Dutch Jews killed by the Nazis. Posters and photographs hanging in the stair well give an impression of Jewish life in Amsterdam and the history of the Hollandsche Schouwburg as a theatre with a Jewish ambience. A permanent exhibition is mounted on the first floor dealing with the persecution of the Jews in the Netherlands. A service of remembrance organized by the Jewish community is held here each year on Yom ha-Shoa and on 4 May, the Dutch Remembrance Day.

5   THE CRÈCHE

The Germans organized a special crèche to look after the babies of people who'd been herded into the Hollandsche Schouwburg. They used the former premises of the Talmud Torah society, which since 1882 had owned the building at numbers 31 to 33, Plantage Middenlaan. In 1924 Talmud Torah moved to Tweede Boerhaavestraat. The director during the war years, J.W. van Hulst, together with Walter Süskind and Felix Halverstad, managed to smuggle hundreds of children out of the crèche across the back yard and into the Dutch Reformed Teachers' Training College, whence they would be taken to secret 'underground' addresses. A plaque on the façade of the school that stands there today remembers '*all those who during the German occupation helped Jewish children to escape deportation, 1940-1945*'. Where formerly the Talmud Torah

had its headquarters there now stands a modern school building designed by the famous Dutch architect Aldo van Eyck (1912-1999).

6   BETH MENUCHA

The building on the corner of Plantage Middenlaan and Plantage Westermanlaan was Beth Menucha (House of Rest), a home for the elderly of the Dutch Israelite congregation of Amsterdam. Beth Menucha was the largest Jewish home for the aged in the whole of the Netherlands. During the Second World War most of the old people were taken from the home and killed. When the war was over Beth Menucha moved first to the empty Portuguese Israelite Hospital on Henri Polaklaan. In 1976 the home was merged with Beth Shalom (House of Peace) in Osdorp, now in Buitenveldert. The building of the former rest home is now used by a hotel.

7   THE CITY REGISTRY OFFICE

The building at number 36, Plantage Kerklaan used to house the city's registry offices. Among other information, it contained index cards listing the city's 70,000 or so Jews. It is generally agreed that this meticulously updated register was enormously useful to the Germans in tracking down Jews living in Amsterdam. In the Netherlands, where the distinctions between Protestant denominations and Roman Catholics were for centuries a very sensitive area, everyone was registered according to their religion. This system made it only too easy to introduce Identity Cards on which a capital letter 'J' was stamped for Jews.
A wall plaque records how on 27 March 1943 a resistance group attempted to set fire to the registry office, with the aim of destroying the card index. Unfortunately the cards wouldn't catch light (they were too tightly packed). The twelve resistance fighters, among whom several Jews, were betrayed and arrested. They were executed by a firing squad. The leader of the group, Gerrit Jan van

der Veen, managed to escape but was arrested later during another operation and executed.

8 PLANCIUS: THE MUSEUM OF THE DUTCH RESISTANCE

The neo-classical building with a striking Star of David enhancing the façade at number 61, Plantage Kerklaan was founded in 1876 by the Jewish choral society 'Practice Makes Art'. The building is named after a former country house, which in turn had the name of the Dutch Calvinist preacher and geographer, Plancius. The society 'Practice Makes Art' was founded in 1854 by Jewish workers in the diamond trade. The first conductor was Aron (Anton) Berlijn (1817-1870). Born in Amsterdam, he was a famous conductor and highly esteemed composer, well-known throughout his life. Over five hundred compositions by him have survived, including operas, oratorios, symphonies, cantatas, lieder and above all splendid music for the synagogue. Berlijn taught music at the Dutch Israelite Seminary and conducted the Jewish choral societies *Amphion* and *Harpe Davids*. The latter had grown out of the diamond workers' fund for orphans.

Wages for diamond workers rose appreciably during the Cape Age, making it possible to purchase the Plancius building and construct a new complex on the site. The first stone was laid on 27 May 1876. The newspaper *Weekblad voor Israëlieten* (Jewish Weekly) wrote enthusiastically that this witnessed 'a step forward for our faith here in the city.' The large auditorium in Plancius, with its thousand seats, was used like the winter garden for concerts by the society 'Practice Makes Art' and the Amsterdam orchestral society – from which later the world-famous Concertgebouw Orchestra was to emerge. Also, Plancius was often the location for parties, and on Jewish festivals religious services were held here. It boasted one of the largest halls in the Amsterdam of its day and was thus also used for major political rallies, especially by the socialists and the trades unions. In 1890 the First of May celebrations in Amsterdam were held in Plancius and the famous Dutch socialist Domela Nieuwenhuis addressed a cheering crowd. But in 1896 the same Domela Nieuwenhuis, who had by then distanced himself from the parliamentary process, was booed out of the hall with cat-calls. Two other socialists, Pieter Jelles Troelstra and Henri Polak, hardly fared better and the police had to intervene to prevent a riot. For many decades Plancius was the fortress of Jewish socialism in Amsterdam until the more spacious Peoples' Palace on Frederiksplein took over the role.

As a music centre too, Plancius gradually lost its star position and particularly so after the opening of the Concertgebouw music halls in 1883. However, in 1898 the building gave an enthusiastic premiere to the Voice of the People, *Stem des Volks*, a choir which was almost entirely composed of Jewish socialists. Among other songs they performed the Socialists' March by Dolf de Levita and Otto de Nobel.

In 1913 Plancius was sold to J.H. Pimentel, who turned it into a garage for his taxi business. It continued in this function until 1999. Then the Museum of the Dutch Resistance moved into the premises from its previous home in a former synagogue on Lekstraat. The aim of the museum is to offer an overview of the struggle against fascism and racism during the Nazi period. The permanent exhibition illustrates the Dutch Resistance under the German occupation of the Netherlands. Following the main museum route, the visitor gets to see how most Dutch people lived through those years. The side alcoves illustrate specific aspects of the war. The museum aims to project something of the personal experiences of Dutch people during those years, and so doesn't tell the story of the major political events or figures. Projected onto the floor of the museum are questions that faced the Dutch people: the ongoing dilemmas of an occupied country.

The whole question of the Dutch Resistance touches a very tender spot in the country's consciousness. Initially, the resistance movement was praised but later it was observed that very few people were

The Plancius building with its striking Star of David, now the Museum of the Dutch Resistance

actively involved. In fact, only a tiny group of about 25,000 Dutch were involved in organized illegal activity. People felt that the majority of the Dutch population supported the resistance. But it cannot be denied that many Dutch people collaborated with the Germans. When the war was over various official bodies produced about 450,000 filed records and based on these 49,920 people were cautioned by the tribunals while 14,562 people were condemned by special courts The vast majority of Dutch people simply tried to survive the miseries of the war years as best they could. The Museum of the Dutch Resistance has a comprehensive documentation department with books and videos providing information about the Netherlands under German occupation.

9 HENRI POLAKLAAN

After the war the street called Plantage Franschelaan was re-named after the outstanding socialist leader Henri Polak (1868-1943). His father had made good in the Cape Age as a diamond polisher and the young Henri was sent to England on several occasions to specialize in the skills of diamond cutting and polishing. There he came in contact with the left-wing Fabian Society and British socialism. In London he also encountered questions dealing with the organization of workers and the trades union movement. There are few people in the history of the Dutch workers' movement who achieved as much as Henri Polak. Together with Jan van Zutphen (1863-1958) he was one of the leading lights when the General Dutch Diamond-Workers' Union (ANDB) was established. Between 1894 and 1940 he was chair of the Union ANDB. He was also one of the founders of the Dutch national trades union, the NVV and of the Social-Democratic Labour Party, the SDAP and indeed, representing this party he was an MP for both of the Dutch houses of parliament (First and Second Chamber).

Polak was a moderate socialist and a pragmatist and as such achieved a great deal for the emancipation of the Jewish proletariat. He gave them a voice of their own with which to confront capitalism, and the means to hold a dialogue as Jews with the municipal authorities. As he said of himself, he was 'a Jew among the Jews and a Dutchman among the Dutch'.

Polak's concern for the improvement of the working class included cultural aspects. For instance, he organized language classes and strove for cultural enrichment, setting up a chamber music ensemble for the diamond workers.

Writing *The Struggle of the Diamond Workers*, Henri Polak described such things as the Cape Age and the temptations that appeared with the sudden sharp rise in wages:

> A few months before they had been living in grinding poverty, scraping together an existence as best they could, negotiating with the peddlers for a few pickles or a couple of apples. Then suddenly money was pouring into their pockets, astonishing amounts, one week's wages now equalled what had been a year's. But hardly had it flowed into the house than it streamed out. People did the most idiotic things. The money had to be spent, and spent it was on the most vulgar, ugly objects…

In 1932 Henri Polak received an honorary doctorate from Amsterdam University. Shortly after the German invasion, he was arrested. During his interrogations he remained full of dignity, and told the Germans exactly what he thought about the occupation. Remarkably, he was set free in 1942. However, his health was broken and a year later he died.

10 ZICHRON JA'AKOV

During the First World War Jewish refuges from Belgium escaped to the neutral Netherlands, giving a notable impulse to the Dutch Zionist movement. Most of these Jews had fled from eastern Europe towards the end of the 19th century, on the run from growing anti-Semitism. Many of them were fervent Zionists. The youth organization Zichron Ja'akov was founded in 1915 to teach Modern

Hebrew – with an eye towards emigration to Palestine. The organization soon became the largest Zionist youth movement in the Netherlands, with over 500 members. The movement supported the ideas of world Mizrachi, that is, religious Zionism, which strove for a Jewish state in the spirit of Torah. Initially the meetings were held at number 107, Amstel. Then in 1933 they moved to Cats House at numbers 10 to 12, Plantage Middenlaan and in 1935 rented a large hall in the building known as the Chess House at number 14, Plantage Franschelaan (today Henri Polaklaan).

On the whole Zionism did not really catch on in Amsterdam among the many socialist-oriented Jews. In his reminiscences titled *Een leven lang* (A Lifetime), the socialist Ben Sajet explains this with great discernment:

> To begin with, that's for sure, I was – we were – cosmopolitans. When I became a student I encountered some ardent Zionists among the other Jewish students and they were often liberals, not socialist. But us Reds knew much better than them how international situations and relations actually work. We were absolutely convinced that socialism would triumph in the end … and so we were cosmopolitan, that is, we felt that the Jewish question would be solved when the social question was … In (1906) Maupie Mendels defended Social-Democracy in contrast to Zionism; then in turn A.B. Kleerekoper defended Zionism in contrast to Social-Democracy. I remember that occasion so clearly and Mendels talking about national heroes and referring to the royal House of Orange and then Kleerekoper yelling in a fury, 'How can Mendels, the Jew Mendels, talk about heroes and name the House of Orange? The Maccabees, those are our heroes!'

Incidentally, a few years later Kleerekoper (1880-1943) rejected Zionism and became a convinced socialist. His life is an excellent reflection of the criss-crossing interaction of a Jewish background, the longing for a Jewish homeland in Palestine and the socialist ideals of a classless society. He was descended from a line of rabbis and thoroughly educated in the Jewish liturgy and history. He became a fervent Zionist because he found the self-satisfied Dutch Jewry failed to understand and sympathize with the persecuted Jews of eastern Europe. Finally, convinced that the class struggle should dominate the fight for Jewish emancipation, he became an active propagandist and representative of the Social-Democratic Labour Party (Dutch SDAP). Interestingly, these different streams remained flowing through his personality, as can be seen in his work *Rebellious Scribbling* written in 1916:

> I've always suffered from the illusion that you couldn't just tell from looking at me that I'm a Jew. I've always been extremely careful trying to hide the bitter secret that my father was a rabbi and my grandfather the Rabbi of rabbis as far back as ten generations.
>
> And what did all this lead to? There it was, staring me in the face from one of the daily newspapers for the Dutch East Indies: I'm called a yid, a kike. The tolerant use the word 'Israelite'. Those on the inside use the term 'Jew'. The honest say 'Yid'. I am a yid. God be praised, the truth is out. Now I can be myself! Tonight I'll eat gefilte fish and matzos and fresh figs and apple strudel – all mixed together – and I'll drink a cup of sugar with a drop of tea in it and I'll put the bottle of spirits in the most obscure corner of the attic. The word of liberation has been pronounced. I was born a yid and that's what I'll die. Comrades, view me with suspicion, but do not reject me! I beseech you to show me your mercy.

It was only later, after the Nazis had come to power in Germany, that Zionism also became popular among Dutch Jewish socialists. In 1934 the Dutch branch of the Zionist Labour Party *Poale Zion* was set up. It never gained a great following but did exert considerable influence on the intellectual Jewish hard core. The radical position taken up by Zichron Ja'akov led, however, to many conflicts with the leaders of the Jewish community. One such example occurred when the society adopted the pronunciation of Hebrew as used in Palestine and

also adapted their Hebrew spelling. This was condemned by the chief rabbi Sarlouis for being 'Zionist
modernism'. However, religious services held in
Modern Hebrew, that is Ivrit, were very popular and
continued to be held into the Second World War.

11 THE A.N.D.B. BUILDING

The castle-like building of the General
Dutch Diamond-Workers' Union, or A.N.D.B., on
Henri Polaklaan played a significant role for many
decades in the lives of the Amsterdam diamond
workers, the majority of whom were Jewish. It was
the workers' fortress, which opponents nicknamed
the Robbers' Castle and from which the trades
union launched its metaphorical rockets. The diamond workers' union acted as the prototype, and
was indeed the forerunner of the Dutch trades union
organization (NVV), which was absorbed later into
the Dutch Trades Union Congress (FNV).
Thanks to the Cape Age the vanguard of the
Amsterdam proletariat emerged from their abject
poverty. Their emancipation expressed itself in the
creation of trades unions for almost every specialty
known to the diamond trade. These groups were
soon riddled with disputes about the relative status
of workers in different branches, and the death
knoll began to sound with the drop in prices that
began in 1876, when the bull market in the diamond
trade was over. Furthermore, there was conflict
between the Jewish and Christian unions. The
Diamond Workers' Union set up in 1890 tried in vain
to unite the warring parties.
The great breakthrough came with the strike in
1894. The Christian diamond-chips workers took
the initiative, quickly followed by other groups of
Protestant diamond workers. Spurred on by Jan van
Zutphen and Henri Polak the strike soon became
general and proved a triumph for the diamond workers. It resulted in thousands of new members for
the union and encouraged Henri Polak to found the
General Dutch Diamond-Workers' Union, or ANDB.
Initially the new union would meet in various
Amsterdam cafes, but before long they bought a

plot of land on Plantage Franschelaan. The famous
Dutch architect H.P. Berlage (1856-1934), known
for his socialist sympathies, was commissioned to
design a monumental building for the union. This is
one of the most impressive creations of the Dutch
workers' movement. Berlage took his inspiration
from Italian palazzi. The grand entrance hall with its
brickwork arches and stately stone staircase wel-
comes the visitor with its powerful architectonic
lines. Berlage's ideas about style are excellently
expressed in the functional ornamentation and the
plastic use of materials, particularly the brickwork.
Undeniably, the building embodied the expectations
of the socialist movement, as appears in the comment from a journalist of the left-wing paper *Het
Volk* (The People) at the opening in 1900:

> *A fortress for the toiling masses. Pressing their
> mighty weight one upon the other, the red bricks
> tower on high. Look at this building – it will stand*

Home of the people, the 'workers' castle', ANDB building

Murals painted by R.N. Roland Holst inside the Diamond Workers Trades Union building

for all eternity. It bears witness to strength immovable as a rock, to determination and gravity of purpose. High above in the lofty heights the tower is crowned with castellated forms and richly-decorated protrusions. Symbol of unity, the tower rises from this structure, a powerful square statement above the entrance well. Beaming afar, the rays from the tower gleam into the sky, proclaiming above the crowded city rooftops, the triumphant light of unity and labour.

In 1904 there was another massive labour strike, which broke once and for all the resistance of the jewellers and the diamond polishers, who were objecting to the actions of the union. From then on the union was involved in many trail-blazing activities in the social history of the Netherlands. Among these were the introduction of a week's annual holiday and an eight-hour working day, but also the 'raising the status of worker to that of a civilized, free individual with a sense of personal worth and

an interest in the arts and culture.'

Although the letters ANDB still adorn the building's tower, since 1991 the 'castle' has been used as the Trades Union Museum. The story of the labour movement and its struggles is presented at length, as well as the role of many Jewish diamond workers in the emancipation of the proletariat. The building is a remarkable piece of architecture and well worth a visit. In the entrance hall is a bust of Henri Polak and a memorial plaque in honour of the two thousand comrades who were murdered in the Second World War. Restored in all their glory are the remarkable murals by Dutch artist R.N. Roland Holst (1868-1938) in the union council chamber, illustrating the struggle of the working masses. Behind the table for the board members, the wall panels symbolize the organized workers' movement. The boardroom, also designed by Berlage, has frescoes by Roland Holst. The interior of the boardroom was presented to mark the introduction of the eight-hour working day. The original thick tablecloth embroidered with Hebrew texts is seldom displayed nowadays.

12 PORTUGUESE ISRAELITE HOSPITAL

The care of the poor and the sick is one of the fundamentals of the Jewish community. The Dutch Israelite Chief Synagogue had on its payroll a special doctor for paupers. Starting towards the end of the 18th century there were plans to build a Jewish hospital. Up until then Jews who were sick had always been tended at home, or, if that proved too difficult, had been admitted to a general public hospital. In 1804 the Ashkenazim opened the first Jewish hospital on the corner of Rapenburgerstraat and Rapenburg. When in 1885 they moved to new premises on Nieuwe Keizersgracht, the Sephardim obtained the old building. By 1916 this had become far too small and a new Portuguese Israelite hospital was opened opposite the ANDB building on Henri Polaklaan. The hospital, designed by the architect Harry Elte, had on its façade – just like the former building on Rapenburgerstraat – a pelican feeding its young, symbol of the Sephardi community. The hospital was in use until 1943. Then the patients were deported. Later, the building was used by the Joodse Invalide, since the fine premises on Weesperplein were too large. The name was changed to Beth Shalom, meaning House of Peace. This too had its curtain call in 1976 when Beth Shalom moved to the Amsterdam suburb of Osdorp. The building was then converted into dwelling units.

13 THE A.C. WERTHEIM PARK

The A.C. Wertheim Park dates from 1898. At the centre of the park is a monument to Abraham Carel Wertheim (1832-1897). He was a prominent banker and a major figure both in Amsterdam and beyond. In 1884 he saved the Dutch Colonial Bank from a financial debacle, and he was director of the

The pelican, symbol of the Sephardi Jewish community

Dutch Credit and Deposit Bank, chairman of the Zuiderzee Committee (which was already proposing and planning filling in the waters known as the Zuyder Zee), he supported De Lesseps in his plans to construct the Suez Canal, he was commissioner of the Dutch Trading Company and of the Bank of the Netherlands, and involved in founding the Bank of Amsterdam. Not only a prominent businessman, Wertheim was also an important figure in encouraging stimulating art and theatre.

It seems likely that Wertheim inspired the anti-Semitic text by the Dutch novelist W.A. Paap (1856-1923) in his work *Jeanne Collette*, written at the end of the 19th century:

He sits enthroned; his puffed-up body reclines slothfully on his throne: the Jew-baron. The short legs crossed, the rolls of fat cascading over each other, there he sprawls, the dollar-baron, puffing smoke from his cigar into the faces of lords and princes, who humbly bow low, cringe full of flat-

tery inspired by dollars, offering the interest on usury and princely favours … high above the shrill cry of old Europe, the howl of hunger and death; high above the De Profundis, the yearning call from the depths, that rustles through this century's dying hour, resounds the shriek: the Jew, the Jew. For the filthiest creature that this nineteenth century, this dollar-century has brought forth – whether it be born a Jew or has the soul of a Jew – is this dollar-baron …before whom princes and prelates and people bend low.

Wertheim was a prominent figure in the Jewish community. Indeed, he was the personification of the Jewish bourgeoisie, concentrating on integration into Dutch society and regarding Judaism as primarily a religion. Thus Wertheim dedicated his energies to his chairmanship of the Dutch Israelite Religious Community although he was not an Orthodox Jew. He explained this paradox with great clarity when in 1854 he gave a lecture to the Freemasons:

A new dawn is breaking for humankind …Now it is no longer only exiles dreaming of a fatherland. Their fatherland is where they live, where their parents and their children were born …Their nationality dissolves into the great nationality where they are living and consists only in their faith which they have managed to preserve through eighteen centuries of persecution …In the synagogue they are Jews; outside they are citizens.

Clearly, not everyone understood this distinction between 'Jew' and 'citizen'. This was seen when the monument to Wertheim was unveiled in1898. In a song written specially in his memory we find the somewhat curious words, 'he was so good, gentle to everyone … full of Christian virtue and a faithful citizen.' With the rise of socialism, Wertheim's reputation among the proletariat declined noticeably.

Wertheim Park with the monument to A.C. Wertheim

The Auschwitz Memorial designed by Dutch writer and artist Jan Wolkers, Wertheim Park

The Jewish workers became aware of their under-privileged social position, which was opposed to that of wealthy bank directors like Wertheim. The right-wing conservative ideology of the Jewish elite contributed to the fact that Jewish emancipation didn't take place within a purely Jewish setting, but rather within the socialist movement – thereby causing a huge rift within the Jewish community.

14 THE AUSCHWITZ MEMORIAL

In the Wertheim Park you can also see the famous Auschwitz Memorial made by the well-known Dutch writer and sculptor, Jan Wolkers. It consists of six large pieces of cracked mirror and the text *Nooit meer Auschwitz* (Never Again Auschwitz). The monument was unveiled in 1977 at one of Amsterdam's cemeteries, Oosterbegraafplaats, and later transported to its present location. The pieces

of broken mirror represent the thought that after Auschwitz the skies were forever scarred. This links up with an old Jewish tradition in which something is left incomplete during the building of a synagogue, to remind people that after the destruction of the Temple in Jerusalem no building can ever be perfect. Jan Wolkers, who was born in 1925, said in this connection:

How can you find the means to commemorate a crime when you have the feeling it could never be washed away, even after two thousand years, when this planet dissolves into the universe. You can beat your brains puzzling for an image that could signify such horror and represent such suffering. You look up to the sky, and cannot conceive that the blue shining there was present while such terrors took place, peaceful and unperturbed as when it shines above a meadow full of flowers. Then in a vision somehow to do

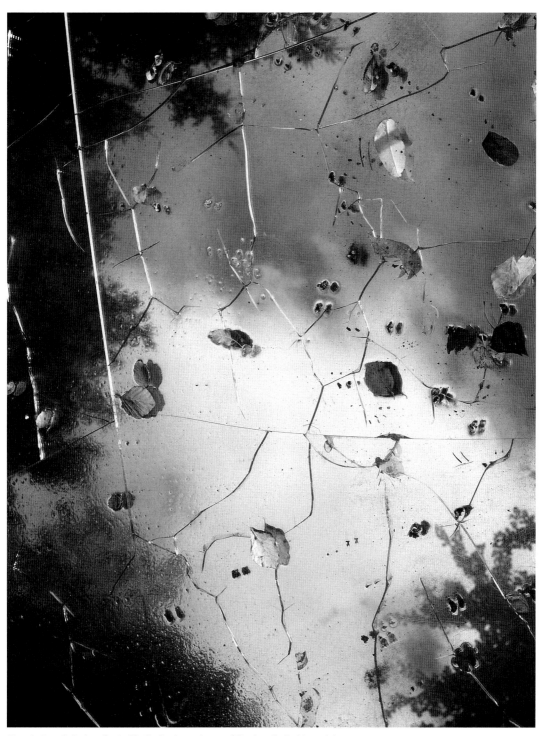

The shattered sky is reflected in the broken mirrors of the Auschwitz Memorial

with justice, cracks and jagged lines appear in the blue sky as if the abominations that took pace on the earth below have seared eternity and can never be forgotten.

Beneath the monument an urn is buried, containing human ashes brought from the death camp at Auschwitz. In Amsterdam the liberation of Auschwitz on 27 January 1945 is commemorated annually, recalling the many thousands of Dutch Jews who were killed there.

15 THE HOME OF DE CASTRO

The fine canal house at number 93, Nieuwe Herengracht is a good example of the attractive dwellings often owned by wealthy Sephardim, lining the so-called 'Jewish' canals. The most famous resident of this house was David Henriques de Castro (1826-1898), scion of a prominent Amsterdam Jewish family who had emigrated in the 17th century from Bayonne and Hamburg. In Amsterdam they soon became highly prosperous merchants. In the Sephardi community several generations of De Castros held important positions. The building was bought by David Henriques de Castro in 1859. It had previously housed a school for Jewish children of well-to-do families, but had not been able to survive when the Education Act of 1857 put an end to state subsidies for private education. David Henriques de Castro had a great appetite for knowledge and was keen to maintain both Jewish and secular traditions. He is chiefly remembered for his comprehensive Jewish library and the trail-blazing research he undertook in connection with the Portuguese cemetery in Ouderkerk just outside Amsterdam. He was also active in the Sephardi community as board member, administrator and member of the Synagogue Council. After his death in 1898, his extensive collection of Judaica and art was auctioned. The major works of Judaica were bought by the libraries of Ets Hayyim and Rosenthaliana, thus remaining in Amsterdam.

Nieuwe Herengracht, called 'Jews Herengracht' because of its many Jewish residents, including De Castro (nr. 93) and Cohen (nr. 103)

In the ceiling on the first storey of the house an attractive Star of David recalls the former Jewish residents. To mark the hundredth anniversary of De Castro's death, his great-granddaughter unveiled a memorial plaque recalling his pioneering work in connection with the Portuguese Jewish cemetery in Ouderkerk.

16 NUMBER 103, NIEUWE HERENGRACHT

The splendid house at number 103, Nieuwe Herengracht has a rich Jewish history going back to 1685. In that year the Portuguese Jewish printer and publisher Joseph Athias (c.1635-1700) and his Roman Catholic partner Widow Schipper built a new dwelling next door to a printer's and type-founder's. Athias was one of the many renowned Jewish print- ers who in the heyday of the Dutch Republic greatly contributed to Amsterdam's fame as a book-printing centre. Here, for the first time in history, Jewish books were published set in Hebrew characters, as well as in Spanish, Portuguese and Yiddish. Both widow Schipper and Athias had been granted a licence from the States-General to print the Bible in English. In 1673 they decided to undertake a joint venture. The enterprise was so successful that they soon required more space. Hence the house on Nieuwe Herengracht. The famous printing shop of Athias, who himself moved into the attractive dwelling, produced many thousands of Bibles in English as well as many Hebrew works and the famous Yiddish translation of the Bible by Jozef Witzenhaussen.

In about 1700 the complex was inherited by the heirs of widow Schipper. In 1728 the dwelling was sold to a certain Samson Salomons, who was forced to sell the expensive property in 1734. The new owner was the successful businessman Aron de Joseph de Pinto (1710-1758), first cousin of the famous David de Pinto of Sint Antoniesbreestraat. This Aron possessed wide cultural interests and had the house fundamentally rebuilt in 1751, giving it its present-day appearance. It has a richly sculptured stone façade in three sections and elegant wrought-iron fencing, providing a unique example of Amsterdam rococo architecture. Inside too was elaborately decorated while the garden was adorned with a delightful rococo garden house. The house was a fitting backdrop for a fast-growing art collection. In a eulogistic poem, Eleazer Uziel Cardozo sang the praises of this mansion:

Who ever saw so many masterpieces in one place?
Who ever beheld such glittering crystal mirrors?
Apollo and Fidias are struck dumb!
All that this house has is remarkable!

In 1787 De Pinto's children sold the house to the wealthy tobacco merchant Benjamin Cohen (1726-1800). He was the great-grandson of Eliokim Cohen, who according to family legend had come to Amsterdam from Italy in 1664. At the end of the 17th century his son Ezekiel set off for Amersfoort, in the east of the Netherlands. The Cohen family was closely bound up with the founding of the tobacco business near Amersfoort and for many years played a prominent part in the Jewish commu- nity there. During the 18th century the descendants of Cohen became scattered throughout Europe, ally- ing themselves with leading Jewish families such as the Gompertzes, Goldschmidts, Montefioris and Rothschilds. Benjamin Cohen succeeded in expand- ing the tobacco business near Amersfoort into a mercantile house that was to acquire a leading posi- tion on the European money market. Besides all this, he was very knowledgeable about Jewish teachings and way of life, and spoke fluent Hebrew. In 1813 the Cohen family sold the house to the dia- mond dealer Elkan Jacob Levie de Vries, a very wealthy and successful Jew. From 1902 to 1921 it became 'Huize Stranders', an elegant Jewish restau- rant and location for parties. It was famous for the many Jewish wedding that were celebrated in it. Later, much of the glitz and glamour was lost, espe- cially after the disappearance of some of the deco- rations on the façade. Sadly, the beautiful garden house was taken down and exported to Ukkel in Belgium; the premises were never quite the same again.

The stylish front of number 103, Herengracht, for several centuries home to Jews

17 LIPPMAN ROSENTHAL, NIEUWE HERENGRACHT

The banking firm of Lippman Rosenthal and Co. was established at 111, Nieuwe Herengracht. Baron George Rosenthal (1828-1909) lived right beside the offices while his partner Leo Lippman lived four houses further along at number 119. During the second part of the 19th century the bank earned itself a good reputation. As told elsewhere in this book, the German occupiers used the bank during World War II as a cover for their anti-Jewish financial transactions. Consequently, the name Lippman Rosenthal today has a bitter ring.

George Rosenthal is remembered above all because in 1880 he donated his father Leeser Rosenthal's (1794-1868) extensive book collection to the Amsterdam municipality. After his father's death, George Rosenthal commissioned the Jewish bibliographer Meijer Roest (1821-1899) to catalogue the entire collection. The beneficiaries didn't want to split up the collection. When no agreement was reached with large libraries in Europe and the United States, the choice fell on Amsterdam. The Bibliotheca Rosenthaliana became part of the university library. After the death of George Rosenthal his widow, Sophie Rosenthal-May (1838-1921) continued his good works, notably through her support for the poor, and founding the Sophie Rosenthal Kindergarten on Nieuwe Uilenburgerstraat and the Rosenthal-May Nurses' Home on Nieuwe Keizersgracht.

THE CENTRE

Amsterdam city centre doesn't have a particularly Jewish character
to it, but in the course of the 19th century it became the backdrop
for a number of activities that arose because of the assimilation of
Jews into Dutch society. Traditionally most of Amsterdam's Jews
lived east of the river Amstel in the Jewish quarter. A small number,
especially the more well-to-do, lived in grand canal houses near the
Amstel. As the 19th century wore on, Jews became increasingly
involved in the general urban life, activities often taking place in the
city centre. They took part in the lively nightlife centring round
Rembrandtplein and in the daytime thronged the large department
stores, founded by Jewish families and still flourishing in the 21st
century – Metz & Co., Maison de Bonneterie, De Bijenkorf, besides
Hirsch on Leidseplein and Gerzon on Kalverstraat.

1 HAMBURGER'S LEAD AND ZINC ROLLING MILL

The premises at 194 to196, Amstel housed the Royal Dutch Lead and Zinc Rolling Mill owned by A.D. Hamburger. The Lead and Zinc Rolling firm also had branches in Delft and Utrecht, run by other members of the family. These three Hamburger family firms had developed from the traditional Jewish scrap metal trade. In the second half of the 19th century Hamburger expanded his business into an industrial enterprise in Utrecht. The Amsterdam branch was chiefly concerned with trading. The Delft factory also had a branch in Amsterdam on Herengracht.

On 30 November 1900 a memorial plaque was set into the façade of the house on the Amstel, by two members of the Hamburger family. Incidentally, one of them, the lawyer J. Hamburger, was a prominent member of the Utrecht Jewish congregation, where he acted as chair of the synagogue board and was also on the board of the society for biblical study, Mischne Torah.

2 AMSTEL DIAMONDS

Just beyond Amstelstraat, opposite the bridge called Blauwbrug, is Amstel Diamonds, the Diamond Polishers. The firm was founded in 1876, towards the close of the Cape Age, by Wolf Streep, who had been highly successful thanks to his monopoly on diamond chips. The new diamond polishing factory lay just outside the old Jewish quarter. The family was proud of the fact that they had 'emigrated' to the other side of the Amstel. Employing 32 diamond cutters, at the beginning of the 20th century Streep had the largest diamond-cutting business in Amsterdam. After World War II the business largely fell into non-Jewish hands. Today the firm only sells

Herengracht, a central canal where prominent Jews would have their homes

diamonds to tourists, and has furnished a showroom where visitors can learn about the process whereby rough diamond is transformed into a glittering gem.

3   HOME OF WERTHEIM

On the last block of Herengracht, almost beside the river Amstel and thus close to the Jewish quarter, a number of wealthy Jews have had their homes through the centuries. They were well integrated into Dutch society and one of them was the prominent banker, A.C. Wertheim (1832-1897). He lived in the grand canal house at numbers 615 to 617, Herengracht, where two 17th-century buildings stretch behind the imposing façade. Wertheim was a man of versatile accomplishments, active in the Jewish community and at the same time a leading figure in the political liberal movement. He made a distinction between religion, which he saw as a private affair, and participation in worldly matters, as a good citizen. Indeed, he was in many ways the personification of the integrated Jewish bourgeoisie in 19th-century Holland.

4   HOME OF SARPHATI

Number 598, Herengracht, close to the river Amstel, is a beautiful late 17th century house with a neck gable. In the 19th century it was the home of Samuel Sarphati (1813-1866). This son of a Sephardi tobacco dealer was an untiring planner and inspired with a great vision for the future of the city of Amsterdam. At the age of 26 he started a doctor's practice in the impoverished Jewish Quarter. Later he was also to work as apothecary, teacher, manager and project developer. He was involved in the founding of the Society for the Advancement of Pharmacy, as well as the Amsterdam School of Trade and the Society for the Promotion of Agriculture and Land Reclamation; the latter dealt with much of the city's refuse and as such was the impulse for organized urban sanitation. Furthermore, Sarphati was the driving force behind the Association of Grain and Bread

Dr Samuel Sarphati's house on Herengracht

Factories, challenging the poor quality of bread in the 19th century, particularly the huge differences in the quality of flour and the weight of this staple diet of the poor. As board member of the Credit and Deposit Bank and the National Mortgage Bank, Sarphati maintained close ties with the Dutch Building Society – another of his initiatives.

All these organizations were forms of private enterprise. In this Sarpahti was a typical example of the 19th-century liberal leaders, who played a major part in shaping social policy. Presumably, Sarphati's motivation can be found in his upbringing. Although he came from a middle-class family, he saw around him the grinding poverty and the appalling hygienic conditions of the old Jewish quarter. His little sister died from an infectious disease when she was six years old. He worked for many years as a doctor in the heart of the Jewish slums. There he concluded that the traditional Jewish zedakah, or charity, was not adequate. Convinced that the battle against poverty was a task for the government, he argued that the poverty of the masses threatened the entire national economy. For him, combatting poverty was in the general interest. Characterized by ceaseless energy, Sarphati, with his combination of private enterprise and service to general social causes, was surely one of the most outstanding figures of 19th-century Amsterdam.

5 BELMONTE COURT

Although he was of Jewish origin, Isaac Nunez Belmonte (died 1705), using the name of Manuel baron de Belmonte, was an agent general of the – generally anti-Jewish – king of Spain. In 1700 Belmonte bought the splendid house at 586, Herengracht. The building, with its double front steps and four sets of large windows, is exceptionally wide. Incidentally, the present façade dates from the 18th century. Belmonte and his family belonged to the Sephardi elite of Amsterdam, who were almost completely integrated into the Dutch way of life. When the Dutch Republic finally signed a peace treaty with Spain in 1648, a wave of 'New Christians' (that is, Jewish *conversos*) left Spain for the Dutch Republic; among them was Belmonte. He lived in Amsterdam from 1656. A few years later he succeeded his brother as agent general to the Spanish king. When Spain and the Dutch Republic allied against France, the Spanish monarch bestowed the title of baron upon Belmonte. Many aristocratic visitors were entertained in Belmonte's beautiful home, notably the Spanish ambassador and his connections. Like a lot of prominent Sephardim, Belmonte – especially in his later years – was active in the Jewish community and from 1681 was representative of the so-called 'Jewish Nation', that is, he appeared on behalf of the Sephardi Jewish community in cases involving the rulers of Amsterdam city, or the Dutch Republic. Manuel de Belmonte was active in literary matters, being patron of the Sephardi literary academies *Temor Divino* (Holy Fear) and *Los Floridos* (The Talented). These academies would hold meetings in his home, when they would recite poetry and per-

form plays. After his death the house was inherited by his nephew Francisco Ximenes Belmonte and then by the latter's son, Manuel Lew Ximenes.

6 KOKADORUS

A bronze statue on one side of the Amstelveld commemorates the legendary barrow boy, Kokadorus. More than anyone else, he came to symbolize the Jewish peddler – through the centuries the most familiar type of Jew in western Europe. His grandpa was called Ko, his grandma Ka and his father Dorus – so Meijer Linnewiel combined the names and became Kokadorus. He was to become the king of Dutch stallholders, a man of brilliant wit and imagination, seller of pens and pencils, pocket knives, spoon and forks, combs and soap, braces, corn plasters, all kinds of wonder cures and above all, master of unceasing banter. Meijer Linnewiel was born in 1867 in Leeuwarden, Friesland. As ten-year-old he was selling matches on Amsterdam's Kalverstraat and four year later he began working on the marketplace of Amstelveld. His silver jubilee was a grand celebration and the citizens of Amsterdam presented him with a silver medal. He died in 1934. Meijer Linnewiel was an observant Jew, who kept the dietary laws, honoured the Sabbath and studied the Talmud. Some of his market orations joke about his Jewish background and refer to widely-held anti-Semitic prejudices:

> 'O, so you think Kokadorus is pulling a fast one? That's right, some of you will say, that Koki is a Jew, and you can never trust a Jew. You know, the Jews just don't stand a chance any longer. Nowadays the Christians are up to so many tricks trying to get the better of each other, the poor Jews are out of the running.'

And on another occasion he said:

> 'Here, listen all tramps, on the spot where I have been feared and famed they will dig a grave for me, and in the same grave they will also lay my assistant, Cheffie. But I'm warning you now about Cheffie – you'll have to lay a massive gravestone on top of him – because he can get away with anything!'

Meijer Linnewiel, alias the market stallholder 'Kokadorus'

Kokadorus had prophesied that after his death a statue of him would be put up in a cross street where no one would recognize him. In fact his statue stands close to the market where he earned his fame – and he is probably the only barrow boy to be immortalized in this way. The statue was made in 1977 by Erica van Eeghen.

7   REMBRANDTPLEIN

In the course of the 19th century, alongside the formal and classical theatrical and musical productions in Amsterdam, there arose more popular form of entertainment, often in the neighbourhood of Rembrandtplein. This new entertainment, so close to the Jewish quarter, attracted a large Jewish public. Together with the many Jewish performers this resulted in a Jewish-Amsterdam ambience in the theatres and cafes on, or close to, the square. A strikingly large number of Jews were engaged as musicians, directors, producers or impresarios in this entertainment world.

Traditionally, Jews did not take up jobs in the entertainment world because it was a pastime of the heathen. Indeed, the Jerusalem Talmud (Benedictions, or Berackhot) says quite explicitly:

> I thank you Lord and God of my fathers that you allow me to sit among those who attend your house of study and the synagogue and that you have not made me to sit among those who go to theatres and circuses. I work and they work; I keep watch and they keep watch; I for the day when I shall enter your Paradise, they eternal destruction.

That despite this centuries-old prohibition of light entertainment the Amsterdam Jews took part in it, is presumably largely due to their extreme poverty. Generally without restrictions, the theatre world offered Jews job opportunities without presenting barriers.

There were many cafes on Rembrandt Square, such as the New Cherry Tree on the corner of Amstelstraat. Jews nicknamed this the *Warme Jad,* or Warm Hand, because courting couples would often sit there hand-in-hand. On the south side of the square, Schiller Café still stands. It used to be a meeting place for Jewish writers and artists, such as Herman Heijermans, who lodged there for a time during World War I. Across the square is The Crown, so called because it opened in the year of the coronation of Queen Wilhelmina, 1898. It too was a meeting place for Jews – the cabaret artist Louis Davids could often be found there. On Mondays in The Crown jobs were doled out to the many unemployed artists. Beside The Crown stood The Mill Café, founded by the impresario J. Gosschalk, while to the right lay the Rembrandtplein Theatre, where operas and operettas were performed under the direction of Max Gabriel; both these places had an enthusiastic Jewish following. The former was pulled down in 1929 while the theatre was set on fire in 1942.

Amstelstraat linked Rembrandt Square with the

Jewish quarter. Thus in the 19th century it became the Broadway of Jewish Amsterdam, though of course neither the public nor the performers were only Jewish. Today you'll find the disco called *It* where at the beginning of the 20th century you could have gone to hear the songs and jokes of cabaret artist Leon Boedels in Flora Café. Formerly the Central Theatre stood on the corner where now you see the large bank building of the AMRO; the theatre started its life in 1881 as a waxworks museum, later to become famous for its performances by the Yiddish Theatre *Potash and Mother-of-Pearl*.

Across the street was the *Grand Theâtre* run by the brothers Abraham and Ben van Lier; it was founded in 1787 as the Ashkenazi Theatre by J.A. Dietrichs. The J.H. Dessauer Jewish theatre company enjoyed huge successes in this venue. Later, the socially engaged plays of Herman Heijermans were often performed here. Finally, just before you reached the corner of the square there was the *Salon des Variétés*, a variety theatre established by Jews in

1844, which was to see its heyday under the direction of Boas and Judels. Specially for its opening, the Jewish composer Aron Wolff Berlijn wrote a cantata. Jewish participation in the Rembrandtplein theatre world was greatly enhanced after the Cape Age with the subsequent rise in wages. In his novel *Jeugd* (Youth), Jos Loopuit (1864-1923) describes how this sudden rise to riches didn't please everyone:

> Saturday evening in the Salon chez Judels or Van Lier's, they would be seated in the stalls or in the boxes, hung heavy with their gaudy gold chains boastfully twinkling on their over-plump middles. The women wore 'shawls-longs' [sic] costing over two or three hundred guilders, necklaces of heavy gold, bejewelled buttons and flashy rings on their fingers. The stones didn't cost a penny, 'just the price of the production', said the men.

In the 1930s Amsterdam theatre life gained a lively input from the many German refugees, most of them with a Jewish background. But the Second

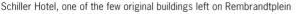
Schiller Hotel, one of the few original buildings left on Rembrandtplein

World War signified the end of the Jewish entertainment world in and around Rembrandt Square. First the German occupier ordered Jews to act in purely Jewish companies and perform to a purely Jewish audience. Thus there was a Jewish Symphony Orchestra under the conductor Albert van Raalte (1890-1952), a theatre section under Elias van Praag (1884-1942) and Eduard Veterman (1901-1946) and the cabaret group led by Heintje Davids (1888-1975). The Germans brought this to an end in July 1942 and began the deportations. Fritz Hirsch was the first to be arrested and sent to Mauthaussen death camp, because early in the war he had made jokes about the Gestapo. Almost all the Jewish performers were killed in the death camps, where they would often have entertained the Germans with their music and their wit.

8 TUSCHINSKI

The Tuschinski Theatre on Reguliersbreestraat was the crowing achievement of the Polish Jew, Abram Icek Tuschinski (1886-1942). This ebullient character arrived in Rotterdam as a young man and threw himself into the theatre world. Hardly was the First World War over, when Tuschinski decided – together with his business partners Gerschtanowitz and Ehrlich – to build a theatre in the heart of Amsterdam. A theatre with a difference. They bought a piece of land known as Devil's Triangle – a slum of dark narrow alleyways – and promptly razed it to the ground. The theatre that rose upon that site is indeed unique. Even today it's hard to say exactly which architectural style it represents – but style it has, that's for sure. Although it was designed by a certain Klaphaak, Tuschinski himself supervised the entire building process and the theatre unmistakeably bears the stamp of his personality. The construction process was beset with problems – for example, Tuschinski had ordered 1,200 wooden piles from Germany but the British stymied all transport from that country. So what did Tuschinski do? He went to Germany in person, found the piles, tied them into rafts and

The striking façade of Tuschinsky Cinema

draped the Dutch flag over them – and sent them floating down the river Rhine to Holland. On one occasion Tuschinski found himself in the middle of a gunfight in troubled postwar Germany, and at another time the factory where he had ordered two million bricks was flooded. Despite this, Tuschinski saw to it that the bricks were delivered to Amsterdam. Perhaps his most remarkable achievement was in persuading the director of the Brussels *Cinema de la Monnaie* to dismantle his splendid Wurlitzer Cinema Organ and give it to Tuschinski because the organ the latter had ordered for the theatre's opening wouldn't be ready on time.

The Tuschinski Theatre was a resounding success. The building, both the exterior and the interior, rejoices in many small, exquisite details. There is something Byzantine about it. Tuschinski was deported to Auschwitz in 1942 and killed. The theatre bearing his name is still the most attractive in Amsterdam – all the more so after a careful restoration in 2001. In the entrance lobby behind the bar a plaque commemorates the three men who dreamed up this beautiful cinema palace.

9 GOUDSTIKKER ART DEALER'S

The firm of Goudstikker was one of the most prestigious art dealers in the Netherlands. Founded in 1845 by the brothers J. and S. Goudstikker, it gradually expanded to become a highly respected business. In 1919 the young Jacques Goudstikker became director. Under him, the company moved to 458, Herengracht. Through the years the Goudstikker Firm gained international fame. The lifestyle of Jacques Goudstikker also earned him an international reputation. He and his wife, the Viennese singer Desi von Halban-Kurz, led a decidedly un-Dutch and almost fairytale-like existence. His home on Herengracht was furnished to suit the paintings it housed. Furthermore, he bought

Title page from one of art dealer Goudstikker's lavish catalogues

CATALOGUE
DES
Nouvelles Acquisitions
DE LA
COLLECTION
GOUDSTIKKER

Exposées à
AMSTERDAM
Heerengracht 458

avril-mai 1930
N° 58

Nijenrode Castle, some distance outside Amsterdam on the river Vecht and restored this medieval building to its former glory. Here he organized a grand opening gala, with the complete Concertgebouw Orchestra playing under their conductor Willem Mengelberg. Goudstikker was particularly famous for his stylish meticulously-produced art catalogues, which he numbered and signed personally. With the Depression of the 1930s he was forced to limit his activities more and more and ended up dealing with a small select groups of collectors.

From the very start of the Nazi rise o power in Germany, Goudstikker distanced himself from them, and after Hitler's putsch he refused to have dealings with Germany. When Jewish refugees began to stream across the border, he organized charity parties and concerts for them at Nijenrode Castle. When war broke out, the 42-year-old Goudstikker fled to England with his wife and child on SS Bodegraven. Goudstikker died as the result of a fall aboard ship and was buried in England. His family were refused entry into the country and sailed on to America. Goudstikker had left behind his art collection, and his elderly mother, pressurized by their non-Jewish staff, sold it to the German art dealer Miedl, on condition that he would protect her. This he indeed did, but the collection fell largely into the hands of the Nazi chief Göring. Goudstikker's magnificent collection was one of the prizes most coveted by the Nazis in their massive theft of Dutch art. After the war 235 paintings were found – a mere fraction of Goudstikker's collection of over two thousand. The Stichting Nederlands Kunstbezit (charged with recovering art stolen from the Netherlands by the Germans during the war) declared that the art collection had been sold voluntarily and thus the works now belonged to the State. Goudstikker's widow accepted a settlement for what had been 'alienated' by Miedl. Many years later the Goudstikker case again hit the headlines, when questions of restitution of property and reparation were being hotly discussed. In 1998 a new claim was submitted by the heirs of Goudstikker, only to be rejected once more by the State of the Netherlands.

10   BIBLIOTHECA ROSENTHALIANA

The library *Bibliotheca Rosenthaliana*, housed in the same building as Amsterdam University Library on Singel, is, together with the Ets Hayyim Collection of the Portuguese Israelite community, one of the cornerstones of Jewish culture both in Amsterdam and far beyond. The core of the library is still formed by the collection of Leeser Rosenthal, a rabbi born near Warsaw in 1794 who later moved to Germany. His collection, numbering over 5,200 books, was one of the largest private collections in Germany. After his death in 1868 the family spent a long time searching for a suitable home for his library. Finally, in 1880, the collection was presented to the city of Amsterdam on condition that it would remain intact as a distinct section of the Library of the University of Amsterdam. Since then the Bibliotheca Rosenthaliana has expanded immeasurably. Until his death in 1909 the banker George Rosenthal financed the buying of volumes, and after that his widow Sophie established the George Rosenthal Fund to deal with this. In 1941 the unique library was closed by the Germans. The librarians and their families were deported and killed. The pro-German mayor of Amsterdam, Voûte, managed for a long time to prevent the transport of the Bibliotheca Rosenthaliana, by presenting it as municipal property. Some of the highlights of the collection were removed for safekeeping. But in June 1944 the books departed for 'scholarly study' to Frankfurt's *Institut zur Erforschung der Judenfrage*. But the swift advance of Allied troops into Germany gave the Nazis no time to unpack the books, and the collection was found virtually intact in a monastery in Offenbach.

The collection comprises books on Jewish culture and the Jewish way of life, journals from many countries, Jewish coins, anti-Semitic posters dating from the Dreyfus Affair in 19th-century France and religious books, the oldest being a prayer book from 1290. One of the four gable stones of the Amsterdam University Library is dedicated to the memory of Manasseh ben Israel (1604-1657), one of the most remarkable figures from the early days of the Portuguese Sephardi congregation in Amsterdam. Manasseh came from the island of Madeira to Amsterdam with his crypto-Jewish father, and was an outstanding member of the young Sephardi congregation. He was a controversial figure in the Jewish community, partly because of his many publications – but he was deeply respected for his learning among non-Jews. One of them was the artist Rembrandt, whom Manasseh commissioned to illustrate several of his works. In 1627 Manasseh ben Israel published the first book in printed Hebrew, suggesting the high degree of (intellectual) freedom that prevailed in the Dutch Republic at that time. Indeed, Manasseh laid the basis for a thriving tradition of Jewish book printing in Amsterdam; he also supervised the very first

Wall plaque in memory of Manasseh ben Israel

Jewish newspaper, the *Gazeta de Amsterdam*.
Manasseh ben Israel held the belief that the
Messiah would only come when the Jews were literally spread 'to the ends of the earth.' This explains
his diligent attempts to gain re-entry for the Jews
into England, which he saw in the medieval Hebrew
terms as *angle-terre*, that is, one of the world's four
corners. In 1656 he wrote the treatise *Vindiciae
Judaeorum* (A Vindication of the Jews) addressed to
the English parliament in order to dispel English
prejudice against the Jews:

> Thus I am compelled to bewail, with bitter tears
> and grieving spirit, those most weighty and heavy
> accusations that certain Christian folk do bring
> against the scattered and downtrodden Jews who
> dwell amongst them, that these same
> Jews…when they are celebrating their Paschal
> Feast, in order to bring leaven to their bread do
> make use of the blood of Christian folk whom
> they have killed for this purpose…Nevertheless,
> how far from the truth this accusation is, ye may
> judge from the following proven judgments.
> It is most strongly forbidden to the Jews to eat
> any form of blood, Lev. 7:26, and Deut. 12,
> where it is most expressly stated and as a result
> of this commandment the Jews do not eat any
> blood of any kind, from whatsoever manner of
> creature…
> The law of the Ten Commandments: thou shalt
> not kill, sums up everything. It is a moral law
> whereby not only is it forbidden to the Jews to kill
> any person from the community in which they
> live, but also, as an extension of that command-
> ment they are even obliged to love them …

Finally, Oliver Cromwell gave permission for the
Jews to settle once more in Britain but Manasseh
had to return to the Netherlands with his son
Samuel, who was gravely sick. Manasseh ben Israel
lies buried in the Sephardi cemetery just outside
Amsterdam, in Ouderkerk aan de Amstel.

11 MAISON DE BONNETERIE, DEPARTMENT STORE

Drawing on their age-old experience in the textile
trade, a number of Jews profited from the growth of
major fashion houses and clothing stores which
developed into department stores selling a wide
variety of goods. In 1889 Josef Cohen and Rosa
Cohen-Wittgenstein opened a small shop selling
haberdashery and knitwear. Josef, born in Germany
in 1860, had come to the Netherlands as a sales-
man in textiles. Once in Amsterdam, he did the
rounds of the new fashion palaces, taking in the lat-
est developments in the readymade clothes industry. He met his wife-to-be, who was also from
Germany, at Hirsch's store. They began their own
store, and business was soon booming. Before long
they bought up neighbouring property, and De
Bonneterie, as their store was called, progressed
by leaps and bounds. The success was partly due
to the fact that De Bonneterie presented its collections in the provinces, supported by advertisements
in local newspapers. When transport improved, and
people could more easily travel to the big cities,
these presentations stopped – but by that time De
Bonneterie had made a name for itself as a quality
fashion house. The furs department, with its own
atelier, was particularly famous.

In 1911 the present elegant building on
Kalvertstraat and Rokin was built. It was designed
by two Dutch architects, A. Jacot (1864-1925) and
W. Oldewelt (1865-1906) in a traditional style with
classical details. Inside there is an impressive open
space into which the daylight floods. The building,
with its simple grandeur, underlines the quality of
the goods marketed by the Maison de Bonneterie.
Rosa Cohen-Wittgenstein is described by Joost
Mendes, alias Emanuel Querido (1871-1943), in his
ten-volume work *The Santeljano Saga*. She is criti-
cally portrayed in the following passage:

> The director's German wife, imported into
> Holland, who with her mentally one-sided and
> physically many-sided heavily-functioning person-
> ality almost always ruled the roost … the unceas-
> ing, unresting impetus pushing her husband on …

Department store *Maison de Bonneterie* with its impressive dome

for the staff she was the highly-feared boss-with-a-bosom whose keen eye saw all, who exploited all, and then of course for the heaven-sent clientele she was the pillar of joviality, friendliness itself and above all the charmingly winsome speaker of broken Dutch, never succeeding in getting the words right – because of some inner contempt – the murderess of her adopted language.

During the Second World War Maison de Bonneterie was placed under German management. Sales were transferred completely to the nearby store De Bijenkorf and the building on Rokin was used only as a warehouse. The owners, Alfred and Max Cohen escaped to Spain, but most of the Jewish staff died in the death camps. Every year, on the Dutch Remembrance Day, May 4, a moment's silence is observed for the 68 victims of the war years 1940 to 1945, whose names are recorded on a plaque by the main staircase. On the other side of the staircase is a memorial plaque to the founders of Maison de Bonneterie, Rosa Cohen-Wittgenstein and Josef Cohen.

After the war Maison de Bonneterie managed to survive as a quality store in Amsterdam's historic inner city. Undoubtedly, the attractive architectural interior plays an important role here.

12 DE BIJENKORF DEPARTMENT STORE

Simon Philip Goudsmit was one of the Jewish retail traders to start up a business of his own in the second half of the 19th century. In the centre of Amsterdam he opened a small shop in 1870 where he sold wool for knitting, and general haberdashery, and where the Jewish Sabbath was strictly observed. When he died in 1889 his nephew Arthur Isaac took over the business. He expanded the assortment of goods and enlarged the premises, buying up adjacent buildings in the street. He also had electricity installed and began advertising campaigns – which were almost unheard of in those days. Meeting with enormous success, Isaac decid-

ed in 1909 to build one large store to replace the smaller buildings. In the meantime, a temporary shop was put up on a piece of wasteland bordering on Dam Square. Several years previously the city council, under pressure from local trades-people, had turned down a request from a German entrepreneur to build a large department store on this location. It was, after all, a time when department stores were being built in all the major European cities. Now, housed in its temporary premises, the Bijenkorf's turnover multiplied by four in just a few months, which made Isaac decide to move the store permanently to that location. This time protests from local traders were in vain and in due course Holland's first department store, De Bijenkorf (meaning Beehive) arose on Dam Square. The architect was J.A. van Straaten (1862-1920). It is a striking building, not only because of its size but also with its Neo-Romantic façade, interesting accentuation of the roof and magnificent use of space. The new Bijenkorf was constructed storey by storey in 1914. Work was completed shortly after the outbreak of World War I.

A daughter branch was opened in The Hague in 1926 and four years later in Rotterdam. Meanwhile another store had hatched under the wings of this fashionable mother – it was a kind of 99-cents-store, run by the Dutch All-One-Price Company, the HEMA. Whereas De Bijenkorf catered for the upper echelons, the HEMA spoke to those who had to be frugal. Initially it only sold articles costing 10, 25 or 50 cents. Rabbi Meijer de Hond, in the opening speech, explained: 'This is a store for everybody: Haman, Esther, Mordecai and Ahasuerus.'

When the Second World War began the Bijenkorf was still a Jewish family firm. The Isaac family managed either to escape or to go into hiding. There was a dramatic moment when the store manager Goudsmit had to select only fifty of the Jewish staff to escape with him by boat to England. He had to decide who to leave behind. Despite attempts to place the business under non-Jewish management, the Germans replaced the board of commissioners with a *Verwalter* (an administrator) and two German

The classical front of department store *Bijenkorf* on Dam Square

collaborators on the staff were appointed to the board of directors. The *Entjudung* (De-Jewification) of the Bijenkorf could then begin. Jews were forbidden to use the lunchroom and members of the *Wehrmacht,* the German army, were not allowed into the building as a precaution against possible disturbances. The deportation of the Jewish personnel, who numbered around one thousand, soon began. Some of them managed to gain stay of execution through the Jewish Council, for the number killed by the Germans is given as 737. By the end of 1943 the huge department store was virtually a hollow shell, with restricted opening hours. After the war the Bijenkorf, despite some initial difficulties, soon revived under the direction of the Isaac family who had returned from exile. In 1980 the last member of the family retired from the company. The store encountered financial problems in the 1980s and was finally taken over by the Vendex concern, owners of the rival department-store chain, Vroom & Dreesman. A relief portrait of Arthur

Isaac in the store witnesses to its Jewish history; opposite on the same landing is a circular relief bearing the text in Dutch: 'Remember and Renew, 1940-1945'.

13 SCULPTURES BY MENDES DA COSTA

Adorning the façade of the former offices of Lloyds at number 30, Damrak are several of the highly characteristic sculptures made by Joseph Mendes da Costa (1863-1939). His work was immensely influential for Dutch applied monumental art in the first part of the 20th century. Mendes da Costa, a scion of an aristocratic Sephardi family, was at the forefront of a revival in Dutch sculpture. He wanted to express the eternal values of art through new style forms. He was inspired by ancient Egyptian work and gave a subjective religious content to his sculptures. The figures on the Lloyds building are a good illustration of his work. The first expresses the

Statue of *Thriftiness* by sculptor Mendes da Costa

'prayer in bronze'. Eternity is symbolized by the circular form. In 'love for children' it is not so much the mother as the child who is central. In connection with this, Mendes da Costa once said, 'We Israelites carry the child in our hearts.' The next sculpture is 'thriftiness', the housewife planning for the days to come. In 'self-deception' he shows a scholar who achieves wisdom in isolation, whereby he suppresses the less laudable characteristics, which are represented by a small misshapen man. The final sculpture is titled 'transience' and shows a chameleon above an hourglass. On the building's side wall, 'domestic fidelity' is represented by a dog. Also, the roof ridge-beams are decorated with animal motifs and sphinx-like figures. Work by Mendes da Costa can be seen in Amsterdam's Rijksmuseum and the Jewish Historical Museum.

14 QUERIDO PUBLISHING HOUSE

The fine house at 262-264, Singel is the headquarters of Querido Publishers, who specialize in Dutch literature. In the 1930s, together with Allert de Lange, Querido published a great deal of the so-called 'literature of exile' notably work of German-language authors who were persecuted by the Nazis either because they were Jews or too left wing. Like his brother Israel Querido, Emanuel Querido (1871-1943) was a well-known writer, whose novels are written from a socialist viewpoint. Emanuel Querido was a highly successful publisher and in the 1930s listed such writers as Alfred Döblin, Lion Feuchtwanger, Bruno Frank, Heinrich, Thomas and Klaus Mann and Arnold Zweig among his published authors. Querido also published the journal *Die Sammlung* edited by Klaus Mann, the son of Thomas Mann.

The *Exilliteratur* (exile literature) published by Allert de Lange included work by Bertold Brecht, Max Brod, Herman Kesten, Joseph Roth and Stefan Zweig. Although including many Jewish writers it was not specifically Jewish literature, but rather, writing that was declared 'decadent' by the Nazis because it was, among other things, too left wing. During the war both De Lange's press *Exil Verlag* and Querido Publishers were closed down. Afterwards, Allert de Lange re-opened and was a well-known bookshop until the 1990s, when it had to close. Querido is still one of the most prestigious publishers in the Netherlands.

15 STATUE OF ANNE FRANK

At the corner where Prinsengracht meets the small square of Westermarkt, stands a bronze statue of Anne Frank. It was made in 1977 by Mari Andriessen on commission from the publisher Blom and some of his friends, and presented to the Amsterdam municipality. It was Blom who had published the account in Dutch now known worldwide as The Diary of Anne Frank. This statue, unlike the brawny Dockworker also by Andriessen, represents Anne Frank as a slender girl. The statue is

Anne Frank's statue by Mari Andriessen

restrained, has no frills, and this gives it great power. Something of the enormous potential of Anne Frank, which emanates from her diary, also radiates from this understated figure.

16 ANNE FRANK HOUSE

In the very heart of Amsterdam, almost beside the large city church Westerkerk, is Anne Frank House, now a museum. Anne Frank, her family and a few of their friends, went into hiding from the Nazis in Amsterdam in the back house of an unobtrusive canal dwelling at number 263, Prinsengracht. Anne Frank's diary, which she kept through the years they were in hiding, gives a vivid account of the trials and sufferings imposed by Nazi rule.

In 1933, to escape Hitler, the Frank family fled from their home in Germany. Anne was four years old when they arrived in Amsterdam. In May 1940 the Nazis caught up with them. The Netherlands was occupied, anti-Jewish measures began. Otto Frank, Anne's father, decided to transfer his business to non-Jews. Just after Anne's thirteenth birthday the family went into hiding on 6 July 1942. They had made a secret space at the back of the office where Frank had been working. With them went the Van Daan family and Mr Dussel. Anne had just begun writing a diary, recording her thoughts and feelings. She addressed the entries to 'Kitty' as if chatting to a girlfriend. She already wanted to be a writer, and was evidently driven by the desire to live on after her death.

With simplicity and sincerity Anne Frank's diary records the thoughts of a young teenager. She sees the world around her and describes it with impressive clarity. She writes vividly both of the people in hiding with her and of her own feelings. She has watched the world in which she grew up change into a horrifying wasteland. Many of her contemporaries seem not to have known what was happening to the Jews, but Anne, having listened to the BBC on their radio, writes on 9 October 1942:

'The English radio talks about people being gassed... I am terribly upset.'

Anne was very conscious of her Jewish identity:

One day this appalling war will be over, one day we'll be able to be people again, and not just Jews. We can never be only Dutch, or English, or whatever, we will always be Jews as well – and that's what we want, to be Jews too.

Anne never lost her ideals and her hopes, and her diary has become a monument to human faith and courage. She has become not just the little girl who was killed by the Nazis, but a voice of hope for a better world. She wrote:

It's really a wonder that I haven't let go of all my ideals because they seem so absurd and impossible to carry out. Yet I keep them because I still believe that in spite of everything people are really good at heart. I simply can't construct everything on a basis of death, misery and confusion ... I hear the approaching thunder grow ever loud-

One of the rooms in the *Achterhuis* (back house) where the Frank family hid during World War II

er, it will overwhelm and kill us. I feel the suffering of many millions and yet – when I look up to the sky I believe that everything will once more turn to good, that once again there will be peace and quietness.

In the meantime, I shall keep my thoughts shored up safely; perhaps the time will come when I can put them into action.

They hid in the *Achterhuis* (the back house) for about two years, but were betrayed on 4 August 1944 and transported first to Westerbork, then further east. Anne died in Bergen-Belsen in March 1945. The only member of the family to survive the war was her father, Otto. On his return to Holland he managed to get Anne's diary published. Before long, Anne Frank was a household name worldwide. Her diary has been translated into more than fifty languages, filmed and adapted for the stage. After the war there was talk of demolishing the house on Prinsengracht, but following widespread protest and then setting up the Anne Frank Foundation, it was saved. Today it has about 600,000 visitors annually. Because of its enormous popularity the house has been expanded to allow a constant through-flow of visitors. The adjacent building at 263, Prinsengracht now forms part of the route through the Anne Frank Museum. The story of Anne Frank is presented using citations from her diary, historic documents, objects, photos and video clips. The back house where the families hid, the *achterhuis,* has been restored as far as possible to how it was during the war years. This includes the originals of the pictures that Anne stuck up on the walls, showing her favourite film stars, and also the map of Normandy shortly after the Allied landing, pinned up by Otto Frank. Drawn on the wallpaper are the lines marking Anne's increasing height, another vivid record of the daily life in the *achter-*

The bookcase hid the entrance to the back house – until they were betrayed on 4 August 1944

huis. Formerly, visitors were treated to a historical account in the attic rooms but this has now been replaced by themes evoking the experiences of those in hiding – for example, there is a metal floor, to emphasize how cold the house must have been in winter. In the neighbouring building visitors can see exhibitions about Anne's diary and its significance in the world today. The modern premises on the corner presents temporary exhibitions, and houses a media room and a museum café.

THE NINETEENTH-CENTURY NEIGHBOURHOODS

In the final decades of the 19th century, as a result of industrial developments, the city of Amsterdam underwent huge changes. Workers flooded in from many other parts of the Netherlands, in search of jobs and fortune. The city grew, but there wasn't much more room in the centre, so new neighbourhoods sprang up beyond the old canals. These new working-class districts also attracted many Jews, all too glad to leave the city slums of Uilenburg, Marken and Vlooyenburg. In the new areas they would often live in a tightly-knit community and in this way many distinctly Jewish neighbour-hoods developed. The first was De Pijp, just west of the river Amstel. The municipal authorities drew up the street plan but left the housing construction to private enterprises. Since there were few regulations stating how the houses should be built, they were put up as close together as possible, to cram in as many tenants as the landlords could permit. De Pijp soon acquired a bad name and the socialist leader Henri Polak referred to it as ragged rows of shoddy housing, wretchedly ugly.' However, the new tenants had little choice and what was on offer in the old Jewish quarter was usually far worse. Many of the streets had a preponderance of Jewish residents, especially around Gerard Doustraat. East of the Amstel the neighbourhood known as Dapperbuurt was created, along with the Oosterpark district. Gradually the city introduced more building regulations and then housing associations began to take charge. After that, the quality of the buildings improved rapidly. Two streets in the Oosterpark district, Ruyschstraat and Blasiusstraat, were notable for the number of Jewish families living there. The same was true of the streets Commelinstraat and Wagenaarstraat in the Dapper neighbourhood. Jews traditionally formed close-knit communities and so it was natural for them to continue this habit. But also, most of them were members of the same socialist housing associations, which allotted them dwellings close together in the new complexes. With their preponderance of Jewish working-class residents, the new neighbourhoods not surprisingly became bastions of the Dutch Labour Party. In 1902 they returned the first socialist member of parliament, Pieter Jelles Troelstra, to the Dutch Second Chamber and also voted in the first socialist city councillor, Henri Polak. As a rule, the Jewish vote was decisive in this electoral district. Probably Henri Polak was the best-known political figure, but there were also David Wijnkoop and Sam de Wolff, both political radicals with a large following. The Jewish voice in this important socialist bastion was so strong that on one occasion at a party conference in the province of Friesland someone asked ironically whether the Dutch Labour Party was in fact Dutch. As a result of this it was voted that Christians and Jews should take turns in speaking in public.

In the 1920s when the slum clearance began in the Jewish Quarter, large numbers of Jews moved out to the so-called Transvaal neighbourhood, beside the Oosterpark district. The East End of Amsterdam retained a markedly Jewish character up until World War Two.

1 GERARD DOU SYNAGOGUE

With the migration of Jews from the rundown, overcrowded areas of the Jewish Quarter into the new working-class districts, new synagogues were needed. The Jews who moved into the new neighbourhoods would combine to form small shuls. The first of these was the society Teshungat Israel (Help of Israel) set up in 1877. Initially this group had a small shul on Quellijnstraat, but this was soon replaced by a roomier building on Jacob van Campenstraat. This in turn soon grew too small and in 1892 the synagogue on Gerard Doustraat was opened. It was designed by E.M. Rood (1851-1929) in neo-classical style, with tall stained-glass windows, which are unfortunately on the rear of the building and so not visible from the street. The front façade, however, with its Star of David and striking decorations adds a certain lustre to the otherwise sober street.

The synagogue was a well-attended people's shul and flourished until the 1930s. It was also used to hold classes in Jewish education. With the continuous movement of most Jews – thus also their synagogues – away from the city centre and into new neighbourhoods, by the time the Germans invaded

Gerard Dou Synagogue viewed from the women's gallery

Inside Gerard Dou Synagogue

the Netherlands the Gerard Dou shul was leading a pretty quiet life. Religious services continued to be held there until September 1944 and the interior was hardly damaged in the war years. However, most of the members of Teshungat Israel, including all of the governing board, were killed in death camps.

After the liberation of the Netherlands the Jewish survivors preferred to live in South Amsterdam and it proved difficult to keep the Gerard Dou synagogue going. It is thanks to the chief rabbi Justus Tal (1881-1954) that it was not closed down. He lived nearby and at an advanced age the only shul he could walk to was the one in Gerard Dou street. Every year, around the Passover festival (Pesah) and the Jewish New Year (Rosh Ha-Shanah) he would give lectures on the halakhic (to do with the legal side of Judaism) teachings about these festivals. Despite the difficulty of dwindling numbers, the

synagogue, after thorough restoration, is still in use today. Its sukkah, used during the Feast of Tabernacles, has also been restored so that the roof opens to the sky. A Youth Rabbi has been appointed specially to deal with youth matters, and this has attracted new families to the shul. During the summer months tourists will often visit the shul, partly because it is, together with the Portuguese synagogue and the Russian synagogue on Nieuwe Kerk street, one of the only three synagogues still in use in central Amsterdam.

2 ALBERT CUYP STREET MARKET

The most famous street market in the Netherlands stretches through De Pijp (The Pipe), along Albert Cuyp street. The market appeared during the last quarter of the 19th century soon after the first streets in The Pipe were built. From the

Hustle and bustle, Albert Cuyp street market; after World War II it has lost its Jewish flavour

Impressive Van Moppes Diamond Factory on Albert Cuypstraat

very start it was the busiest working-class market of Amsterdam. Because of its popularity there were sometimes rambunctious episodes and in 1905 the municipal authorities found it necessary to impose a little law and order and even, in 1922, to place it under the supervision of the municipal market inspectorate.

For centuries Jews in the Netherlands had been prohibited from undertaking many jobs, but market stallholder was one position where they excelled. The majority of the almost three hundred stalls on Albert Cuyp Street were run by Jews. The competition was immense and the barrow boys had to slave away in order to make a living. However, the stallholders earned a reputation as persuasive and amusing speakers.

The Depression of the 1930s drove many Jews to peddling, which only made street trading more competitive. At the same time, people's spending power fell. The hawkers and barrow boys suffered extreme poverty. To cap it all, came the horrors of the Second World War. First, Jewish stallholders were ordered to work in a separate 'Jewish' market and later on most of them were deported and killed. When the war was over, the market revived once more and has now become one of Amsterdam's tourist attractions. However, the Jewish element is almost entirely gone.

3   VAN MOPPES'S DIAMOND FACTORY

Of all the Amsterdam diamond-polishing factories Van Moppes's is one of the few where you can still find something of the atmosphere of skilled craftpersonship. With the murder of thousands of the Jewish diamond workers in World War II, Amsterdam lost it leading position in the European diamond business. Most of its diamond-polishing firms have gone and those that remain concentrate on selling gems to tourists and in fact do little cutting and polishing. Incidentally, it was Van Moppes who in the mid-1950s was the first diamond-polishing factory to begin offering guided tours. Today it attracts around 150,000 visitors annually.

In the 19th century during the Cape Age, Van Moppes was one of the polishing firms to break the monopoly of the Diamond Cutting and Polishing Society. The demand for diamonds was more than the Society could keep pace with. In 1828 Levie van Moppes had begun as apprentice in the diamond-cutting trade and it was his son, David Levie, who in 1875 decided to build a large steam-powered diamond cutting and polishing factory on Plantage Middenlaan. In fact, when three years later the factory opened, the glory days of the Cape Age were past tense. Nevertheless, things prospered for Van Moppes. Within a few years the factory expanded twice and set up branches in London, Paris, Brussels and New York. The firm offered an excellent training for its apprentices, thereby ensuring that high standards were maintained.

During the war the Van Moppes brothers lived in Brazil, where they founded that country's first diamond industry. Immediately after the war they returned to Amsterdam and started a new diamond-polishing factory in a building near the corner of Albert Cuyp Street. This had been a diamond factory run by non-Jews before the war and the German occupiers had taken it over to turn it into a training school for diamond workers. The Germans were expecting to defeat Britain and thus acquire the diamond supply from South Africa; then they would need skilled workers. They weren't planning to use the Jewish labourers. However, the German expectations never materialised. They didn't invade Britain and they never took over the diamond trade. After the war the building on Albert Cuypstraat became state property; first it was rented and then in 1951 sold, to Van Moppes. The Van Moppes diamond works, one of the oldest in Amsterdam, continued to flourish and once more established branches in

many other countries. Over the past few decades, diamond cutting and polishing has considerably declined although there are still a few polishing wheels in use. Today Van Moppes is chiefly involved in producing jewellery and had set up a special department for this. There is also a genuine factory tour for visitors, when they are shown the many stages in the production of diamonds.

4 SARPHATI PARK

Surrounded by the streets of The Pipe district is a park called after Dr Samuel Sarphati. His involvement in the construction of the park illustrates his keen interest in the urban development of 19th-century Amsterdam and the importance of private initiative.

The working-class neighbourhoods that went up towards the end of the 19th century tended not to flaunt much greenery – space was at a premium, and green parks were costly. Sarphati Park forms an exception to this rule – though it took a lot of discussions before it could be allowed. In fact, the park is a remnant of Sarphati's plans for the neighbourhood around Amstel Hotel and the People's Palace on Frederiksplein. Sarphati dreamed of an elegant district with a spacious park. In 1862 he was granted permission by the municipal council and at the same time – at no cost – given the land he required. Three years later Sarphati transferred his rights to the property to the Dutch Construction Company, which he had founded himself; shortly after his death they sold the ground at vast profit. Factories were then built along the Singel canal.

In the years that followed there were frequent discussions about what to do with the rest of the land and finally part of it was returned to the city council, to use for a park. The Dutch Construction Company urged the building of the park because they planned to erect houses around the square for the more well-to-do and a park would increase the value of the property. The park was eventually built in 1886 and named after Samuel Sarphati. A small pavilion was placed at the centre in honour of Sarphati with

Monument to Dr. Samuel Sarphati in the park named after him

a bust of him surrounded by eight pillars and four lions' heads. The text commemorates Sarphati as the Founder of the New Amsterdam. During the German occupation the park was (temporarily) renamed Professor Bolland Park: he was a professor at Leiden University who in around 1920 saw fit to air his anti-Semitic views during lectures.

5   THE JEWISH BOOK CENTRE

Although Dutch Jewry was characterized by its high level of integration into Dutch society, in the 1920s and 30s there was an increased number of specifically Jewish organizations. Their aim was to support and encourage Jewish culture. The Jewish Book Centre was one such body. It was founded in 1931 and had its own quarters in a new public library building, the Cooperatiehof, a magnificent example of Amsterdam School architecture.

Frequent lectures were held in the book centre both by the curator of the Bibliotheca Rosenthaliana and by the librarian of the Ets Hayyim Seminary. These two last-mentioned bodies emphasized scholarly study, while the Jewish Book Centre preferred to keep alive the Jewish traditions and way of life. They also tried to inform the non-Jewish public about their religion, 'especially now, when we are regularly hearing voices from certain newspaper sources that are trying to encourage anti-Jewish feeling.'

The plaque in the façade, which adorned the library of those days, showing books and the key to knowledge, was typical for the socialist ideal of those decades, of educating the proletariat.

6 COCO'S ICE-CREAM PARLOUR

A simple plaque on the house at number 149, Woustraat recalls the dramatic events that took place there in February 1941. Coco's Ice-cream Parlour was run by E. Cahn and A. Kohn, two Jews who had escaped from Germany in the 1930s. Their ice-cream parlour was very popular with both Jews and non-Jews. During the occupation the behaviour of the Nazis was a source of great irritation. Together with some of their regular clients, Cahn and Kohn formed a kind of 'resistance gang'. On 19 February 1941 some members of the German police in Amsterdam were sprayed with ammonia. This resulted in Cahn's arrest and execution – he was the first Dutch Jew to be openly shot. The Germans, after their initially cautious approach, seized upon the incident to toughen up their policy. The first roundups were held on 22 and 23 February. During these, 425 Jews were arrested and deported to Mauthaussen death camp. These roundups in turn provoked the February Strike in Holland.

7 ASSCHER'S DIAMOND FACTORY

One of Amsterdam's most imposing diamond-polishing factories stands in Tolstraat, right opposite 'Diamond Street' – Diamantstraat. The Asscher factory was built in 1907, designed by the famous Dutch architect G. van Arkel (1858-1919). The streets that surround the factory take their names from precious stones such as diamond, sapphire or emerald. The buildings are in the solid brick style of the Amsterdam School of architecture, fine examples of which may be seen particularly in the working-class dwellings. This unity of architecture emphasizes the proletariat nature of the neighbourhood, which is crowned by the splendid and unpretentious Asscher factory. The simple workers' dwellings in Diamond Street were designed in 1891 by the architect A.L. van Gendt (1835-1901). The diamond trade was very important in the Jewish proletariat's growth towards socialism. The writer

Front of the Asscher building, seen from Diamantstraat

A.M. Reens (1870-1930) puts into words the subsequent break with Jewish tradition that came as a result. In his work *The Arrest of Solomon Hangcoat*, he says:

Solomon Hangcoat was miserable. His only son, his little Abie, had joined the socialists. A bitter blow for a pious father. To think that he'd lived to see this day. And he'd given the boy such a good example. He sent him to the Talmud Torah school. He's always gone together with him to shul. Made sure he put on his phylacteries every morning; checked that he recited his morning and evening prayers, and yet in spite of all this, the boy had ended up with the socialists. It was all the fault of those diamond polishers. That ruins all the young people nowadays. How on earth does a Yehuda, a Jew, turn into a socialist? ... Who ever heard of such a thing in the old days? ... A Jew shall not be a wise guy... That's alright

for the plebs who don't understand a thing...
Asscher's was one of the most successful diamond-polishing factories in Amsterdam. One year after the opening, Asscher was given the commission by the British royal house to cut the Cullinan diamond, the largest stone of its kind ever to be found (it was 3106 carats). The story goes that the diamond was brought to Amsterdam on a special torpedo boat, but in fact it was quite simply in Abraham Asscher's coat pocket. Only after he'd studied the stone for two weeks did Joseph Asscher muster the courage to cleave it.

Abraham Asscher (1880-1950) was a leading figure in the Jewish community. He was one of those selected by the Germans to direct the Jewish Council. Together with Professor David Cohen he chaired the council. It first met on 13 February 1941 in Asscher's office, in the diamond factory. Another nadir came when Nazi chief Göring visited the factory. People managed to ensure that he didn't sign the visitors' book. During the Second World War the Asscher factory occupied an exceptional position, which appears from the fact that it is the only Jewish business to be listed among Amsterdam firms in 1943.

After the war the diamond-polishing factory continued but more and more sections of the building were used for other purposes. Today only a small part of the side wing is used by Asscher's. The factory is no longer open to the public. But you may catch sight of a relief sculpture in the entrance hall, portraying a sorrowing woman, in memory of 'our colleagues and friends who died in the years 1940 to 45.'

8   CINETOL

Opposite Asscher's factory stands a remarkable circular building, first used as a centre for theosophists. It is a fine example of the Dutch *Nieuwe Bouwen* style of architecture, which corresponds to the strictly functional designs that were so popular in the1920s. Before the Second World War the theosophy building was used as a synagogue by the still-young and modest Liberal Jewish community of Amsterdam. German-Jewish refugees also attended this synagogue, including the family of Anne Frank.

The Liberal Jewish community was also decimated during the war. After the war this liberal branch appeared to be the only Jewish community to experience a growth of any kind. It had various 'homes' including the Kleine Zaal in the Concertgebouw concert halls. Since 1966 the liberal Jewish congregation of Amsterdam has had its own synagogue, the Jacob Soetendorp shul in Amsterdam's River Neighbourhood. The Theosophical Centre functioned for some time as a cinema called 'Cinetol' until in the 1990s it was converted into a public library.

9   BLASIUS SHUL

Fleeing the vicious pogroms of eastern Europe at the end of the 19th century, many Jews sped westwards, often heading for America. But some of them paused in the Netherlands, where they encountered a welcoming atmosphere. Thus in Amsterdam a small eastern-European community developed. In contrast to the more emotional Hasidim, these Jews, known as Misnagdim, had a more intellectual approach to their religion. For them, *lernen* and the study of the great teachers were the keystones of their faith. In 1890 they formed the community of Jacob, *Kehilla Ja'akov*. Its members came from Lithuania, Latvia, Poland and Russia but the community was referred to as 'Russian'. In 1907 a shop on the corner of Swammerdam street and Blasius street was converted into a shul, by bricking in the windows. As well as being a synagogue, there was also a study room, for *lernen*.

In her book *Een eigen plek* (A place of one's own) Sera Anstadt recalls the Polish-Jewish atmosphere in the Blasius shul:

The Polish shul stood on the corner of Blasiusstraat and Swammerdamstraat. On a Saturday, if it was warm weather, people would

Former Blasius Shul , home to Jews from eastern Europe

come outside between the prayers, to catch a breath of fresh air. The men would often keep their prayer shawls on. You'd see fathers paying extra attention to their children, whom they'd been too busy to attend to during the week. The women enjoyed being free to chat with friends, without the constant harassment of small children. ... I didn't like Saturdays. As soon as I woke, I could sense the atmosphere. No noises from outside. The barrow boys who on weekdays would be calling 'Ripe apples and pears for sale' now walked past our street. And even though I didn't have to go to school, I wasn't allowed to play outside because the children had to wear their best clothes.

The shul was used for a short while after the Second World War, partly because the members of the Russian shul *Nidchei Yisrael Yechanes* on Nieuwe Kerkstraat joined them. In 1967 the congregation moved to Gerrit van der Veenstraat in South Amsterdam, and the shul on Blasius street was registered for residential purposes.

10 HOME OF VICTOR E. VAN VRIESLAND

The Jewish poet, journalist and literary critic Victor Emanuel van Vriesland (1892-1974) lived at number 25, Weesperzijde close to the river Amstel. Van Vriesland's writing addresses a wide range of topics and his poetry examines in depth the borderlands between life and death. As a young man he was an active Zionist and supported the idea of expelling people from the Jewish community if they married a non-Jew. Indeed, he wrote:

> The mixed marriage is the most subversive action of the Goloes (that is, Jewish life in the diaspora) for it threatens to an increasing extent the future of our people, through assimilation.

Ironically, in the very same year that he wrote these words, Van Vriesland became engaged to marry a non-Jewish young woman and consequently had to leave the Zionist movement. This is a striking example of the discrepancy between theory and practice in the prewar Netherlands, where Judaism was walking a tightrope, balanced between assimilation and the restatement of Jewish identity in the face of the growing threat from Nazi Germany.

11 THE IJSBREKER

The history of the café called the IJsbreker on Weesperzijde beside the river Amstel dates from the 17th century. The name comes from the boats used to break the ice on the rivers, so that barges could transport fresh water for the Amsterdam breweries, who paid for the costs of the icebreakers. Soon a café was built where the boat lay moored and this developed into a favourite spot for Amsterdammers to meet over a drink. In 1885 the present building was erected. The architect, Van Gendt, designed a building to reflect Dutch Renaissance style, with many classical elements.

כשר

David Wijnkoop and Sam de Wolff in a cartoon over 'the kosher element in the party' for the Dutch Labour Party congress of April 1907

Café The IJsbreker, still a lively centre today

Shortly after this, the surrounding Swammerdam neighbourhood was built, and the café became its bubbling centre. In his book *Van het groene laken* (Green Baize) Israel Querido describes the IJsbreker as a veritable billiard-player's paradise:

The IJsbreker became, without question, the meeting-place of all the best billiard players …The much-envied publican would permit the master players to perform on his beautiful Wilhelminas [the most expensive make of billiard table] and from then on really top-rate playing in all its subtle variations could only be seen in the IJsbreker. The publican understood perfectly well that everyone had their favourite drink and snack; and he abolished class differences because in that café there was a complete mix of people – Jew, Christian, Catholic, Protestant, freethinker, socialist, the boss and the worker …

It is not surprising that Querido first mentions the Jew, while his reference to the boss and the worker refers implicitly to the diamond trade – for the Swammerdam neighbourhood had a predominantly Jewish population, most of them employed in the diamond business. These people also gave a social-ist tone to the whole neighbourhood and to the IJsbreker. The café often witnessed political debates among members of the Social Democratic party. Sam de Wolff (1878-1960), who represented the radical wing of the party, recounts in his *Voor een land van belofte* (For a Land of Promise) how together with the later communist David Wijnkoop (1876-1941) he fiercely attacked the socialist leader Troelstra, after which the latter:

When it was over, still in the IJsbreker, our party's corner café, he [Troelstra] tried to calm us down and persuade us to be a little less extreme, and to learn the virtue of patience. For hours, assist-ed by many glasses of beer, he would talk to us, like a father with his children. Alas, we weren't the sort of kids to listen to advice. But he could sit there chatting on, it was fascinating, often till past closing time and then we would just contin-ue, sitting on the bench outside the café until about three in the morning. Then Wijnkoop and I would often accompany him to his home a little further along on Weesperzijde …

In 1941 the IJsbreker Café was closed by the

'Talmud Torah' in Hebrew characters

given downstairs under the Uilenburg shul, later in Rapenburgerstraat and after 1882 in a special school building on Plantage Middenlaan, later to become a crèche. When large numbers of working-class families moved into new districts, in 1924 the Talmud Torah school also moved to number 7, Tweede Boerhaavestraat. The school's name still stands there written in Hebrew characters vertically upon the façade. Formerly it could also be read in the fence, but was removed during the German occupation.

Sera Anstadt describes how in 1930 she was sent to the Talmud Torah school, shortly after she and her family had arrived in the Netherlands, and she still hardly spoke a word of Dutch:

But after a few weeks a letter arrived from the Jewish authorities. They were displeased that we had been sent to a Christian school. My parents understood their attitude. They simply hadn't real-ized that in Holland there were Jewish schools and they were quite prepared to send us to one straight away ... One week later we were at the Talmud Torah school. No one paid any attention to us. The teacher didn't say anything to me and showed me a place in the first class. He couldn't keep order and shouted at the kids who simply yelled back. At playtime there was such a din I was scared and went to stand in a corner and just stayed there until the end of recess.

Talmud Torah didn't have a long life in its new loca-tion. The school shut down in 1943. Today the building has been converted into apartments. In the entrance hall a plaque records the silver jubilee of Queen Wilhelmina of the Netherlands and the laying of the foundation stone in 1923.

Germans. Shortly after, the Jews who lived in the neighbourhood were taken away. After the war the future of the café was unclear for some time. Then in the 1960s The IJsbreker Foundation was set up, and the café became a centre for contemporary music, with an attractive bar on the street side. Although quite soon the music centre will be moving to the banks of the IJ, the café will live on, as it has done for centuries, a lively meeting point for local residents.

12 TALMUD TORAH

The study of the law, or Talmud Torah, lies at the heart of the Jewish religion. The Talmud Torah school was one of the earliest to offer Jewish education, aimed especially at children from poor families who couldn't afford private schooling. At the beginning of the 19th century lessons were

13 MONUMENT AT MUIDERPOORT STATION

The somewhat dingy railway station of Muiderpoort played a significant part in the deportation of Jews to the death camps. Most of the Jews who were sent from the Hollandsche Schouwburg were first transported by tram to Muiderpoort Station and

Monument by artist Karel Appel at Amsterdam's
Muiderpoort Station

14 THE TRANSVAALPLEIN MONUMENT

Although before the Second World War the Transvaal neighbourhood had a largely Jewish population there is little in today's street scene that recalls this past. The reason is, the Transvaal was largely a residential neighbourhood, and most of the Jews who went to live their were socialist-oriented members of a housing association. In the 1920s no less than 17 percent of the General Housing Association and Building Fund the Handworkers' Friendly Society were Jewish diamond workers. Those who were still religious would go to the synagogue on Linnaeus Street, no longer there. During the war the Transvaal neighbourhood and especially the large square, Transvaalplein, was used by the Germans as assembly points for the Jewish families who were driven out of their homes. On 20 June 1943 loud-speaker vans drove through the district ordering Jews to wait on their doorsteps with the prescribed amount of baggage, until they were picked up. Most of them obeyed the orders, were deported and killed. The Jewish socialist proletariat of East Amsterdam ceased to exist. On 4 May 1987 the mayor of Amsterdam, Ed van Thijn, unveiled a simple Star of David on one of the buildings at the corner of Transvaalplein. Designed by Mieke Blits, it is in memory of all the Jews who were taken to their death from these streets of Amsterdam.

thence by train to Westerbork concentration camp. In 1991 a monument commemorating this was erected in the square in front of the station. The monument has three sections. In the middle of the flowerbed a text has been created stating that between 3 October 1942 and 26 May 1943 about 11,000 Jews were sent to Westerbork and later deported to the death camps in eastern Europe. At the end of the flowerbed is a statue by Dutch artist Karel Appel (born Amsterdam 1921) titled *Flowers*. It shows three flowers with broken heads and one unbowed, standing on a grey socle. Some seats are placed at the edge of the flowerbed. A text is punched with holes into the middle seat, titled 'Muiderpoort Station'; a memory by the poet Victor E. van Vriesland (1892-1974):

> *Through their faint forms*
> *does there shiver*
> *a long, long list of*
> *long-forgotten names,*
> *long-forgotten eyes?*
> *Will they still remember*
> *that we have forgotten*
> *our immense forgetting,*
> *our forgotten ones?*

SOUTH AMSTERDAM AND THE RIVER NEIGHBOURHOOD

Even back in the 17th century the southern part of the city was the most prominent. This was still the case at the end of the 19th century when there was an explosion of new working-class districts beyond the Singelgracht. Unlike De Pijp (The Pipe) and East Amsterdam, the South evolved into an elegant neighbourhood, with important cultural buildings such as the Rijksmuseum and the Concertgebouw music halls. The famous Plan Zuid (the urban plan for the new southern district of Amsterdam) developed by the renowned architect H.P. Berlage (1856-1934) also embraced the more popular River Neighbourhood (so called because its streets are named after Dutch rivers), where housing corporations have left their mark on the architecture. The hallmark of Plan Zuid was its dwellings, which were spacious for that time, its layout of wide streets and the dominant architectural style of the Amsterdam School with its abundance of brickwork detail. South Amsterdam and the River Neighbourhood have never been genuine Jewish neighbourhoods; nonetheless, thirty percent of the population of the latter was of Jewish origin at the end of the prewar period. A number of synagogues were built in these two quarters and a large part of Jewish life in Amsterdam gradually concentrated there. In the 1930s many Jewish refugees from Germany ended up in the new dwellings being completed in South Amsterdam. During the German occupation these refugees were persecuted by the notorious Sicherheitsdienst, the Nazi secret service, and by the so-called Zentralstelle für Judische Auswanderung, euphemistically known as the Central Office for Jewish Emigration. The extermination of the Jewish proletariat has largely wiped out Jewish Amsterdam. Only in South Amsterdam and the southern River Neighbourhood and, beyond that, in Buitenveldert and Amstelveen do some traces remain. The Dutch writer and critic Ischa Meyer (1943-1995) wrote a moving poem about the return of his father Jaap Meyer after the Second World War:

> South Amsterdam, the river neighbourhood
> The streets flow though my mind…
> My father was a man
> who returned from the war.
> They had damaged him,
> broken his spirit.
> We walk down the street
> where he should not have been.
> He smoked his cigar
> and seemed highly pleased.
> An old coat, ash of a cigar
> along the streets of an imaginary city.

1   THE RIJKSMUSEUM

The Rijksmuseum, opened in 1885, is internationally renowned for its immense collection, particularly of works by Rembrandt and other Dutch masters. The museum owns some art works by Jewish artists and some of these portray scenes of Jewish life. Apart from this, non-Jewish artists have also included Jewish elements in their art.

For part of his working life Rembrandt lived in the heart of the Jewish Quarter and he depicted many Jewish characters, especially in his Old Testament scenes. From a Jewish perspective, his *Jeremiah lamenting the destruction of the Old Temple in Jerusalem* is especially interesting, as is his portrait of the physician Ephraim Bueno. Rembrandt also made etchings of the latter, which can be seen in the Rembrandt House Museum. Also in the Rijksmuseum is one of his most famous works, known as *The Jewish Bride*. It has been suggested that this painting was a portrayal of the married couple, Daniel Levy de Barrios and Dona Abigael de Pina. Influenced by his wife, De Barrios, a poet and captain in the Spanish army, converted to the Jewish faith in Amsterdam. As a poet he refused, however, to renounce the ideas of the Renaissance, and so remained somewhat isolated in the Sephardi Jewish community.

Also in the Rijksmuseum are *The Interior of the Portuguese Synagogue* by Emanuel de Witte (c. 1617-1691/2) and *Mary Magdalene* by Jan van Scorel (1495-1562), with Hebrew letters emphasizing the Jewish origins of the Magdalene. In Protestant Holland there was a great interest in the Jewish background of the Old Testament and of Jesus's own Jewish origins. The Calvinists saw the study of the original texts as a way of arriving at the pure source of the Bible, free of Roman Catholic dilutions. Comparisons were also drawn between the chosen Jewish people and the Dutch Republic that had liberated itself from the yoke of Catholic Spain. Amsterdam was often called the second Jerusalem. The most important Jewish artists whose work is to be seen in the Rijksmuseum are Jozef Israels (1824-1911) represented by his *Jewish Wedding*, based on Rembrandt's painting; *Children of the Sea* and *After the Storm*. Works by his son Isaac Israels (1865-1934) include *Shop Window, Donkey Riding on the Beach, Two Girls in the Snow* and *In the Bois de Boulogne*. Also represented is Joseph Mendes da Costa (1863-1939) known as the father of modern Dutch sculpture, with the figurines 'Three Old Women Gossiping', 'A

Painting *The Jewish Wedding* by artist Jozef Israels

nature with trees and water. You didn't really need to paint something like that. If you climbed over the dike in Tuindorp, you could also see it ... What I didn't understand was that *The Jewish Bride* was allowed to be painted. 'Rembrandt painted a great number of Jews,' my aunt told me. But Titus wasn't one. Titus was his son. If you took a good look at the boy you could see that he'd soon be dead, he had such a sad look on his face ... What I saw here was marvellous, I'd never seen anything so beautiful before. An extremely old man, Jeremiah lamenting the Fall of Jerusalem was written underneath. His face looked lonely and so sad I'd have hugged him to cheer him up if I'd been able to.

Ceramic Duck', 'The Sick Monkey' and 'Two Monkeys Grooming Each Other'. Partly due to the Second Commandment, 'Thou shalt not make any graven images', the visual arts have long played a subordinate role in Jewish culture. The prohibition on membership of the Dutch artists' guild of St Luke was also an obstacle to Jews making a career for themselves in this field. This only changed after the Jews were granted civil rights in 1796. Before then, only a few Sephardi Jews had distinguished themselves as portrait painters or illustrators, due to their contacts with Southern Europe and the Renaissance. Since the 19th century some Ashkenazi Jews have also made a name for themselves as artists. The conflicts that this gave rise to among Jews who had had a traditional upbringing is discussed in the autobiographical work *Jullie is Jodenvolk* (Youse guys is Jews guys) by the Jewish socialist author and political activist Sal Santen (1915-1998). In his book of short stories *De kortste weg* (The shortest route) he describes a visit to the Rijksmuseum:

> I followed (Aunt Fien) up the stairs towards the paintings ... The first name of one of the painters was Salomon. Did that mean that Yids could paint too? My father had told me that that wasn't allowed, that you weren't allowed to make any image of living people. This painting was admittedly not a portrait. It was just a scene from

2 COSTER DIAMONDS

Coster Diamonds is one of the oldest surviving diamond-cutting firms in Amsterdam. Since 1970 its premises have been in two elegant villas on the corner of Paulus Potterstraat and Hobbemastraat, but the firm started out in Vlooyenburg, in the old Jewish quarter. In around 1845 the jeweller Martin Coster opened a diamond-cutting shop on Zwanenburgerstraat, where the polishing wheels were turned by horsepower. In no time at all he enlarged his factory and introduced steam. The founding of diamond-cutting businesses like that of Coster marked the transition in the industry from one that was home-based to a large-scale enterprise. Together with the Diamantslijperij Maatschappij (the Diamond-Cutting Company), that also owned a steam-powered factory, Coster dominated the Amsterdam diamond industry for a number of years. In the so-called 'Cape Age', when the industry boomed, his monopoly was broken by others, but Coster diamonds remained one of the leading establishments. During the Second World War the firm was closed down, but it started up again afterwards. In 1970 with the demolition of Vlooyenburg, Coster moved to Paulus Potterstraat in South Amsterdam, where little now recalls the company's Jewish past.

Painting by Marc Chagall: *Inside the synagogue in Safad*

3 THE STEDELIJK MUSEUM

The Stedelijk Museum is one of the major modern art museums in the Netherlands. It was founded in 1895 as a result of the will of Sophia Adriana de Bruyn, the widow of Lopez Suasso. She stipulated that her extensive collection of applied art and antiques should become the property of the city of Amsterdam on condition that it was given the name The Sophia Augusta Foundation and that the trustees should be Protestant. She also gave a considerable donation, which helped to build the present museum. Soon it was being referred to as the Suasso Museum and once a special new building had been erected, it became renowned as the Stedelijk (or Municipal) Museum. Despite an expansion after the war, the Stedelijk Museum is still not in a position to show all the major works it owns. Furthermore it focuses mainly on the art of the second part of the twentieth century. The paintings of the most important Jewish artists, such as Jozef and Isaac Israels and Sal Meyer, are therefore virtually never on view. Besides that one can only really speak of Jewish art when it is both made by Jewish artists and when it contains definite Jewish themes. In this sense Jozef Israels is a Jewish artist. As one of the most famous painters of his day he remained true to the Jewish religion. A decisive figure in the Hague School of painters, he acquired great fame with his seascapes and beach scenes in which poor fishermen usually play a central role. Jewish history is also an important theme in his work. The collection of the Stedelijk Museum contains, for instance, *Saul and David* and the portrait of Eleazar Herschel. Jozef's son, Isaac Israels developed a distinctive Impressionist style at the end of the 19th century in which specifically Jewish elements are scarcely to be seen and indeed often are quite absent. The Stedelijk owns a number of characteristic works of this artist, such as *Two Girls in the Snow*, *Seamstresses' Workshop* and *At the Dressmaker's*. With a father and mother who were respectively a cutter and a polisher of 'rose' diamonds, Sal Meyer (1877-1965) was born in the heart of the Jewish Quarter and also chose the profession of diamond cutter. From 1914 he became a professional painter and etcher, specializing in scenes of Amsterdam and producing a number of paintings of the old Jewish quarter. The Stedelijk Museum also owns a number of works by Marc Chagall (1887-1985) that contain many Jewish religious elements as well as personal memories of the Jewish shtetl in Russia. These include *Ida in the Window*, *Motherhood*, *Bella in Green*, *Portrait of the Artist with Seven Fingers*, *Love Idyll*, *Circus Rider*, *The Violinist*, *Rabbi with the Scroll* and *Interior of the Synagogue of Safad*. They show the great originality and mystical character of his work in which his Russian Jewish background is a dominant element. Finally, the Stedelijk Museum owns Chaim Soutine's painting *The Slaughtered Ox* and works by Barnett Newman and Mark Rothko.

4 ETTY HILLESUM'S HOUSE

A simple plaque tells us that the premises at number 6, Gabriël Metsustraat was the address of Etty Hillesum (1914-1943). In her diary *An Interrupted Life*, she gives a detailed and intimate account of her personal life in the war years till she was deported to Auschwitz in 1943. Her diary is often compared with that of Anne Frank. Since the 1980s it has been published in many countries and it now has a readership of hundreds of thousands. Meanwhile a complete and unabridged edition of her work has been published. Etty Hillesum, born in Middelburg, was the daughter of Levie Hillesum and Rebecca Bernstein, who was Russian in origin. She spent her childhood years in the historic town of Deventer and went to Amsterdam University at the age of eighteen. At the beginning of 1941 she went into therapy with J. Spier, and it was presumably he who encouraged her to keep a diary. From her diaries we learn that the war had taken her by surprise, just at a point when she had decided to take control of her own life. As a member of the staff of the Jewish Council, she tried to avoid deportation, but when she could no longer stomach that work, she requested to be transferred to Westerbork in July 1942, where she tried to give support to people preparing for deportation. In July 1943, however, she lost her protective status as a member of the Jewish Council and was herself deported. On 30 November 1943 she was gassed in Auschwitz. Etty Hillesum's diary is first and foremost a deeply personal document, in which she lays bare her complex personality. Her own experiences and the terrible reality are constantly intertwined, as for instance, when she describes the moment when it became obligatory for Jews to wear the Star of David:

But we were so happy there, the three of us. Precisely on the evening when the Yellow Star was enforced. And I said: it's maybe still worthwhile being present at a moment when history is being made. Then one can see what else there is, besides what we read in our books at school. The gentleman on Beethovenstraat this afternoon definitely deserves a mention. Like a first crocus, peeping out of the ground, and which you look at with such joy. He wore a huge golden star triumphantly on his chest. All by himself, he was like a one-man procession or demonstration. And he looked so satisfied cycling there. And with all that yellow, I suddenly got a poetic insight, that a sun was rising over him, he looked so terribly radiantly yellow and pleased with himself. Ah well, dear sister, in reality there's not very much to be pleased about, though you really seem to be able to make everything sound poetic.

A little while later she showed that she realized all too well what was going on:

We'll have to suffer a great deal. We'll be impoverished and if this process goes on much longer we'll end up destitute and everyday we experience a decline in our powers, not just through the terrors and uncertainties, but through perfectly ordinary small things, like being increasingly refused admission to shops and having to go great distances on foot, that is already utterly exhausting for a lot of people I know. Our extermination draws closer from all sides and the ring will very soon be closed around us, making it impossible for people of good will to help.

Etty Hillesum's great achievement was to bear witness to the struggle of a young woman trying to make her way in life in a time when others had decided that, because of her origins, she no longer had any right to be alive.

5 THE CONCERTGEBOUW

Entirely in the spirit of the 19th century, the Concertgebouw music halls, like the Stedelijk Museum, was also the product of a private initiative. A design of A.L. van Gendt (1835-1901), the building opened in 1883 and at once acquired a reputation for its wondrous acoustics and especially for the superb quality of its resident orchestra, later to become the Concertgebouw Orchestra. It originated in the Amsterdam Orchestral Society that up until then had given concerts in the Plancius building, the premises of the Jewish choral society *Oefening Baart Kunst* (Practice Makes Art). In its early years concerts were often held in the gardens around the building, which was still situated amid open fields. Poor Jews who couldn't afford a ticket often stood by the railings to listen. Many Jews also attended the cheap popular concerts. The Concertgebouw is not a Jewish institution, but Jews have always produced a proportionately large number of musicians and have always been well represented in the orchestra. Eduard van Amerongen (1912-1992) editor of the *New Israelite Weekly*, describes the pious

Jews who went on Saturdays to hear performances of Bach's *Matthew Passion*, a work that was regarded in Orthodox circles as anti-Jewish or even anti-Semitic:

> There were a great number of pious Jews who were extremely interested in music and who went there on Saturday evenings. But the performance began at half-past seven; the Sabbath was not yet over, and they were therefore still subject to the laws of the Sabbath. So they went instead to the closest synagogue, on Jacob Obrechtstraat, and performed 'havdalah' there, that is they celebrated the end of the Sabbath, after which they could do what they liked. But they were usually too late for the opening numbers with the introductory chorus. Shortly afterwards, however, the doors were opened and in they went. The deputy head of the Jewish seminary, Dr de Jong led the way, followed by the students, the cantors, extremely pious individuals with beards. There were some ten to twenty of them; it was most interesting to see it, this procession of pious Jews attending the Saint Matthew Passion on Saturday evening. It was something quite unique and at the same time typical of Amsterdam Jewry.

After the war the Small Hall of the Concertgebouw was used for celebrating the High Days of the Liberal Jewish Community. Wanda Reisel (born 1955) recalls them in *Een paar brieven aan R* (A few letters to R):

> On high holidays the little shul on De Lairessestraat was too small to accommodate all the Jews who wanted once every year, on Rosh Ha-Shanah or Yom Kippur, to celebrate their ties with Jewry. Before the larger Liberal Synagogue was built, near the New RAI conference centre building, the high holidays were celebrated in the Small Hall of the Concertgebouw. A religious service was thus held in the temple of Culture, there was singing, which was suitable in the concert hall, and the old rabbi Jacob Soetendorp did a bit of play-acting. (...On Yom Kippur when he started singing and chanting praise with the tallith

> over his head and white gym shoes on his feet [he's not allowed to wear leather shoes on Yom Kippur], and raised the shofar to his lips, I dreamed I was in the desert.) A religious service in the concert hall and a rabbi in white sneakers, there was enough unconventional behaviour there for me to think that it was no bad thing, this sort of Jewishness.

6   JEWISH YOUTH HOUSE

At the end of 1998 the Jewish Youth House was opened at number 13, De Lairessestraat. Since1979 the Meschibath Nefesch Society had run a student restaurant at this address, serving cheap kosher meals to Jewish students and working young men. The conversion of the building into a fully-fledged youth centre met with the growing demand for activities with a distinctly Jewish character. The Jewish Youth House was thus an important expression of the vitality of Jewish life in Amsterdam. There had long been a need for a youth centre but differences between Liberal and Orthodox Jews had formed an obstacle to setting one up. As owner of the premises, The Netherlands Israelite Institute for Social Work (NIISA) was only too pleased to give its backing to the new youth centre. The breakthrough occurred when the Jewish charity, Cefina, received a bequest from Mrs Vilbach, who had decided that the money should be spent on Jewish youth. The youth clubs Iyar, Shuche, MOOS! and Meschibath Nefesch combined to organize joint accommodation there. On the ground floor the centre contained the cafe-restaurant NashViel that has a kashrut certificate and where kosher food can be consumed every evening except the Sabbath. There are also numerous cultural activities and a club that is open every evening. The Shuche Foundation organizes regular social and cultural activities and parties for Jewish youth in the activities hall on the first floor. The second floor has a study centre with a reading room and a lounge with a large reading table. The building is also the premises of the Jewish student union, Iyar.

7 JOODS MAATSCHAPPELIJK WERK

Joods Maatschappelijk Werk, Jewish Social Work or JMW, located at 145, De Lairessestraat, was founded in 1947 to coordinate the various social aspects of the postwar Jewish community in the Netherlands. This organization has come to assume an ever more important place in Jewish Holland. Immediately after the war the survivors were mainly concerned with restoring the old institutions, and particularly the Netherlands Israelite Community, the Portuguese Israelite Community and the League of Liberal Jewish Communities. Parallel to developments in Dutch society as a whole, secularization led to society's increasingly evolving outside religious institutions. This was expressed in various legal tasks and subsidized activities in the domain of social work. The Jewish community also had to deal with family situations most of which had been tragically disrupted, and the great issues of the war and the Holocaust. The orientation on Israel forms a particular problem for a large number of people, who always feel Jewish to a greater or lesser degree. Secularization has certainly not meant that having a Jewish identity is no longer important. The Jewish experience should be seen in a much broader context and has to do with aspects such as having a worthwhile social life, meeting people and sharing and debating specific aspects of Jewish culture and history and topical issues such as Feminism, homosexuality and anti-Semitism. The JMW is active in all these fields, with something like twenty-thousand people being involved in one way or another. In *Vol als Fisj* (Full as fish) the writer Jessica Durlacher (born 1961) describes how a sense of one's Jewish identity was a factor for the postwar generation even if one only had a father, and not a mother, who was Jewish:

I'm not even Jewish. My father is Jewish. Even gefilte fish is only a word for me. It sounds like a word that's full of history, full of culture and nostalgia, but is it my history and my culture? And why should it be my nostalgia? Even so the culture of gefilte fish is more my culture than that of other people. The others who don't have any Jewish father ... There are words that can evoke whole worlds for me without my having even an approximate knowledge of these worlds ...chicken soup, honey cakes, Hanukkah, yarmulka and a mezuzah on the doorpost. They are the cosy kitsch clichés for some people like me, but they belong to the awareness that one has a past much of which has disappeared, in which these words – it's not a coincidence that many of them have to do with comfort food – are a remedy for anger and fear. Even the cosy nostalgia you get in klezmer music or in the hypocritical shout of joy, 'Next year in Jerusalem', or in the rare choppe [Jewish wedding] I've attended, are in this sense reasonably legitimate, ritual utterances of emotion that in the end touch on a sense of abandonment and a lack of any close previous family. Because that family is dead, indeed it was already dead before I arrived on the scene.

De Lairessestraat leads to Krusemanstraat where at number 50 the hot pitta bakers Pita Nash set up shop in the early 1990s. The business was started by a Russian Jew who left the Soviet Union after the fall of Communism. Pita Nash also sells Jewish and Israeli specialities such as aubergine and humus salads, and it has a small area where these dishes can be consumed on the premises. It is closed on Saturdays and Jewish holidays but open on Sundays. The same goes for the Carmel Restaurant at number 224, Amstelveenseweg. With its generous menu of Jewish dishes, it has had a kosher licence, or hechsher, since the mid-1990s.

8 THE JACOB OBRECHT SYNAGOGUE

The Jacob Obrecht Synagogue on the corner of Heinzestraat is one of the places of worship symbolizing the departure of the Jews from the old Jewish quarter to the new neighbourhoods in South Amsterdam. The Ohel Ja'akob (Tent of Jacob) Society opened a house shul in Cornelis Schuytstraat, but rapidly growing interest made it

Jacob Obrecht Synagogue: stylish interior designed by Harry Elte

necessary to build a large synagogue. First of all a temporary synagogue was built in wood on the grounds next to the Central Israelite Hospital. In 1928 the Jacob Obrecht Synagogue was consecrated. The architect was Harry Elte (1880-1944), one of the representatives of the Expressionist style in Holland. It is striking for its extremely expressive forms and volumes. Despite its massive exterior, the inside is light with a fine sense of space. The most impressive features are its large arches and superb stained glass. In twelve windows, the number of the tribes of Israel, biblical scenes are depicted, while behind them are seven small windows with scenes from the Book of Genesis. The Jacob Obrecht Synagogue was one of the most popular in Amsterdam at the outbreak of the German occupation. In an exchange of prisoners from Bergen-Belsen, rabbi Philip Coppenhagen was able to travel to Palestine, but he died there shortly after arrival. Most of the members of the community and the architect Elte were deported and killed. The synagogue itself suffered little damage during the war. After the war most of the survivors moved to South Amsterdam, so that the restored building of the Jacob Obrecht Synagogue became the centre for Orthodox Jewish life in Amsterdam. This is still the case today, partly due to the presence of a ritual bath or mikweh, despite the creation of a new Jewish centre in Buitenveldert and Amstelveen. In 1997 the building was restored. Since then it bears the name of the Chief Rabbi of Amsterdam in the postwar period, Dron Schuster.

9 ZENTRALSTELLE FÜR JÜDISCHE AUSWANDERUNG

During the Second World War the headquarters of Nazi terror against Amsterdam Jews was situated

Today's Gerrit van der Veen School was the HQ of the German Secret Service, SD, during World War II

on what today is called Adama van Scheltemaplein. The *Zentralstelle*, the Central Office for Jewish Emigration and the *Sicherheisdienst* (the SD) were housed in school buildings fronting on this square. The former institution, with its premises on the north side of the square, was the apparatus that prepared and coordinated the extermination of the Jews – on Göring's orders, its task was to take 'all the preparations required to achieve the final solution of the Jewish question in the German occupied territories in Europe'. Officially, the Central Office for Jewish Emigration was responsible for the 're-housing' of the Jews, issuing 'permits' for this purpose; in fact of course that was just a euphemism for deportation to the extermination camps.

Jews were expected to report here for a whole range of matters. The square was also one of the assembly points for people arrested during roundups. They had to stand there herded together in large numbers in the open air until their forms were filled out. To deal with the office work involved in the deportations, the staff of the *Expositur* department of the Jewish Council were brought in. They had to check out whether any of those arrested had valid exemption papers. The vast majority had nothing of the kind and were transported to the former theatre, Hollandsche Schouwburg, or else directly to the railway station for deportation. The Central Office for Jewish Emigration was the administrative centre for all deportations from Holland. In the words of the historian Presser,

'The Central Office was ... the enemy citadel in Amsterdam, the crater from which all calamities were spewed out over (the Jews). It was there that, in the German expression "the essential task of *Entjudung*" – that is, purging the country of its Jewish population – took place.'

Towards the end of 1944 the Central Office for

Jewish Emigration was destroyed during an English bombing raid, but by then the deportations were largely complete. The Netherlands was almost entirely *Judenrein* (purged of Jews). The director of the Central Office was W. Lages. After the war he was arrested with his assistant F.H. Aus der Fünten and sentenced to death. He received a royal pardon from the Dutch queen however, and the sentence was commuted to life imprisonment. They were held in Breda Prison, in the south of the Netherlands. Lages died in captivity; Aus der Funten was released in 1989 on grounds of his advanced age.

On the facade of the new school building erected on the site of the Central Office, a relief has been set in the wall showing two figures going down fighting. There is also a memorial stone on the corner house at 26, Rubensstraat, recalling Gerhardt Badrian (1906-1944), a German Jew who fled to Holland and was active in the resistance movement. He was shot dead 'as a fighter for the freedom of the Netherlands'.

10 HEADQUARTERS OF THE SICHERHEITSDIENST

On the south side of Adama van Scheltemaplein is the Gerrit van der Veen School, named after the famous freedom fighter of that name; he was involved in the attack on the municipal registry office and was the brain behind the centre that produced false identity cards. He was betrayed in the course of one of his operations. While awaiting execution he wrote in words that are typical of the man:

'I have always known the risks I have taken, so I cannot complain, but even so I think it's a pidy.'

The school that bears his name today was a high school for girls used by the Germans as HQ for the dreaded Sicherheitsdienst, or SD, the German secret service. Since the SD's archives have been lost one can only guess what went on in this building, how many people were tortured during the interrogations and the kind of terrors prisoners were subjected to in their cells. The victims were then sent on by the SD to the prisons in Amersfoort or Scheveningen. Some were executed on the spot or died during interrogation. Jewish prisoners were as a rule sent straight on to Westerbork and from there to the death camps in Poland. The former cells in the basement of the building are today in use as a bicycle shed.

11 EXPOSITUR

Not far from the central office, at numbers 15-21, Jan van Eijkstraat, was a special department of the Jewish Council known as the *Expositur*. When the Central Office for Jewish Emigration was instituted in 1941, the Jewish Council was assigned the task of escorting Jewish people there and assisting them with filling in their papers. Officially the task of the Expositur was to maintain 'contacts between the Jewish Council and the German authorities in every area'. Possible exemptions from deportations, that were given 'until further notice', made the body into the most important link between the Jewish Council and the Germans: it was the gateway to the Central Office for Jewish Emigration and the deportations.

12 BEETHOVENSTRAAT

Today a fashionable shopping street, Beethovenstraat was a new development in the 1930s with houses that were hard to rent. This was where many of the refugees from Germany who tried to shape a new life in the Netherlands after the rise to power of Hitler and the Nazis, made a home. Besides Jews, there were many artists and intellectuals among these refugees, resulting in a thriving 'exile literature'. A great number of these refugees were Jewish tradesmen, so that in no time some twenty Jewish shops were opened in Beethovenstraat. Leo Pollack set the trend, with a delicatessen shop and lunchroom, opened in 1934; he was soon followed by Hergershaussen butcher's shop, the De Leeuw Cigar store and Isidor Kaiser who opened a butcher's shop-cum-restaurant. A meeting point for German Jews was Café de Paris. Etty

Beethovenstraat, home to many Jews in the 1930s and World War II

Hillesum often spent time there. Due to this German Jewish atmosphere in Beethovenstraat, Amsterdammers nicknamed it Brede Jodenstraat (Broad Jews Street), parodying the name of Jodenbreestraat (Jews Broad Street) in the old Jewish Quarter; while tram number 24 was referred to as the Berlin Express. The conspicuous presence of this German Jewish community was a cause of some irritation, witness the liberal weekly *Liberaal Weekblad* in May 1938:

> It has to be said that this was due to the provocative behaviour of a number of German emigrants, particularly in Amsterdam, who never fail to raise their voices when speaking their German, with the inevitable remark, "bei uns war es besser" (we were better off at home), praising the people who had rejected them rather than those who shared their bread with them.

It must be stressed that these feelings were more anti-German than anti-Jewish. To refute any notion that it might be anti-Semitic, the *Liberaal Weekblad* declared some months later:

> The natural affection that we feel for the Jewish immigrants, our total readiness to help them, is obfuscated in this country by those immigrants, who are unsympathetic to us, not because they are German Jews, but because they are German Jews. Their preference for the German language, for German customs, their praising of everything German over everything Dutch is repugnant not just to our national pride but also to our philo-Semitic feelings.

The German refugees were followed only a few years later by the German occupiers. Due to the proximity of the SD and the Central Office, Beethovenstraat swarmed with Germans during the war years and heart-rending scenes were witnessed there. They were described among others by Grete

Weil. She was born in Germany in 1906 and had fled to Amsterdam in 1935. Weil was a typist for the Jewish Council for a while but managed to go underground in time, thus surviving the war. Her husband Edgar Weil was arrested in a raid in June 1941 and later liquidated in Mauthausen. Her book, *Tramhalte Beethovenstraat* (Beethovenstraat Tram Stop) is all about the deportations in South Amsterdam:

Below us we saw four trams, each with an extra car, while behind them an obscure crowd of people swarmed around; there must have been a few hundred of them; pale faces in the gleam of the blue torches held by young men with white armbands. To one side there were a few men in uniform – maybe soldiers or police officers – with huge Alsatians on short leads. Sharp muffled orders: 'Get a move on, move, move. Car number one, number two, number three.' The men with the armbands dragged suitcases and rucksacks and helped the older people. A child cried and a woman slapped him, shouting: 'Behave yourself.' They pushed forward into the trams, in a frightful hurry, like chickens running squawking to the feeding trough, shoving each other aside with their elbows, afraid of being left behind, stumbling as they climbed onto the running boards. One man fell to the ground, but the others just moved on over him, trying to get into the car as quickly as possibly so as to get a seat, and make it as comfortable for themselves as possible. The dogs kept on barking, set on by the men in uniform with a blow of the lead. In an amazingly short time they'd all got in and, after someone had waved his torch around, the trams drove off; only the men in uniform and the men with armbands stayed behind, standing there stiffly in two separate groups, finally disappearing in different directions without saluting each other at all.

13 GERRIT VAN DER VEENSTRAAT SYNAGOGUE

The new synagogue of the Kehilla Ja'akov Society (the Congregation of Jacob) in the dwelling at 26, Gerrit van der Veenstraat was consecrated in 1967 on Rosh Ha-Shanah, the Jewish New Year.

The congregation had had a shul in Blasiusstraat since 1890, which was not adequate anymore and was also too far away for the members, most of whom had gone to live in South Amsterdam. With its exterior like an ordinary house, one would hardly suspect that the Gerrit van der Veen Synagogue was one of the most important Jewish venues in Amsterdam. Apart from a space for services, it also houses the classrooms of the Hakham Zwi Foundation, which also carries out many educational, social and cultural activities. The successor of the now vanished Netherlands Israelite Seminary in Rapenburgerstraat has its premises here. While there is no longer any training provided for rabbis, it does offer a curriculum for Jewish adult education.

14 THE HENNEICKE GROUP

One of the darkest episodes in the persecution of the Jews during the war was the work of the Henneicke Group, which had its headquarters in the house at number 244 on the present Churchillaan. From March to October 1943 this group of some fifty Dutch men, led by an Amsterdam resident Wim Henneicke, supervised the arrest and deportation of an estimated 8,500 Jews; they received a fee of seven-and-a-half guilders for each arrest. The extermination of about 10 percent of all the Jews in Holland can thus be attributed to the Henneicke Group. The group was particularly active in Amsterdam, but it also hunted down its victims throughout the Netherlands. To achieve their ends, they threatened informers and people supplying safe addresses, resorting to physical force when required. In their pursuit of Jews the group made no distinction between rich and poor, men or women and even little children were taken away from their 'underground' parents, as one of the

Sal Meyer's sandwich shop – still a meeting point for wandering Jews

men, a certain Schipper snarled at Mrs Schoonderwoerd in Zuilen when she refused to surrender André, a boy aged two and a half: 'He's a Jewish child, but a Jewish child grows into a Jewish boy and later he'll grow up to be a Jewish man'. These Jew-hunters were primarily concerned with the rewards that the Germans paid them from the assets of the Jews themselves deposited in the Jewish bank of Lippman Rosenthal. The group was a branch of the *Hausraterfassungsstelle*, a body supervised by the Central Office for Jewish Emigration, which registered the household effects of Jewish families with the aim of stealing them and transferring them to Germany. In October 1943 the Henneicke Group was disbanded, since the majority of Jews had been deported by then. After the war twenty-five death sentences were passed on members of the group, but only three of them were upheld after the appeal hearings. All three had already taken refuge in Germany. Wim Henneicke

himself did not survive the war. He was shot dead by members of the Dutch resistance on 8 December 1944, after trying to save his skin by passing on information about the SD when he saw which way the war was going.

15   SAL MEYER'S SANDWICH SHOP

Sal Meyer's sandwich shop is a byword in Jewish Amsterdam. Sal Meyer was one of the butchers who rented a spot in the former Jewish covered meat-market on Nieuwe Amstelstraat. Some years before the Second world War, however, he set up shop independently outside the market building, first on Lepelstraat and after the war on Jodenbreestraat. Due to the redevelopment of this street, the business moved to Nieuwmarkt square where people came from far and wide to enjoy one of Meyer's sandwiches.
The Nieuwmarkt quarter grew gradually scruffier

Theeboom, Jewish grocer's in Diemen

16 THEEBOOM GROCER'S SHOP

Theeboom is the only baker that still supplies kosher wares under rabbinical supervision. The bakery dates back to the 19th century when it had its premises in the heart of the Jewish quarter on Jodenbreestraat. Due to the redevelopment of the street, Theeboom was forced to move in 1962, and a site was chosen closer to the postwar Jewish neighbourhoods on Tweede Sweelinckstraat in the Pijp district. In 1969 a grocer's shop with a wide selection of products was opened on the corner of Churchillaan and Maasstraat; since the closure of the bakery in the Pijp, it has become Theeboom's main premises. A great range of kosher groceries imported from throughout the world can be purchased there. The best-known products of Theeboom are the small ginger and almond cakes sold in many shops and catering establishments. Special products are made and imported for Jewish high holidays, and in particular for the 'Pesah shop' that is only open for ten days a year.

Theeboom Grocery's is closed on the Sabbath and open on Sundays. There is a branch of the store in Buitenveldert.

17 MARCUS BUTCHER'S SHOP

Due to the regulations connected with the kosher slaughtering and preparation of meat, many Jews traditionally took up the trade of butcher. Especially in smaller towns where there were no other butchers, Jewish butchers could support themselves by providing meat to the non-Jewish population as well.

Marcus is the sole remaining kosher butcher in Holland. The firm originated in Zwolle. After the war it was only in Amsterdam that there was a large enough Jewish community to support a ritual butcher. For a long time the firm had its premises on Ferdinand Bolstraat, but in the mid-1990s it moved to number 19, Waalstraat in the River Neighbourhood. Marcus is under rabbinical supervision, with a shomer, or kashrut inspector, attending in the slaughterhouse, to make sure that the meat

and demolition operations in preparation for the new metro line made the shop increasingly hard to reach. In 1982 Meyer moved to Scheldestraat, where his son Nico had already reopened the butcher's shop. Both butcher's and sandwich shop were thus again housed in premises close to Amsterdam's Jewish population. In the year 2000 the butcher's shop had to shut down. As the only remaining kosher sandwich shop in Amsterdam, Sal Meyer's has a vital social function. On Sundays many people meet there to enjoy the sandwiches and meat products prepared in the traditional way. The typically Jewish salt beef, beef sausage and liver and salt beef sandwiches are highly popular. Sal Meyer's is closed on the Sabbath and high holidays, but is open on Sundays.

Headed notepaper of a historical nature, from Marcus the butcher's

is prepared according to Jewish dietary laws. Only meat with a Dutch hechsher, or kosher certificate, is sold here.

It is proving increasing difficult to maintain ritual slaughter. In recent years shehitah, or kosher slaughtering, has been stopped more than once because the rules that apply for slaughter in the Netherlands cannot be complied with. With ritual slaughter in particular, cattle are often not killed immediately. This has led to emotional discussions about which has priority – the legal prescribed requirements for the well-being of animals, or Jewish customs, and religious freedom. This is a sensitive issue particularly because shehitah is one of the traditional pillars of the Jewish community. Kosher meat, moreover, is relatively expensive due to the numerous ritual regulations and it also costs a great deal to have a shomer to supervise it. Competition with groceries such as Theeboom and Mouwes, who import cheaper kosher meat from abroad, has therefore become increasingly intense. Furthermore the number of families that still maintain the kashrut dietary laws is noticeably declining. Marcus has found a new market by providing airlines and supermarkets such as Albert Heijn with kosher meat. The shop is closed on Saturdays and Jewish holidays.

De Leeuw's, the only pickle shop in the Netherlands still using the traditional recipes

18 DE LEEUW'S PICKLES

Pickled gherkins and onions can be obtained in many different places in Amsterdam. It is the commonest thing in Amsterdam to serve raw herrings with onions and gherkins. Almost nobody realizes that it was the Jews who introduced this habit to Amsterdam. They had learned the method of pickling onions, cucumbers and gherkins in central Europe. Before the war many Jews made a living for themselves in the pickling trade. De Leeuw, situated today on Vrijheidslaan at the corner with Vechtstraat, is the only remaining traditional Jewish pickle dealers in Holland. This pickling firm was founded in around 1850 by Isaac de Leeuw, on Rapenburg in the Jewish quarter. The pickled preserves were put in oak wood barrels and sold all over the city from a cart. Before the war De Leeuw had its premises in Jodenhouttuinen. Due to the redevelopment of this district, De Leeuw had to move, first to Elandsgracht and from there to Vrijheidslaan. Since then everything is only sold on the premises. Today De Leeuw remains a family firm, and is now run by the fourth generation. The pickles are made in the traditional manner, being saturated in brine and then made more bland with a marinade of wine vinegar and herbs – the recipe is a closely guarded secret. In the shop window is a model of the 19th-century barrow that Isaac de Leeuw trundled through the streets selling his wares.

19 MONUMENT ON GAASP STREET

Next to the playground on the square on Gaaspstraat is a monument built in 1986 to record that the Jews were separated from the rest of the Dutch population during the Second World War, amongst other things by setting up special Jewish

Monument in Gaaspstraat records the segregation of Jewish and Dutch school-chums during World War II

markets and isolating Jewish children. Besides the one on Gaaspstraat, there were Jewish markets on Waterlooplein, Minervaplein and on Joubertstraat in the Transvaal neighbourhood.

Shortly after the market was opened during the German occupation, the local residents destroyed the fence and hung up a banner with the text, 'We want to go shopping in the market together with the Jews'. Only Jews could use the market and they had no alternative, because all other markets and shops were 'forbidden to Jews'. The Jewish market stall-holders mainly came from the Albert Cuyp market. Many of them went into hiding. In summer 1943 both customers and traders disappeared. On 9 August of that year the market was closed.

The monument was unveiled on the day that forty-five years previously, in 1941, the board of the playground association sent a circular announcing that Jewish children were no longer allowed in the public playground. The sloping wall separates two non-Jewish children at play from two Jewish children fearfully awaiting deportation. The playing children are a black boy and a white girl. The monument not only aims to recall the past, but also points to the future. The inscription reads: 'Playing together, living together' and goes on to state that on 3 November 1941 a 'market' was opened exclusively for Jews.

The journalist Martin van Amerongen (1941-2002) recorded this shift from the specifically Jewish to a more general approach to minorities in 'Dat kan hier niet gebeuren. God zij dank' (Thank God, this cannot happen here):

It is a waste of time to be sentimental about this issue …In the Jewish Hospital one rarely sees a Jewish invalid any more; the District Health Authority (the GGD) currently has its premises in the building and in the polyclinic departments, you get a splendid cross-section of cultures, you can have a broken wrist set by a doctor from India, who is assisted in turn by a nurse from Kalebaskreek in Surinam. Smaragdplein, where the celebrated socialist alderman De Miranda, surrounded by proud neighbours and co-religion-

ists, opened the public baths in 1926, is now full of Turkish, Moroccan, Surinamese and Caribbean children. The same is true of the playground a couple of blocks further on Gaaspstraat. There you will find a monument to the children, commemorating the fact that the Jewish children were forbidden with a hideous matter-of-factness to play with non-Jewish children. Today the playground has adopted this children's monument, as a symbol for its efforts to teach children through play to socialize with each other in a tolerant fashion no matter what the colour of their skin. Not without emotion I take note of this.

20 LEKSTRAAT SYNAGOGUE

The Congregation of Benei Teimon, or 'Children of the South', opened on Lekstraat in 1937 and was the last Jewish place of worship to be consecrated before the war. The synagogue adopted the Yiddish motto *Nicht in der Goloes, oen nicht in der Heem* (Neither in exile, nor in our home) taken from the novel by Chaia Raismann (1890 –1936), later the wife of Ben Sajet the socialist.

It is typical of the ambiguity that Jewish Netherlands felt under the threat from Germany. The synagogue was designed by Abraham Elzas (1907-1945). This socialist-minded architect had freed himself from the Orthodox environment of his parents in Alkmaar and had worked in Paris under Le Corbusier. As a functionalist he always opted for the most efficient solutions, so that the synagogue does not have a single item of ornamentation and consists solely of space, materials and light.

The main building has a severe, closed façade and houses a large synagogue. The Hebrew text on the facade reads: 'And I will live among the children of Israel and will not leave my people of Israel' (1 Kings 6:13). The simple, light interior has an intensity that one would not suspect from its exterior. In the annex there was a small synagogue, or young people's shul, as well as meeting rooms and communal areas. The building attracted many comments right from its consecration. The *New Israelite*

Lekstraat Synagogue: the last shul built in Amsterdam before World War

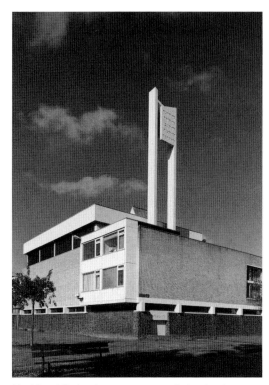

The Liberal (Reform) synagogue named after Jacob Soetendorp

Weekly described it as: 'a new monumental place of worship... (that) will testify to the strength and energy to be found in our 300-year-old community; to the unbroken courage and will to live of the Jewish people in a day when gathering storms are battering against our stronghold'. On the other hand, the great socialist Henri Polak expressed his dislike for this place of worship that he saw as a monstrosity and not fit to serve as a shed to store tulip bulbs. After the war, services were still initially held in the main space that had now become much too large. In the 1970s demolition was decided on. Widespread opposition to the decision resulted in the building's being offered to the Museum of the Dutch Resistance, while the former young people's shul was converted into an adult synagogue. At the outset of 1999 the Resistance Museum moved to the Plancius Building in the Plantage district; the Jewish community then sold the former synagogue

to the city of Amsterdam. Since then the auction house of Glerum has set up shop in the monumental building. The former young people's shul is still let to the Jewish community, for religious services.

21   JACOB SOETENDORP SYNAGOGUE

The Progressive Jewish Centre with the synagogue on Jacob Soetendorpstraat has accommodated Liberal Jews since 1966. The synagogue was named after Rabbi Jacob Soetendorp (1914-1976), who did so much to encourage the growth of this congregation after the war. Liberal Judaism, also known as Reform or Progressive Judaism, emerged in the 19th century as a result of ideas about emancipation. In the 20th century it also began to gain a following in the Netherlands. Liberal Jews have pushed innovations through in the religious services

Service in the Jacob Soetendorp Synagogue

and they support equal rights for men and woman. In doing so, they endeavour to give Judaism and Jewry greater vitality. In the domain of religion, they see the Torah mainly as a guide on how to live. They regard the five books of Moses as being inspired by God but not as representing any divine decree. This means that they can also lay more emphasis on the evolution of Judaism, a process that continues up to the present, and they are open to present-day social conditions. As such the liberal movement is a continuation of Liberal or Reform Judaism as it became popular in Germany in the 19th century. The reform idea can also be seen in the synagogue's interior. In the design of L.H.P. Waterman (1912-1988), the bimah, from which the Torah is read, is placed next to the Ark. Traditionally the rules require it to be at the centre. Another major difference with Orthodox synagogues is that there are no separate areas, or galleries, reserved only for women. During the services men and women sit side-by-side. On the outside the most striking feature is the two pillars that support the table on which the Ten Commandments are carved. On the facade that faces Europa Boulevard is a large glass menorah, or seven-branched cande-labrum, forming part of a glass mosaic in the front wall. The brickwork by the entrance consists of bricks brought from Amsterdam's redeveloped Jewish quarter. Owing to lack of space, especially for the currently expanding social and cultural activities, and because of major building operations taking place in the immediate vicinity, the Liberal Jewish Community has advanced plans for a new development on a site nearby.

THE BUITENVELDERT AND AMSTELVEEN NEIGHBOURHOODS

Up until well into the 19th century almost the entire Jewish population lived in the eastern part of the city. Since then they have gradually left for the new neighbourhoods in the south – a development that continued in the postwar period. The decimation of Jewish Amsterdam in World War II mainly affected the poor proletariat, and the survivors tended to come from the relatively better-off classes. The decay in the old Jewish quarter reinforced this migration of the survivors to the better neighbourhoods in the south. To find Jewish Amsterdam today, one has to go to Buitenveldert, and neighbouring Amstelveen. This is where the most important Jewish institutions have ended up, such as the chief rabbinate and the Jewish educational institutions. Because these developments are recent, there is not much Jewish history in these neighbourhoods. Due to their modern premises moreover, Jewish institutions here are hardly distinguishable from their surroundings, so that contemporary Jewish Amsterdam is not a particularly noticeable element in the city

1 JEWISH CULTURAL CENTRE IN THE VAN DER BOECHORST-STRAAT

The Jewish Cultural Centre at 26, Van der Boechorststraat provides accommodation for the Netherlands Israelite Religious Community (NIK) and the Chief Netherlands Israelite Synagogue of Amsterdam. Various Jewish foundations also have premises here. With its unobtrusive exterior, the building is therefore not only the administrative and organizational hub of Orthodox Jewish Netherlands; it is also the cultural centre for Orthodox Dutch Jewry as a whole. For instance, the Jewish Cultural Centre organizes kosher catering throughout the Netherlands. After the war the many buildings in the traditional Jewish neighbourhoods had become derelict and were no longer suitable for the drastically reduced community. Most of them were abandoned and lost their function. After much negotiation with the city council of Amsterdam, however, a few were provided with a fitting purpose (such as the Ashkenazi synagogue complex), or were preserved as memorials (the Hollandsche Schouwburg). Initially the Jewish community took up residence in the building of the Beis Israel association in the Plantage district. With the move of much of the Jewish population to the South, the Netherlands Israelite Religious Community also moved to Van der Boechorststraat in 1970. The building was designed by the famous Dutch architect, Gerrit Rietveld (1888-1964) as the Buitenveldert Pavilion of the Vrije Gemeente, a Dutch Protestant group. There are therefore no specific Jewish features on the exterior.

2 JOACHIMSTHAL BOOKSHOP

Joachim Loser and Jonas Salomon Joachimsthal started a company in 1867 in Jodenbreestraat, specializing in the book and paper

'Buitenveldert Pavilion' today the Jewish Cultural Centre, designed by the architect Rietveld

Joachimsthal Bookshop has an extensive collection of books on Jewish subjects

trade, and which was also a bookbinder's. In 1892 the publishing rights of the weekly *Nieuw Israëlitisch Weekblad* were passed on to the company; thereafter business boomed to such an extent that it acquired a steam-driven press in 1895. During the war, like all the other Jewish businesses, Joachimsthal was placed under a German administrator and it was plundered and liquidated in 1943. Nevertheless, the business opened again immediately after the war. From 1957 onwards, it continued, but only as a bookshop, since the publishers of the NIW split off and became independent. In the 1960s the business moved first to the River Neighbourhood and then, in 1997, to Gelderlandplein. Over the years Joachimsthal has had a large department of Judaica, including literature, Jewish history, philosophy, religion and books on Israel. Most of the businesses in the shopping centre on Gelderlandplein provide services to the local Jewish clientele. Supermarket Albert Heijn for example has a large assortment of kosher articles, including meat from Mouwes. The Jewish atmosphere in the shopping centre is emphasized every year, with Hanukkah being celebrated with lighted candles in the menorah.

3   JEWISH PRIVATE EDUCATION

After the war, Jewish education as a whole moved to Buitenveldert. 'Jewish Education' (JBO) was instituted there in 1947. It replaced the schools of the Knowledge and Piety Society, wiped out in the war, except for a small kindergarten-cum-elementary school, Rosh Pina in the Pijp and the Maimonides High School in the Stadstimmertuin. In 1973 Rosh Pina moved to Buitenveldert, followed in 1980 by Maimonides. Both schools were given new accommodation on Noordbrabantstraat. Two new

Cheider, school for Orthodox Jews in the Netherlands

kindergartens have now been added to Rosh Pina primary school, Ganon Judith and Ganon Hagamadin. Under pressure from parents and competition from Cheider schools, the Jewish curriculum was expanded in the 1990s. The aim is that the diploma for religious education teacher should be available via the Jewish curriculum at the Netherlands Israelite Seminary in Gerrit van der Veen Synagogue. In the Rosh Pina elementary school, there is instruction in Jewish traditions, such as the high holidays and the parasha, the weekly Torah portion. The Hebrew alphabet is also taught. Maimonides school offers classes in Jewish history and Hebrew. These classes are optional however, because not everyone appreciates this extra strain on the curriculum. One of the rooms of Maimonides is also used as a shul. Because the number of pupils at Maimonides has risen to roughly two hundred, partly due to the school's excellent results, the building needs enlarging. Asbestos was discovered in the buildings of Rosh Pina at the end of 1998 and it had to be demolished. Rosh Pina moved to a provisional building on Leijenberglaan. The new premises of Rosh Pina, combined with the expanded premises of Maimonides, will be completed in mid 2004. In the 1990s a small sculpture was set in the rear corner of the school building on Van Boshuizenstraat, showing a man with a suitcase and a child; it symbolizes the children who went into hiding and their protectors from 1942 to 1945.

4   BETH SHALOM

Early in the 1990s the Jewish old people's home, Beth Shalom, opened a nursing home at 80 Kastelenstraat. The old people's home was the product of a fusion of Beth Menucha, on Plantage Middenlaan and the Joodse Invalide nursing home, that had moved from its premises on Weesperplein to the former Portuguese Israelite Hospital on Henri Polaklaan. Beth Shalom also houses 125 residents of the old people's home and it has 60 in the nursing home in Osdorp. There are also 40 sheltered accommodation units for old people who can still cope by themselves, and who can make use of the facilities of Beth Shalom. Round the central hall are a number of facilities and establishments, such as a grocer's shop and the offices of Joods Maatschappelijk Werk (Jewish Social Work, JMW). The JMW also organizes a refectory for the residents. The atmospheric synagogue with its modern stained-glass windows is well attended, including by people living in the neighbourhood – among them many of the younger generation who like the easy-going atmosphere in Beth Shalom. Because the women's gallery is on the ground floor, there is a curtain to separate the sexes, as required in Orthodox practice.

5   CHEIDER

The private school of the Cheider Foundation for Social Welfare of the Jewish Children's Community is located on Zeelandweg. This strictly Orthodox school opened in 1974 with only five pupils. In the 1980s two adjacent buildings were incorporated in the premises on Van Nijenrodeweg in Buitenveldert. Initially the education provided by the Cheider was merely tolerated by the Ministry of Education, but in 1988 the school's status was recognized and from then on the school had meet with legal requirements. Besides a general curriculum, Cheider offers a wide range of Jewish studies, with four hours of Jewish history and traditions and the Hebrew language. At the beginning of the 1990s, the school had more than 200 pupils

Main hall in Cheider, also used as a synagogue

and was moved to the new building on Zeelandweg, where there is also space for a crèche, a kindergarten and a secondary school. The large room in the middle of the building can be closed off and used as a synagogue.

6 MOUWES DELICATESSEN

Mouwes, with its premises in the gallery at number 261, Kastelenstraat, is a kosher delicatessen under rabbinical supervision. The business dates from the end of the 18th century, when an ancestor started selling groceries from a barrow. During the Napoleonic occupation, he set up shop in Rapenburgerstraat, and the firm remained there till the Second World War. In the postwar period it moved to Utrechtsestraat, later proceeding from there to Buitenveldert. Mouwes sells a large selection of traditional Jewish delicatessen products; it is closed on the Sabbath and high holidays, but open on Sundays. One corner of the shop is used as a simple coffee bar where delicatessen can be enjoyed on the premises.

7 THE BUITENVELDERT BRANCH OF THEEBOOM

Like Theeboom's main store on Maasstraat, the branch at 45, Bolestein is under rabbinical supervision and deals exclusively in kosher wares. Apart from pastries from their own bakery, there is also a general selection of kosher groceries, including frozen meat products from Marcus. In the front of the shop are a couple of tables where one can enjoy Theeboom's products. This branch of Theeboom is also closed on the Sabbath and high holidays, but open on Sundays.

Various delicatessen are virtually synonymous with Jewish culture. Johannes van Dam (born 1946) has written a story about the kugel with pears:

> It was only on reaching the age of Christ's crucifixion, that I felt ready to taste kugel with pears. An older woman friend thought it was high time I stopped keeping everything I saw as too Jewish at arm's length ...We found the original kugel at Saartje Vos: it is a custard steamed in a bain-marie with raisins, cinnamon and cloves, and eaten with stewed pears or apples that are prepared separately... I still cherish a publication from the terrible silence of the war years that you can't really call a cookery book: Pesah in times of rationing...with intensely moving texts such as: 'It is a more weighty task than ever before for the Jewish housewife to preserve a positive atmosphere, that unfortunately is hardly present at all in many Jewish families today. But she can and must do so ... The traditional invitation at the beginning of the Seder to the hungry to come and take part in the festive dish testifies strikingly to how the meal has always been seen as the key to the festive mood.'

8 SEPHARDI SYNAGOGUE, AMSTELVEEN

On 11 January 1995 in a former shop at number 82, Texelstraat in Amstelveen, a new Sephardi synagogue was consecrated, with the ritual affixing of the mezuzot, to the doorposts. A mezuzot contains two short portions of text written on the parchment, taken from the biblical book of Deuteronomy reading:

> 'And thou shalt write these words upon the doorposts of thy house and upon thy gates.'

The last consecration of a Sephardi synagogue, or esnoga, in Amsterdam was in 1675, more than three centuries earlier, when the great edifice on the Mr. Visserplein opened its doors. For Jews of Portuguese origin, the distance between Amstelveen and Buitenveldert and the city centre is too great to cover on foot on the Sabbath, so that a synagogue in the neighbourhood had become essential.

The new esnoga has a sober ground plan. There is a tevah (Ashkenazi bimah) from which the Torah is read, an Ark in which the Torah scrolls are stored, in front of which is an eternally burning lamp, or ner tamid – all from the former synagogue of Scheveningen.

9 JEWISH CULTURAL CENTRE, AMSTELVEEN

The first shul of the Orthodox Jewish community in Amstelveen was consecrated shortly before the war, only to be closed again in 1941. After the war, a flourishing community of Jews sprung up there, so that a new, larger place of worship became essential. In 1961 provisional premises were opened, after which the shul moved to Straat van Gibraltar. In 1981, however, an entirely new synagogue was built on Straat van Messina. When it was opened, this modern eight-sided building was seen as a symbol of optimism about the prospects of the Jewish community in Amstelveen. The centre contains community rooms and an octagonal synagogue. The Ark is situated on the east side – facing Jerusalem, as prescribed. Above it are the tables with the Ten Commandments and in the middle is the bimah, the platform on which stands the desk from which the Torah is read, between two large candelabra. Two light shafts provide constant daylight on the Ark and the bimah. The section for women is on the ground floor and is separated from the male section by a trellis. The synagogue has movable walls so that the space can be enlarged on high holidays. Nonetheless, space has again become a problem, so that plans are being laid for replacing the synagogue with a new development and with the addition of a ritual bath, a mikweh.

10 CENTRAL ISRAELITE HOSPITAL

The only hospital in the Netherlands that complies with the rules of the rabbinate is located in Amstelveen. Before the war there were three Jewish hospitals in Amsterdam alone – the large Netherlands Israelite Hospital (NIZ) on Nieuwe Keizersgracht, the Portuguese Israelite Hospital (PIZ) on Henri Polaklaan and the Central Israelite Hospital (CIZ) on Jacob Obrechtstraat. The two former hospitals were destroyed in the war, leaving only the private CIZ.

Since the beginning of the 19th century, the care of the sick was a task of the Netherlands Israelite Poor Relief Board, that was directly linked to the Jewish community. Gradually the task of funding was taken over by the public authorities, making the care of the sick less dependent on the Jewish community. Another important factor was the emergence of health insurance schemes, especially in socialist circles. The largely socialist-inclined Jewish population of Amsterdam joined the Health Insurance Scheme of the Artisans' Society of Friends. This development made it possible to found a private hospital in 1916 in the middle of the new urban development on Jacob Obrechtstraat. During World War II the German occupiers left it open for a long time, amongst other things to carry out their policy of 'voluntary' sterilization. An *Ärtzliche Verbindungsstelle*, a medical centre, was set up to deal with requests for sterilization. Eventually the CIZ was evacuated by the Nazis and the majority of the patients were liquidated.

After the war the CIZ was the only Jewish hospital to reopen. The building was by now antiquated and no longer had adequate facilities for caring for the few patients. After the opening of a special wing for Jewish patients in the Nicolaas Tulp Hospital in Amstelveen, in 1978 it closed down. Maintaining a Jewish atmosphere in the hospital is a challenge, because it is not easy to obtain enough Jewish staff. An impetus was given by the arrival of the Sinai Centre psychiatric hospital, from Amersfoort. By now the hospital is completely kosher and the Jewish high holidays and the Sabbath are observed.

An important contribution is made by the shul that was reopened in 1997. The Christian patients of the Amstelveense Hospital – who, incidentally, sit with their backs to the Holy Ark during their services – share the use of this sandy-golden interior with its cupboard to hold the Torah, and bright colourful murals.

THE JEWISH CEMETERIES

The burial ground is an important feature of the Jewish community. In expectation of the coming of the Messiah the dead await in solemn quietness. The cemetery is given various names, including Bet Hayyim, or House of the Living, emphasizing the Jewish belief in life after death. In the Netherlands, Jewish cemeteries are silent but significant witnesses to the centuries of Jewish history in this country.

Jewish laws prohibit alterations being made in cemeteries. In particular, the regulation that trees and plants may not be pruned produces over time a scene in which nature runs its own course and creates an atmosphere of hushed mystery. The oldest sections will often provide picturesque effects, with the tombstones half hidden beneath rambling plants.

However, it should be said that the atmosphere in the Portuguese Jewish cemetery in Ouderkerk on the Amstel is different from that in the other Jewish graveyards, which are used by the Ashkenazim. For instance, Sephardim have gravestones that lie horizontal, often beautifully carved, a witness to the wealth of the deceased. The Ashkenazim generally could only afford simple stones, which they stood upright on the grave. Indeed, the very poor – most of them buried in Zeeburg – couldn't even pay for a gravestone. During the Second World War the graveyards of the Jewish dead were rarely violated. Nowadays there are seldom visitors to these places of quiet, since there are very few surviving relatives.

1 ZEEBURG

There are not many tombstones marking the soggy grasses of the Jewish cemetery in Zeeburg. So it is perhaps surprising to learn that around 100,000 Jews are buried here. As the only graveyard close to Amsterdam, Zeeburg became the final resting place of the poverty-stricken Jewish proletariat. Many of them lie in unmarked graves. Generally, poor Jews could not afford the contribution to the Jewish community and were thus not officially listed members. This meant they couldn't be buried in Muiderberg. So in 1714 the cemetery in Zeeburg was opened for them; it had the additional advantage of being within walking distance of the city. The Dutch-Jewish writer Pelouni Almouni (1889-1954) describes in *Een spookgeschiedenis in het Amsterdamsche ghetto* (A Ghost Story from the Amsterdam Ghetto) the feelings of remorse of the

Gravestones in the neglected Jewish cemetery of Zeeburg

rich and avaricious Itzak who let his brother Maayer – who had fallen on hard times – be buried in a pauper's grave in Zeeburg. One of the leaders of the Jewish community decides to teach Itzak a lesson for abandoning his brother in this way:

Maayer Beer lay at rest in …Zeeburg. Although his forefathers slept in the gently rolling countryside of Muiderberg and even (his brother) Itzak, as the sole luxury of his life, had permitted himself the expense of being buried there also when his time came. …

The next day, first thing, Itzak made a request that Maayer might be 'disinterred' and transported to Muiderberg. He received the answer that the necessary conditions in order to perform this action – which was very rarely permitted – had not been met. When Itzak heard this disappointing answer he turned pale, his eyes glazed, his hands trembled and he fell off his low shivah stool and lay unconscious on the ground. When he came round he found the parnas, the leader of the community, was beside him, and he gave Itzak the following advice. Since Itzak's stinginess was well-known in the community, the parnas suggested that he compensate his dead brother in another way: he should give up his plans for a luxurious grave in Muiderberg and buy himself a grave beside his brother Maayer…in Zeeburg.

Early in the 20th century the cemetery of Zeeburg was full up. A new piece of land was consecrated in Diemen, just outside Amsterdam, and the Zeeburg cemetery fell into disuse. Over time most of the gravestones became overgrown or sank into the soggy ground. The cemetery was closed in 1942 and fell into oblivion. Then in 1956 a new highway was constructed running through part of the ceme-

Simple gravestones stand close together in Diemen cemetery

tery. Under rabbinical supervision a section was cleared to make room for the Flevoweg. The human remains were reburied in Diemen. Today the 'Former Jewish Cemetery' lies between Flevoweg and Flevo Park, split in two by the entrance to the park. Recently the fencing was restored and now once more the final resting place of many thousands of Amsterdam Jews is a home of quiet.

2   DIEMEN

The Jewish cemetery in Diemen is split down the middle by a railway track. The oldest section, opened in 1914, lies beside the rail track running from Amsterdam to the east of the country. The more recent section lies on the outside of the track. Diemen cemetery, burial place of the Jewish proletariat, is a sobering sight. Row upon row of gravestones stand, their texts – usually written in Hebrew – facing the entrance. There too is the small house for the ablution of the dead, the bet tohorah, and the caretaker's home. Around the outside is the path for the Kohanim, who are forbidden to enter except for the burial of their close kin. The Kohanim are the descendants of Aaron, the first High Priest of Israel. At the far side, a narrow path runs alongside allotments and across the railway track to the new section of the cemetery. When the new section was given its own entrance the path was closed off, thereby actually creating two separate cemeteries. The new section has its own ablution building, which is used from time to time. The cemetery ground that lies behind this displays a few solitary gravestones where the remains from the Zeeburg cemetery were re-interred. A large stone is inscribed with the hope 'May this resting place remain undisturbed.' Unfortunately the peace of this cemetery is seriously disturbed by the traffic zooming along the highway, which with the recent new building now blocks the view across the fields.

Tombstones from the oldest part, now a woodland, in Muiderberg cemetery

Weathered tombstones in the old cemetery of Muiderberg

3   MUIDERBERG

The most impressive cemetery belonging to the Ashkenazim of Amsterdam is that in Muiderberg. It is also, apart from the Portuguese Jewish cemetery in Ouderkerk, the oldest in the Netherlands. Entering the grounds, visitors are immediately confronted by a low hill overgrown with trees, with many old gravestones jutting from it. At the beginning of the 17th century the first Ashkenazi Jews who died in Amsterdam were buried in the Sephardi Portuguese cemetery. Then in 1639 the Ashkenazim bought their own plot of land just outside Amsterdam near Muiderberg. Menachem Man (?-1767) writes about this in *Seerith Jisrael*:

We bought the cemetery in Muiderberg in the year 5399 and the first deceased to be buried there was the mother-in-law of Meijer Zwart. When the funeral procession carrying the body approached the Hakkelaars Bridge, the church bells began to toll as is the custom among the Christians; for the Christians thought in this way

to honour the deceased; however, we besought them to cease tolling the bells and not to do so in the future under similar circumstances; with which request they concurred.

Shortly after the German Jews began using the cemetery, the Polish Jews bought the adjacent plot of land to use as their cemetery. When the two congregations united, the cemeteries were also combined. Over time it has developed into the largest Jewish cemetery in the Netherlands, although more Jews lie buried in Zeeburg. The Jewish cemetery of Muiderburg, lying on the edge of the town, holds more than 40,000 graves.

The small hill on the right as you enter, with its luxuriant plant growth, is the oldest part of the cemetery. None of the gravestones survive from the earliest period because they were all taken during the French invasion of the Netherlands in 1672 to construct defence works. Even before this it had become apparent that the cemetery should be guarded against vandals, and in 1658 the sheriff of

Muiderberg instituted a guard whose task was 'to intercept and quench all wickedness and mischief.' Since 1724 there has been a Jewish watchman guarding the cemetery.

The cost of transporting the deceased from Amsterdam was high, and also, people could only be buried there if they were 'paid-up members' of the Jewish community; consequently, the many poor Jews have been buried in Zeeburg since 1714. For a long time also no children were buried at Muiderberg because they were not paid-up members of the community. In past centuries the funeral procession usually came by barge via Weesp, a town near Amsterdam, but later on people also began to use coaches and carriages and then the steam train which ran from the city into the countryside, stopping close to the cemetery. Then the solemn procession filed in, towards the tohorah at the end of the pathway.

Muiderberg is the only Jewish cemetery of Amsterdam that is still regularly used. The former distinctions between children, parnasim (leaders of the community), paid-up and not-paid-up members of the community, and Kohanim, are no longer observed. The deceased are buried in the ground behind the mortuary, or tohorah, in the most recent section of the cemetery. Beside the mortuary is a simple monument bearing 28 nameplates of Jews who died during the Second World War and a commemorative tablet recalling the horrors of the war. The more recently-used parts of the cemetery are well cared for and present a simple, orderly sight. In the older sections, however, moss covers many gravestones and indeed trees and plants hide many of them. This lends an air of mystery to the place and particularly in the twilight hours it speaks to the imagination. Also most remarkable are the carvings on some of the stones. Two hands in an attitude of blessing indicate that a kohen lies buried here; as descendants of the High Priest Aaron, the brother of Moses, they could give the priestly blessing in the synagogue and elsewhere. The carved ewer and basin adorn the gravestone of a levite, the Temple servants who poured out the water to wash the priests' hands. With the destruction of the Temple this function virtually ceased. Traditionally, Kohanim and Levites have these symbols of their tribe engraved on their tombstones. In her book *Afscheid van oom Eli* (Farewell to Uncle Eli) Dutch novelist Marianne Philips (1886-1951) describes how Henri Godschalk accompanied uncle Eli to Muiderberg:

At the entrance gate a group of miserable Jewish beggars crowded in wait and the mourners held their gifts ready, because it is a praiseworthy deed to give charity when attending a funeral – it is written: 'The benevolent shall be saved from death.' But it seems as if the beggars feel useful and necessary – if they weren't there, people wouldn't be able to gain blessings for themselves by offering alms.

'The gravestones here are at least three hundred years old,' pointed out the chazzan Polak. 'A levite is buried there!' He indicated the grave and showed Henri the carved symbol on the stone, showing the ewer, the holy objects used by the Levites in the Temple in olden days to wash the hands of the Kohanim, the priests. 'And there's the grave of a kohen.' Carved upon the tombstone were the spread fingers indicating the priestly blessing. 'Why is that always chiselled onto the gravestone?' asked Henri, 'I thought all Jews were equal nowadays.' 'Well, yes,' answered the chazzan, 'because we live in exile. But when the Messiah comes and takes us all back to Jerusalem, then everyone must know his appropriate place.'

Henri tactfully made no response. He knew that old pious Jews like the chazzan Polak still believed in the coming of the Messiah. He'd heard about the Zionists too, a small group of young Jews, who longed to return to Palestine, just like that, without the Messiah, something that pious Jews thought was blasphemous. … He himself loved the Amsterdam folk so much, and the houses and canals of the city, in fact everything about Amsterdam, that he certainly wouldn't leave even if the Messiah himself were indeed to come and lead the Jews back to Jerusalem.

4 OUDERKERK ON THE AMSTEL

A short distance outside Amsterdam in the small village of Ouderkerk on the river Amstel, lies the oldest Jewish cemetery in the Netherlands, opposite the Dutch Reformed church. It was consecrated in 1614 by Portuguese (Sephardi) Jews, which was in fact the first formal recognition of the Jewish community in Amsterdam. Up until then the Sephardim had buried their dead in Groet, a small place north of Amsterdam near Alkmaar. In 1616 the graves in Groet were disinterred and the remains were taken to Ouderkerk.

As the Jewish cemetery became more frequently used, the people of Ouderkerk started to object. The States-General of Holland granted permission to go on using the cemetery, on condition that the funerals were conducted in utter silence, without any pomp or ceremony that might cause offence to the honest citizens of Ouderkerk. In 1618 the States-General issued a reprimand to the authorities of Ouderkerk, saying that they should quash the opposition of certain intolerant members of their village. In spite of this, in 1621 a recalcitrant villager refused to open the barriers to allow a funeral procession to enter, so that the bailiff had to intervene. The Jews also had to pay every toll along the way, and a special tax when they passed a Christian church. These fines were rescinded by the States (parliament) of Holland in 1721.

The Sephardi community of Amsterdam had some most illustrious members who lie buried in Ouderkerk, bringing this cemetery international fame. Here lie, for example, Manasseh ben Israel, correspondent of Oliver Cromwell Lord Protector of England; the famous surgeon Dr. Efraim Bueno; the parents of the philosopher Spinoza; the extremely wealthy Suassos, sponsors of King William III of England; the Teixeira de Mattos and the De Pintos. The recumbent tombstones of the prominent Sephardi Jews are often beautifully decorated,

The deceased were formerly transported by barge to the mortuary on the Bullewijk

The old section of the Portuguese (Sephardi) cemetery with the Catholic church in the background

which makes this cemetery unique. There is no other Jewish graveyard containing so many sculpted figures. This wealth of images breaks the second Commandment which states, 'Thou shalt not make unto thee any graven image, or any likeness of any thing that is in the heaven above, or that is in the earth beneath, or that is in the water under the earth.' Although this Commandment is never strictly interpreted, nevertheless the cemetery at Ouderkerk certainly presents an extravagant exception. It looks at first sight as if this might be an extreme example of adaptation to the non-Jewish milieu, but further study has shown that these tombs should be seen as a conscious effort to make a statement of Jewish identity. When the Sephardim first arrived in the Netherlands their graves had a distinctly un-Dutch look about them. They built sarcophaguses with three-sided lids or cylinder-shaped tombs surmounted by a three-sided prism resting on a flat surface, both of these deriv-

ing from the Mediterranean world. Having lived many decades as crypto-Jews the first Sephardim in the Netherlands now wished to openly express their Jewish heritage. Their tombs belong to a specifically Jewish tradition and differ greatly from the Christian designs and decorations of graves. In the course of the 17th century the earliest signs may be observed of adaptation to the Dutch style of building tombs and decorating graves, particularly in the compositions using of family coats of arms. A frequently-seen feature of 17th- and 18th-century tombstones would be the armorial bearings blazoning the family's fame and fortune. Other decorations borrowed from contemporary Dutch art were the symbols of life's transience, such as a skull or an hour-glass. After the northern Netherlands became predominately Protestant and Calvinist, images of the dead were no longer made but instead symbolic shapes were used to represent death. This, of course, fitted in with the Jewish Second

Commandment and made it easy for the Sephardi Jews to adapt to the usage. A specifically Jewish decoration was the inverted double 'U' shape, symbolizing the Tables of the Law given to Moses.

The Jewish cemetery in Ouderkerk has inspired many with its solemn beauty. The Dutch 17th-century master Jacob van Ruysdael made a painting of it which in all likelihood inspired the famous German poet and playwright Goethe (1749-1832), to write, *'Many important, remarkable graves, some of them partly reminiscent of coffins as far as their shape is concerned, partly characterized by large upright flat slabs of stone. These testify to the importance of this religious community and suggest that those who lie buried here are people of eminence, from noble and wealthy families.'*

The oldest part of the cemetery comprises a park-like open space dotted with ancient trees, where the mortuary, stands in its beautiful setting. Here are the imposing monumental tombs. Unfortunately most of them have sunk into the swampy soil and only a few can be seen in detail. In the cemetery behind, many thousand Sephardi Jews rest beneath simple gravestones. Here too, vast numbers of the gravestones have sunk below ground level. In total about 27,000 Jews lie buried in Ouderkerk on the Amstel.

The cemetery was bordered on one side by the river Bullewijk so it was customary to transport the deceased from Amsterdam by barge. So the old entrance to this House of Life, or Bet Hayyim, lay at the water's edge. Immediately behind the old wooden gateway was the building for the ablution of the dead, the bet tohorah. The Sephardi Jews speak of the *Rodeamentos*, or House of Circumambulation, a reference to the custom of walking seven times

The many horizontal tombstones of the Portuguese (Sephardi) cemetery in Ouderkerk

around the coffin of a male deceased, before lowering it into the earth.

In the 19th century this Bet Hayyim was thoroughly charted by David Henriques de Castro, drawing worldwide attention to the cemetery on account of the many distinguished figures who lie buried here. De Castro rescued them from oblivion. He uncovered almost six thousand gravestones that had sunk into the ground, inventoried and wrote descriptions of them. He also had about one hundred tombstones restored at his own cost.

A project got going in the 1960s to inventory all the graves and a thorough restoration took place at the turn of the century, organized by the Henriques de Castro Fund, which was set up for this purpose. In the cold Dutch winters the most beautifully carved tombstones are covered, to protect them from the effects of frost and ice. Today the entrance to the Bet Hayyim is opposite the Dutch Reformed church. The documentation centre is at number 9, Kerkstraat, run under the auspices of the Foundation for Maintenance and Preservation of Historic Jewish Cemeteries in the Netherlands.

5   GAN HASHALOM IN HOOFDDORP

In the 1930s the still young Liberal-Jewish community of Amsterdam gained its own cemetery in Hoofddorp, just outside the city in the flat polderland that was once the Harlem lake. It is called Gan Hashalom, meaning Garden of Peace. It is used both by the Liberal Jews of Amsterdam and their kindred spirits from other places in the west of the Netherlands.

Beside the entrance, in memory of the victims of the Nazi period, stands a monument consisting of a wall bearing the names of those who died, crowned with a Star of David.

The Liberal Jewish community in the Netherlands is gradually expanding and Gan Hashalom, as the main cemetery for this group, sees considerable use. But its name 'Garden of Peace' no longer applies, because Amsterdam airport Schiphol is nearby, and the noise-pollution is enormous. So a new Liberal-Jewish cemetery has been consecrated in the Amsterdam suburb of Amstelveen. Gan Hashalom in Hoofddorp is now only used for the deceased who are to be buried in family graves reserved for this purpose.

6   GAN HASHALOM IN AMSTELVEEN

Early in 2003 the new cemetery of the Liberal-Jewish congregation, Gan Hashalom in Amstelveen, was consecrated. It is the first Jewish cemetery to be opened in the Netherlands since the Second World War. A still-empty field lies beside the street called after Rembrandt's wife, Saskia van Uilenburg. There is a brand new reception hall designed by Dutch architect Jaap Walvisch. It has a triangular shape, suggesting the Creation and the eternal elements of fire, air and water. The side wall of the hall is built from rough unhewn pale-coloured stones, brought from the caves behind the Kotel, the Western Wall of the Temple in Jerusalem. The cemetery has eight fields and several strips of ground where urns may be placed. This is never found among Orthodox Jews, who for religious reasons do not cremate their dead. Beside the hall is a circular terrace, where a monument is to be placed in memory of those who perished in the Holocaust.

Index

text: Jan Stoutenbeek and Paul Vigeveno
translation: Wendie Shaffer
(chapter 7&8 Donald Gardner)
photography: Sjaak Henselmans
design: Gijs Dragt
typesetting: Annelies Mikmak
printing: Die Keure, Brugge

ISBN 90-76588-57-0
NUR 693

No part of this publication may be reproduced, stored in a retrieval system, or transmitted, in any form or by any means, electronic, mechanical, photocopying, recording, or otherwise, without the prior written permission of the publishers

© 2003 Ludion Amsterdam-Ghent, the authors